HOUSING, PEOPLE, AND CITIES

HOUSING, PEOPLE, AND CITIES

Martin Meyerson

DIRECTOR, JOINT CENTER FOR URBAN
STUDIES OF THE MASSACHUSETTS
INSTITUTE OF TECHNOLOGY AND
HARVARD UNIVERSITY

Barbara Terrett

DIRECTOR OF RESEARCH ACTIVITIES,
ACTION

William L. C. Wheaton

DIRECTOR, INSTITUTE FOR
URBAN STUDIES, UNIVERSITY
OF PENNSYLVANIA

McGRAW-HILL BOOK COMPANY, INC. 1962

New York Toronto London

Drawing © 1952 by Saul Steinberg

HOUSING, PEOPLE, AND CITIES

III
41760

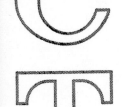
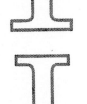

SERIES IN HOUSING AND
COMMUNITY DEVELOPMENT
Directed and Edited by Martin Meyerson

Foreword

Housing, People, and Cities is the culmination of a five-year investigation of impediments to the improvement of housing and the urban environment. The study, made possible by support from the Ford Foundation, has resulted in this Series in Housing and Community Development.

The eight books in the Series, of which this is the last, and many articles and other publications stemming from them, are part of a two-pronged effort of ACTION, the national council for good cities, to help achieve a superior level of living in urban areas. The eight volumes analyze many facts about the present condition of communities and their housing in the United States and propose ways to overcome the problems and achieve the potentialities that the facts reveal. The other part of AC-TION's effort consists of activities which encourage and help communities and their citizens to meet requirements of housing, transportation, and community services in a time of rapid urban growth. Thus research and action are used to reinforce each other.

The Series was designed to deal with important issues in housing and community development. During the past five years its analyses have stimulated many changes in policy and practice. Rehabilitation as a profitable industry was presaged by *Residential Rehabilitation: Private Profits and Public Purposes*. The recent rise in rental housing construction was anticipated by *Rental Housing: Opportunities for Private Investment*, which pointed out market potentialities in the field. Virtually everything that has been written about rental housing since its publication has quoted from or drawn upon this book. *Government and Housing in Metropolitan Areas* has contributed to the wide recognition that metropolitan consolidation would not provide an easy solution to many of the problems of urban America. The arithmetic of

Capital Requirements for Urban Development and Renewal has become a basis for local and national policy debates on a feasible scale of investment in public renewal programs. *Housing Choices and Housing Constraints* has alerted public officials and builders to the possibilities and limitations of the return of families to central-city residence and to the kinds of housing units which will be attractive. The publication of *Federal Credit and Private Housing: The Mass Financing Dilemma* has prodded officials, investors, producers, and others to review the conflicting aims and impact of government programs in housing. Nor has the influence of the Series been confined to the United States. *Design and the Production of Houses* has been cited in several countries in the search for technological and managerial advance in residential building and planning.

Each of these studies contains factual analyses and the interpretations and ideas of its authors. Each, however, contains more. In each case an *ad hoc* committee of thoughtful and knowledgeable businessmen and specialists reviewed the research materials and made suggestions for policy and action.

The interplay between the authors of the studies and the *ad hoc* committees on the investor, the producer, the consumer, the government, and the community was most fruitful. Not only did the authors benefit from the suggestions and advice of the committees, but the insights, information, and recommendations of the authors were widely circulated and discussed and sometimes incorporated into policy, even before publication.

I deliberately sought this combination of research and policy activities in the Series and found it helpful as well for this final volume. My colleagues and I have been able to draw upon the previous studies in our presentation of an over-all view of housing and community development, and we have had the benefit of the cumulative give and take of the *ad hoc* committee meetings. Moreover, we have had the good fortune to see many suggestions from our work adopted by government and private enterprise.

Throughout this book, my colleagues and I have tried to search for ways to improve the housing market and community development within the framework of a mixed economy with its mingling of private and public decisions. We believe that the agents who determine the effectiveness of housing and community services—the investor, the producer, the consumer, the government, and the community—must understand their own conflicting demands and requirements as a basis for contributing to a better market system. The very nature of housing and community development makes it almost inevitable that both the products and the mechanism of the market should come under criticism. Unlike most other goods, housing is also a social commodity. As such, it is overlaid with attributes that blur the lines between supply and demand, need and preference.

In sponsoring the Series, the ACTION Board of Directors hoped to encourage the widening of the choices available to the American people for improved urban living through a larger supply of housing, of better quality and at lower cost. At the least, this means the realization of the following objectives:

1. The elimination of slums that cannot be economically rehabilitated

2. The improvement of properties that can be economically rehabilitated

3. The preservation of currently sound housing and neighborhoods by slowing down their rates of obsolescence

4. The provision of new housing on both cleared and vacant land in sufficient quantity and of satisfactory quality to meet requirements of the large urban growth expected in the years ahead

5. The accomplishment of the above objectives with a high level of community services and in such a manner that all income, racial, and other groups in the population will be served

6. The effective distribution and planning of urban functions in order to correct the costly imbalances which now exist among them both within the central city and between it and its surrounding metropolitan area

The expert and the student in the United States and abroad should find this study a useful addition to the literature on housing and community development, but it is also a purpose of this book, and the Series as a whole, to inform and stimulate the growing body of influential businessmen, professionals, and citizen leaders whose opinions on many facets of urban life are having a profound effect upon policy and action for housing and community development.

Despite its close ties to the other seven books in the Series and to the sponsorship by ACTION, this book is a product of its authors, the selection and interpretation of findings being our own. My close involvement with ACTION—I have been at various times research director, executive director, vice president, board and executive committee member—in no way makes ACTION's Board of Directors responsible for the conclusions Barbara Terrett, William Wheaton, and I have reached. To say that our findings and views do not necessarily reflect the attitude of ACTION or of its Board of Directors is also to underline the Board's intention that the Series should provide fresh points of view on some of the most complex and controversial problems of housing and urban development in America.

Because of my long association with ACTION, this book owes a special debt to the attention and criticism of Fred Kramer, president of ACTION and former chairman of its research committee; Andrew Heiskell, first chairman of ACTION's Board of Directors; Joseph W. Lund, chairman, *ad hoc* Committee on the Investor; Roy W. Johnson, chairman, *ad hoc* Committee on the Producer; Ben Fischer, chairman, *ad hoc* Committee on the Consumer; Philip L. Graham, chairman, *ad hoc* Committee on the Government; and Guy T. O. Hollyday, chairman, *ad hoc* Committee on the Community. The members of these *ad hoc* committees served with patience and wisdom; they are named in volumes on which they gave specific advice. Clifford J. Backstrand, Thomas P. Coogan, Joseph A. Grazier, Philip M. Klutznick, Robert B. Mitchell, James C. Rouse, Robert C. Weaver, James E. Lash, ACTION's executive vice president, and the other members of the research committee of ACTION's Board of Directors were superb critics and stimulators. Henry T. Heald and the late Emanuel M. Spiegel were on the research committee at the time this Series was begun, and aided in initial formulations.

This book owes most to the research and writing of the other authors in the Series. The authors of this book drew heavily on their findings. Two of the authors in the Series, Edward C.

Banfield and Louis Winnick, helped in the revision of three chapters, and my coauthors and I thank them. Through Louis Winnick we also had access to the pioneer work in which he collaborated with Leo Grebler and on which we drew for early chapters.

Documentation of the references appears in the section of the book on sources. Because the Housing Act of 1961 was adopted while this book was already in press, we have added a legislative note, briefly describing the main provisions of the Act which are relevant to the discussion in this book.

Among many other persons whose knowledge and experience I called on frequently for the Series were Neil J. Hardy, now Commissioner of the Federal Housing Administration, and Arthur S. Goldman of *House and Home* magazine. Helen Kistin assisted in the early research for three chapters of this book. Professor William Alonso prepared initial drafts of the charts. Leonard Silk helped greatly by editorial suggestions and substantive questions. Barbara Terrett shared with me the responsibility for directing and editing the Series. In addition to his collaboration on this book, Professor William L. C. Wheaton advised on other books in the Series.

Martin Meyerson

Contents

THE SETTING

Chapter 1

HOUSING AND COMMUNITY DEVELOPMENT

The people of the United States have more housing space per person and better equipped housing than do the people of other countries. But imbalances in the market combine with contradictory public goals for urban development to make the housing of many people a less satisfying product than it can be. This book explores principal problems and potentialities of housing as they affect people and cities.

Cities continue to stir excitement and ambition and to exert their magnetism. Metropolitan areas are growing in numbers and in size; more and more people are finding that the kinds of work they can get, and the kinds of lives they can lead, in or close to the cities, are far more attractive to them than life in the small towns and on the farms.

The metropolis is an elaborate mix of people, uses of land, levels of income, economic activities, social values, private and public decisions. The new and the old, the rich and the poor, the homogeneous and the heterogeneous meet and coexist here with skills, activities, and values that are specialized and general, complementary and competitive. Communities grow and change; people and establishments shift their locations and others fill their vacated places; some activities come into being and others are abandoned. During all the changes and shifts, the burgeonings and shrinkings, people in cities are fed, housed, educated, employed, transported, clothed, amused, and protected from crime and fire, sometimes well, other times less well. Crises in production, employment, or social organization may jolt the intricate interplay of business, industry, recreation, cul-

3

ture, services, education, and residence, causing readjustments of the moving equilibrium that is the community.

The metropolis may be thought of as a stage on which many dramas are being played simultaneously: the drama of families, of business competitors, of political rivals, of artistic and literary movements, of conflicts between criminals and the protectors of the community. These and many more go on together, each cast of characters extemporizing its lines, the players all trying to occupy the center of the stage to make their roles the leading ones, while the stage sets and properties of each get in the way of the others. To the observer, the spectacle is a wild confusion; but if the stage is watched long enough, elements of order appear. One drama becomes distinguishable from another and thus each becomes to some degree intelligible.

Housing and community development are two such dramas played largely in the metropolitan setting. They influence each other, conflict with each other, adjust themselves to each other, limit and constrain each other, and, in the end, bespeak each other.

Everyone has a stake in housing: some only as consumers and taxpayers; others as builders, building laborers, mortgage lenders, landlords, building materials and equipment suppliers, building code and zoning officials, Federal appraisers, housing inspectors, public officials responsible for schools, highways, public works, fire and police, and, finally, as businessmen—merchants and industrialists. Sometimes their interests converge and sometimes they diverge.

Housing is intimately related to every community problem. Because it is the major source of revenue for local governments, housing is also the major reason for expenditures by them. It is the pivot on which turn the location and character of community facilities and services (streets and street lighting, sewers and water lines, schools and libraries, parks and recreational places, police and fire protection), all of them expensive to install, expensive to maintain, and expensive to change. When the character of the supply and demand for housing forces shifts in land use, the community must adjust this complex of services and facilities to different levels of use. A huge wave of families pouring into tract houses in the suburbs, for example, may empty school rooms in the central city, while the raw, new suburbs often fail to provide a single-shift school. Transit lines may flounder for lack of customers. Normal tax sources may suddenly dwindle.

Changes in density patterns are a familiar accompaniment of social changes. Obviously it makes a great deal of difference whether people cluster together in town houses, row houses, walk-up apartments, or elevator buildings, or spread out in single-family and perhaps single-storied dwellings. Density patterns directly affect the circulation system of the community and the cost and character of its facilities. Now that motorcars and shorter work days have freed them from the necessity of living close to their work or close to mass transportation lines, many Americans are choosing to live in the less crowded suburbs. Many other Americans, usually low-income Negroes and Puerto Ricans with a narrow latitude for choice, are converting the older residential areas to more intensive use. Where this has happened, the cities have been caught in a squeeze: at the very time that assessed values and tax revenues have fallen, the increased density of population has added to the costs for schools and other community facilities.

When old areas are rebuilt and renewed, there is always a financial and social problem. It is expensive to buy land and buildings, and then tear down the buildings in order to make the land usable again. This means that land costs will be high, and accordingly there will be pressure to rebuild at higher densities whether or not doing so will provide housing most suitable to family living.

The housing market is subject to limitations of many kinds which hedge the builder, the community, and the consumer. The consumer cannot buy housing apart from a package of related goods and services: with the house go schools, churches, shops, visual environment, places to play, neighbors, status attributes, a municipal administration, a journey to work (perhaps with it a commitment to a particular form of transportation), and even an orientation toward cultural, social, and commercial activities—in short, a way of life.

The consumer may wish to spend a relatively large share of

his income for some items in this package and a relatively small share for others. He must buy the package as a whole, however, and as a rule all items in it are correlated to one general standard of taste. If he desires both a new single-family house and a central-city location, for example, he will undoubtedly have to relinquish one or the other want, unless he is very rich.

The consumer finds that the community and its local government circumscribe his housing choices in other ways. Community tax rates, assessment practices and zoning controls, building codes, housing codes, and their enforcement, all figure into the tally of local housing costs and kinds. Houses almost identical in size and quality may vary as much as $1,500 in cost between adjacent localities because one jurisdiction has a more rigid set of building and related codes than the other. Low-income families, especially Negroes, are often confined to central-city locations because suburban municipalities have adopted building regulations and zoning ordinances requiring high-cost houses.

If the city constrains the consumer in certain ways, so does the consumer constrain the city. The condition of the city largely depends upon how much of his income the consumer (viewed now in the aggregate) is willing to spend for the goods and services the community provides and for the housing which looms so large in its fabric. If consumers do not choose to spend enough for initial residential construction and subsequent maintenance and rehabilitation, neighborhoods will rapidly deteriorate to slums. Moreover, the community depends in the long run upon the consumer's tastes. Many houses that today are entirely acceptable by the prevailing standards will shortly become slums for no other reason than shifts in taste. In a country like ours, where people are moving up the economic and social ladders at a lively rate, cultural obsolescence may be as important as physical obsolescence: structures cease to be fashionable, or even acceptable, long before they actually wear out.

The movement of our fathers and grandfathers from the country to the city constituted a great revolution in American living. But, even as this movement continues, the parallel movement to the outskirts of the metropolitan areas now constitutes a greater trend. Today's transition is from corner groceries to suburban supermarkets, from central department stores to their outlying branches, from acquaintance with diversified populations to associations that are mostly with persons from one's own income level. All of this is unprecedented, and in making these transitions Americans are creating new customs, laws, patterns of economic behavior, and new social outlooks.

We cannot readily predict future patterns of housing and community development. We know that many forces are involved. But which are the fundamental ones? Even if we know what questions are most relevant (which is by no means certain), we cannot know the precise answers. Where will industries locate? Where will people settle? What will be the birth rate? Will the population be more or less mobile? What will be the average family income? How much of their incomes will families spend for housing? How much leisure will people have, and how will they use it? Will privacy be more or less important than it is now? Will people have decided tastes for or against one or another form of transportation, or for or against transportation in general? Will antagonisms of class and race be greater or less? And will middle-class ways be diffused more or less quickly than at present? How much of the national income will be spent for public, as against private, activities? How much investment will be encouraged in urban areas by government? By business? How much will the consumer be willing to pay in taxes for community facilities and services?

Such questions overlap, of course. Where people settle will be determined in part by where industry settles. Industrial location will be determined in part by where people live. And both in turn will be determined by national income, by the activities of government, and by many other factors. Whether the principal metropolitan areas will be more or less crowded than at present will depend upon the kinds of jobs and other opportunities and satisfactions that may be available in smaller places and upon the kind of transportation, communication, and distribution facilities that connect the small places with the large.

Industry, it seems likely, will in the future be less closely tied to sources of power. Automatic factories and automatic warehouses will make it less dependent also upon concentrations of labor. Decentralization is more technologically feasible than ever before. But decentralization, of course, even if possible, need not occur. If it takes place, it will not be perfectly even: some regions will always have more industry than others. Perhaps the location of raw materials will be decisive. Now that we depend more upon foreign sources for raw materials, greater concentrations of industry may occur along the coasts. Perhaps population shifts will be decisive. If more people choose to live in areas of equable climate or easy access to recreation, industry and commerce may follow to be close to consumer markets or even to managerial talents.

One thing, however, is predictable. Patterns of community growth and development will be different in the future. The result will have deep significance for every aspect of community life, and certainly for the way America will be housed.

Housing Markets—Perfect and Imperfect

The perfect competitive market system is a model for the distribution of society's goods. In its ideal operations, the choices and decisions of consumers interact with those of producers and investors to reach an ultimate satisfaction of most, if not all, of the aims of those who meet and bargain in the market place. In theory, each competitor in the market has perfect (or near perfect) knowledge of opportunities and the actions of others, and acts in his own self-interest. In a sensitive, reciprocal relationship, the investor, the producer, and the informed consumer are responsive to each other's actions, and the whole system of supply and demand is ordered by self-adjusting individual decisions—as though guided by an invisible hand—without the necessity for any central direction.

But a perfect market system does not exist; the best inevitably has some shortcomings. The satisfaction of one consumer usually depends on the behavior of other consumers. By letting each consumer judge his own welfare, the welfare of some other consumers may be impaired. For example, one consumer may choose to run a business in a residential district and in so doing will detract by noise and smell and traffic or other annoyances from the satisfactions of his neighbors.

Today's market for housing and for other commodities is interlarded with governmental sanctions and incentives. Adam Smith presupposed little governmental intervention in his ideal market, although the market had never been free of it. So far as housing is concerned, the reality of the market is a poor approximation of the logical construct. There are many special circumstances which prevent the market from working competitively with respect to housing.

For one thing, housing has characteristics which prevent it from moving easily in trade. It is rooted to the ground. It is durable, expensive, and complex. And it is only semi-industrialized, and it is poorly mechanized. The successes of many industries in lowering costs by technological and organizational improvements have not been equaled by the housing industry. The technology of housing is still primitive. So is its organization. Nor is there effective communication between the producer and the consumer of housing. Housing also has social significance of a special kind. In our values as well as in our vernacular, the house is the home. The well-being of the society is not at stake with respect to cigarettes or even automobiles, but it is at stake—perhaps crucially—with respect to the amount and character of the housing supply. If millions of people live in unsuitable housing, or if millions are prevented by race from living where they choose, the quality of our national life will be affected.

Another special characteristic of housing as a commodity is that it is not used up and discarded. Instead, as it becomes less desirable through aging, deterioration, or change in the neighborhood, it is passed on to a lower-income user. Because it is handed down in this way and over many years, there is not as big a regular demand for new construction as there would be if housing were taken off the market altogether. Nor are consumers incited by the production each year of a vast number of "new models" to replace their old houses with new ones as they are stimulated to replace their old automobiles.

If this "filtering down" process worked gradually and smoothly in housing, accompanied by faster cultural obsolescence of structures, there would be constant demand for new houses at the top of the demand pyramid. But it does not work this way. The appeal of some dwellings does not decrease with age, and the prices of aging houses do not always decline. Having large investments in their houses and anticipating continuous price increases, many owners will not accept losses of even normal depreciation. Car owners do not expect to get anything like the original price of their cars after they have driven them for a year. Homeowners, however, expect to sell their houses for more than they paid for them, even though they may have lived in them for many years. Furthermore, families develop neighborhood ties, to friends, churches, schools, which they are reluctant or unwilling to disrupt by moving to a new home.

Even if the filtering down process did function without impediments, it could not work adequately if new construction were confined to high-income families for the simple reason that the income pyramid is so narrow at the top compared with its middle and base. Filtering down could be made to work only if the market for new construction were extended to many groups now unable to enter that market by virtue of income or race, and if a reasonable number of exhausted units were entirely removed from the supply.

Thus demand and supply do not readily come together in the classic sense of reaching a compromise of mutual satisfactions. Even in the best years of housing construction, only 3 per cent of the housing stock is newly built. The result is that much of the old and exhausted stock continues to be used and often doubly used through overcrowding.

Since World War II, however, our accomplishments in housing have been considerable. If a substantial minority is dissatisfied enough so that government intervention in housing is still a constant political issue here as in most of the world, a majority of our people are probably fairly well content with their housing.

Some of the defects in the housing market cannot be changed. Houses today are complicated structures tied to particular plots of land in particular localities. Thus there can readily be scarcities in some localities when there are surpluses in others.

Housing remains relatively expensive. No other single consumer good is as costly. The purchase of a house is normally the biggest expenditure in the lifetime of a household, and the monthly cost of a house is for most middle- and low-income families the biggest item in the budget after food. This is not likely to change.

Few families can buy a house with cash. Few builders have the working capital they need. The housing industry and the consumer are therefore both peculiarly dependent upon credit, and the cost of financing is an important part of the price of a house. As for the rental market, relatively few investors are willing to put their money into a housing investment that is so slowly amortized, and so subject to the vagaries and uncertainties of taxation, maintenance, operation, and the business cycle.

The prospect for technological improvement in housing is better than that for removing the market complexities of a bulky, durable, immobile, and expensive commodity. Housing has not, on the whole, shared in the general technological advance; it has been organized on too small a scale to secure economies of purchasing, off-site assembly, mechanized site preparation, research in design and materials, and market analysis and merchandising. Thirty years ago the typical builder built only one house a year. Today about half the houses are built by organizations that build more than fifty houses a year. The techniques of mass production and marketing have now moved beyond the prototype stage, although it is still a rare builder who innovates, simplifies, standardizes, or improves technology at rates corresponding to those of other industries. Some large builders and prefabricators have made considerable reductions in construction time and in cost by using standardized elements and component units. Large-scale builders have ironed out the seasonal irregularities in building activity by doing assembly work during bad weather, and they have avoided the restrictive practices of subcontractors, dealers, labor unions, and manufacturers by providing a high level of demand, something the scale of their operations makes possible. Although mechanization has not yet changed the basic nature of the housing industry, the directions it will take in the future have already been laid down.

The merchandizing of housing can also be improved. Small businessmen tied to particular localities cannot sell housing the way big businessmen sell soup and soap, aspirin and automobiles. The housing industry has not, as have other industries, systematically studied the tastes of its market. It has been slow to engage in national advertising and marketing. Consumers are spending proportionately less income on their dwellings and more on washing machines, air conditioners, television sets, and other things to put inside of houses. The industry's inability to conduct consumer research has slowed up technological advance and the bringing together of techniques and materials in new ways that might appeal to the many and diverse consuming publics.

If the industry gets and uses the information it needs about housing design and consumer tastes, and if it adopts effective marketing methods, its rewards should be great. Consumer spending nowadays is so large that even a small increase in the share that goes for housing would have dramatic results. If, at the 1960 level of consumer spending, consumers devoted an additional 1 per cent of their income to housing, the result would be an increase of about $3 billion in annual housing demand, or a tenth of present housing expenditures.

Of course the market will not be made perfect for housing any more than for other commodities. But improvements in technology and in merchandising methods are a present possibility, and there is much promise in new credit aids and fiscal policies, and new patterns of consumer expenditure.

Public Intervention in the Housing Market

If the housing market has not worked as it should, the reason is not lack of interest or criticism by participants and observers or lack of intervention by public bodies. Housing has long been bombarded with reforms proposed from both right and left. The analyses that have been made of its problems have rarely produced agreement on solutions.

Every group of would-be reformers has had some fixed ideas. These ideas have survived and flourished although the conditions which gave rise to them have in many instances ceased to exist. There is, accordingly, an oversupply of obsolete ideas about housing.

One school of thought particularly popular in depressions and recessions maintains that housing should be employed essentially for purposes of offsetting swings in the business cycle—that is, housing should be a "countercyclical" industry. When general business is expanding, according to this view, and inflationary pressures develop within the economy, housing construction should be contracted to make way for other expanding industries; but when general business is sluggish, housing should be expanded, through liberal money and credit policies, to sustain income and employment and to generate economic recovery. Opponents of this position contend that continuous and wide swings in housing construction are responsible for inefficiency, high costs, and spasmodic and inadequate progress in raising housing standards. Many builders complain that it is unfair to single out one industry for this countercyclical role. And some economists consider that a policy aimed at achieving a stable and rising level of housing construction would contribute more to general economic stability than would a policy intended to make housing the balance wheel of the economy.

Another widely held idea is that people should be encouraged by public policy to buy rather than to rent houses. Public programs, particularly those of the Federal Housing Administration, have in fact so greatly favored the building of houses for sale that many consumers who would prefer to rent are virtually forced to buy because of the shortage or low quality of rental accommodations. Some people even advocate making homeowners of the people near the bottom of the income pyramid. Believing that the transition of the United States to a country of homeowners is the most significant of the social revolutions which has taken place in this generation, they would sell public housing units as cooperatives to low-income families. Or they would have public authorities buy and improve used housing for a subsidized resale to persons who would otherwise be tenants in public projects.

Still another idea is to eliminate risk for the producer of housing in much the same way that it has been eliminated for the commercial farmer. This, it is argued, will bring about the introduction into the housing industry, as it has into agriculture, of capital-intensive, labor-saving devices and, in general, of technological advance. With guaranteed profits, easy credit, a kind of "crop" insurance, and technical assistance in the form of publicly supported materials testing and market analyses, the builder can, according to this theory, offer a superior product at the present price or at a price not much higher.

Others point out that our policies to date may have only subsidized marginal producers who might have gone out of business. Perhaps it is impossible to increase the competence of the producer while at the same time relieving him of the spurs of risk and competition. What is needed, this reasoning goes, is a policy that helps the consumer more directly; for example, a yardstick of the TVA type by which the government would build houses, if necessary at uneconomic rentals, wherever the private market failed to provide standard quarters.

The Changing Aims of Housing Policy

A changing economy has changed the concerns of housing policy. In the depression years public housing programs were developed for the poor. With prosperity, public concern about the poor has diminished. Public housing serves increasingly only the relocation needs of the households which are being displaced by public works and by slum clearance. People who once were preoccupied with the effects of slums on the physical well-being of the slum dwellers—with slums as a factor in the spread of tuberculosis, for example—now have become more concerned with the effects of slum clearance on the morale and attitudes of those torn from social institutions and neighborhoods to which they were attached.

Similarly, in the last generation, concern for the housing of foreign immigrant groups has turned into concern for the Negro and other minorities, the newest wave of urban immigrants. Whether these newcomers to the city will follow the route of their predecessors, moving out of the tenements and shacktowns as their incomes rise, is a question which policy-minded people must somehow answer. It may be that the mark of color makes these minority groups a special case and that prejudice will follow them however high they climb on the economic ladder. If so, it seems probable that public policy will be used increasingly to restrain or reverse the forces of prejudice.

What policy intends is one thing; what it actually accomplishes is often something else. Effects that were entirely unanticipated by the policy makers frequently prove eventually to be more important than others which *were* intended.

The postwar government-subsidized slum clearance and renewal programs, for example, were intended primarily to provide new housing in the central cities so that their middle-income residents would not all be lured to the suburbs. But slum clearance has in fact done something different. A considerable part of redevelopment has gone to industrial, commercial, institutional, or public uses. And most of the housing that has been built is at a scale too luxurious for most middle-income pocketbooks. Cities need industrial and commercial revitalization and luxury housing, too. But it was not the intention of those who supported the housing renewal acts of 1949 and 1954 to serve the middle-income housing market so slowly.

It is easy to find other instances in which policies and programs have produced effects different from what was intended. The advocates of public housing did not mean to foster racial ghettos in public projects. Nor did people who hauled slum landlords into housing courts intend to force up the price of housing to the lowest income groups. Those who drew up the first zoning codes had no notion that they were creating an instrument by which segregation along income lines would be enforced in residential communities. The framers of building codes expected to protect the community and the consumer, but they did not intend to imprison the building industry in a legal vise or to protect particular building products or construction methods. Congress wanted to stimulate home building in the Depression through the Federal Housing Administration; there is no indication that it intended to create row after row of suburban boxes in the name of insured mortgages.

Not only have some housing programs produced effects contrary to what was intended, but some have canceled out or been canceled by another public program. In the next few years, for example, the Federal highway program will probably displace more people from slum (and non-slum) areas than will the housing program, but little was done to coordinate the two before the inauguration of the Kennedy administration. It appears that public demolition of housing for low-income families has considerably exceeded provision of housing for such families in recent years. All urban renewal projects to date have had but little effect in attracting families to remain in the city, compared with the massive migrations to suburban areas engendered by government mortgage insurance.

The Central Issues

Despite these anomalies and confusions, few people want to get government out of the housing market entirely. The trend in housing, as in everything else, is in the other direction. And there is no reason to suppose that it will change. The experience of all modern industrialized societies demonstrates that some sort of new mix of the responsibilities and functions of government, of economic organizations, and of individuals is inevitable. The practical problem is to find the right place for government in the complex of activity called "housing." In the chapters that follow, the place of housing in the national economy is examined, and consideration is given to the magnitudes of demand and supply of housing and to the postures of the major actors on the housing scene: the investor, the producer, the consumer, the Federal government, and the local community and its citizen leaders. The question to be answered is: What can *each* do to improve the quality and quantity of housing?

This book presupposes that the answers rest upon five general assumptions, the appropriateness and significance of which are developed at length. The first is that there exist neglected opportunities for profitable enterprise in housing. The second is that the time is ripe for the industrialization of housing—that is, for its heavier capitalization, for increases in labor productivity, and for decreases in costs. The third is that the consumer will respond to improvements in housing by spending more of his income for it. The fourth is that the Federal government can play its most effective role by fostering competition on the part of producers and investors, by widening the range of effective choice open to consumers, and by experimenting with and testing its own policies in housing and community development. The fifth is that the impulse for change and the vitality to bring change about do exist in the mind and actions of public and private leaders of the country and of its urban communities.

Throughout this book, the aim is to view housing and the American city as interlocking parts of the same national growth pattern and in doing so to clarify their relationships and pinpoint impediments to the achievement of higher goals for both. Along with this aim goes the further one of specifying ways and means to lubricate the market system for housing and community development. Sole hope must not rest in that twentieth century *deus ex machina*, more and more Federal funds. But neither should government abandon its responsibilities for the disfranchised consumers of housing. What is required is a better mix of private enterprise and governmental effort brought about by a reappraisal of governmental policies and private practices to spur the quantity and improve the quality of housing. The complexities of the situation and the difficulties that stand in the way of improvement are great indeed, but this book views them with pragmatism and optimism.

There is no reason to doubt that men of understanding, will, and energy can create more satisfying patterns of housing than we now imagine. In doing so, they will at the same time create vastly better communities. For, to revert to the image with which this chapter began, the way the housing drama is played most profoundly affects everything that is done on the vast stage that is the metropolis.

Chapter 2

HOUSING AND THE NATIONAL ECONOMY

Housing is of crucial importance to the national economy. Residential construction provides jobs for over a million on-site workers—and for nearly as many workers in supporting industries. Expenditures on residential building account for half of all construction outlays, and a third of total new private investment. Accumulated investments in housing constitute a third of our national wealth. Family expenditures on housing are second in size only to those for food.

Nonetheless, during the last half century, the housing industry has not maintained its proportional share of the national economic growth. Although the dollar amount of housing investments has risen, per capita expenditures for housing have declined from a fifth to an eighth of consumer expenditures, and the average value of homes, measured in stable dollars, has also declined. The decline in per capita expenditures reflects the more effective competition of other industries for the consumer dollar, and technical and geographic changes in home building.

The home-building industry has always been unstable: its booms are higher and its depressions lower than those of other industries. Fewer than 100,000 units were begun in 1933, contrasting with a peak of almost 1,400,000 in 1950. While housing construction has often led the economy up or down, it appears to accentuate economic cycles rather than precipitate them. Expenditures for maintenance, modernization, and operation of housing may compensate for wide fluctuations in new home production.

The next two decades will provide unparalleled opportuni-

ties for the housing industry. The population swell following World War II suggests a huge market for new homes in the 1960s and 1970s that may exceed two million a year. Rising real income, the increased number of aged able to afford separate accommodations, a growing number of young married couples and single persons, and a boost in large families should expand demand for both urban and suburban building, sales and rental housing, apartments and single-family houses.

If these opportunities are to be realized, however, the industry requires changes in scale, organization, management, and technology. Such changes are unlikely if the industry is manipulated by Federal credit policies to counter changes in the business cycle. A national policy of stabilizing residential construction and rehabilitation would also contribute to general economic stability.

As an industry, housing is of major importance to the national economy because of its sensitivity to and influence on the course of business cycles, and because of its relationship to national economic development. As the product of an industry, housing is a vital welfare good; and our concerns about the housing industry and the housing market focus on their failure to provide a standard of living compatible with an expanding economy, and with growing personal and national income and wealth.

The importance of housing in the economy can be measured in terms of employment, production, investment, or consumer expenditures.

Residential areas provide at least 50 per cent of the major source of local tax revenue, the property tax; and they are the largest single item of local capital investment. Nationally the value of residential land and buildings is well over twice the value of the country's 500 biggest manufacturing companies. Housing is almost the sole support of some industries. Two-thirds of all bricks, for example, go into housing.

In the peak postwar home-building year of 1950, according to the Bureau of Labor Statistics, 1,175,000 workers were employed on-site in new nonfarm residential construction alone. Off-site employment in the building materials and supply industries was nearly as great. A very large proportion of all private investments, whether in the form of equity or debt, goes into housing. New residential construction is half of all current new private investment in construction and a quarter to a third of total new private investment. Finally, in terms of family expenditures, and despite its decreasing share in their total, housing still remains second only to food in economic importance.

New homes generate demands for other types of construction and for other services, particularly roads, public utilities, and schools, three of the most important forms of nonresidential construction. School building lags several years behind residential building; but local roads and public utility services must be installed at the same time that new houses are built.

Residential building generates still other kinds of economic activity. Consumer durable equipment such as furnaces, hot-water heaters, dishwashers, washing machines, and air conditioners make up an increasing proportion of residential construction costs, and the production of consumer durables rises or falls with the volume of residential building. There is also a link between housing construction and the output of other consumer goods, such as home furnishings.

Fluctuations in Housebuilding

The output of housing is exceptionally vulnerable to economic fluctuations. Sudden changes in family income or income expectations will alter the demand for housing more drastically than comparable changes in the economy will affect long-term investments in other fields. For example, the Depression of the 1930s reduced the production of various manufactured goods by anywhere from 20 to 50 per cent, but it cut down the volume of housing construction by more than 80 per cent. The causes of the wide and violent fluctuations in the building and marketing of houses are complex. Housing is a capital good, but it is also a consumer product. Unlike factories or mines, which are developed by investors in anticipation of future nation-wide demand, housing is built in response to a fairly immediate and localized consumer demand.

The durability of housing also tends to accentuate cyclical fluctuations in residential construction. Because the supply of housing consists mainly of used homes, and new construction rarely amounts to more than 3 per cent of supply in any year, a 5 or 10 per cent decline in total demand, minor in other industries, can sharply reduce the demand for new houses. On the other hand a 10 per cent increase in total housing demand cannot be satisfied by a 300 per cent increase in production. In consequence, housing prices tend to rise faster than other prices in periods of rising income.

The demand for new housing can be postponed; this accentuates instability in the housing market. During periods of rising prices, families may seek to buy or build as soon as possible, even at prices slightly above current market levels. If buyers expect prices to increase substantially during the years ahead, as many did in the first few years following the close of World War II, they may decide to purchase at once even if it is necessary for them to pay a premium, since the debt they incur will be paid off in cheaper dollars in future years. This anticipation of price increases accelerates and increases demand on the upswing of the construction cycle. But if buyers expect price declines, home purchase may be deferred in anticipation of a lower price, thus accelerating a downswing in the construction cycle.

There are, however, other forces in the housing market that tend to soften the impact of cyclical influences. Housing markets are local in character, and the volume of building can vary widely in different metropolitan areas. Of course, in the depths of depression, such as that of 1929–1937, all areas suffer. But at other times some areas may experience a severe decline in residential construction while other areas enjoy a comparative boom. In recent years, the fast-growing cities of the South and West have had a far higher level of building activity than the older communities of the North and East. As long as cities continue to grow at a rapid rate, they are less vulnerable to sudden downturns in residential building.

Another corrective influence on the building cycle can arise from the expenditures made for additions to and alterations of existing dwellings. During the last half century, expenditures for additions and alterations amounted to an average of 11 per cent of expenditures for new residential construction, varying from boom period lows of 6 per cent to depression highs of 20 per cent. Recent statistics which include repairs indicate that total maintenance, alteration, and repair expenditures may be as much as 75 per cent of new construction volume, a stabilizing force. (Unfortunately, housing data suffer from errors and omissions in reporting the number of housing starts, the level of demolitions and other removals from the housing stock, and the expenditures for alterations and repairs.)

Fluctuations in new residential construction are shown in Chart 1. In the building boom following World War I, a peak was reached in 1925 when 937,000 new residential units were started. At the bottom of the Depression, in 1933, less than 100,000 new homes were put under construction. In the peak prewar year of 1941, residential construction climbed back to over 600,000 units. During the war, housing was cut back to a low of 139,000 in 1944. During the postwar building boom, residential starts reached a high of 1,352,000 new units in 1950. The wide variations are often described as "long building cycles." Since the Civil War these cycles have had their peaks in 1871, 1887, 1892, 1902, 1909, 1925, 1940, and 1950. Each has been succeeded by a trough in which building volume has dropped to low levels.

The cyclical pattern in residential building appears to accompany a similar pattern of prosperity and depression in the economy generally. However, residential building fluctuates far more widely; its peaks are higher and its depressions deeper than those of other industries. Some observers conclude that a decline in housebuilding, if not an important cause of the onset of business depressions, is certainly an important contributor to their severity.

A Shrinking Sector of the Economy

The cyclical swings in residential construction obscure secular changes which affect the present strength and future possibilities of the housing industry. Since the start of this century, a proportionately smaller part of the nation's resources has gone into residential building. Moreover, housing expenditures have declined in real terms, in relation to gross national product, capital investment, and consumer expenditures.

America's gross national product rose from an annual rate of $17.7 billion in 1900 to $503.2 billion in 1960. Investments in residential construction went from $800 million per year, during

Chart 1. New private nonfarm housing units started, 1889–1960, and gross national product, 1909–1960

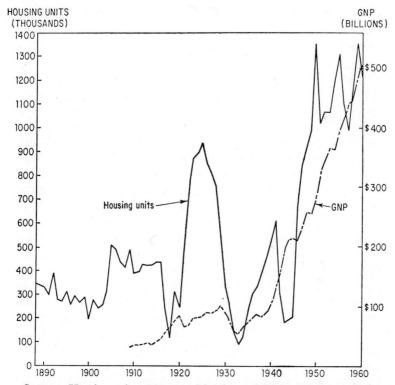

Sources: Housing units, 1889–1960: Housing and Home Finance Agency, *Housing Statistics*, March, 1961, table A-2, pp. 6–7. Gross National Product, 1929–1960: *Ibid.*, table A-30, p. 33; 1909–1928: J. F. Dewhurst, *America's Needs and Resources*, Twentieth Century Fund, 1955, appendix 4-2, p. 958.

the early years of this century, to a peak of $24.7 billion in 1959. When measured in constant dollars, the proportion of national income expended on housing actually declined. For every $100 invested in new capital assets about $30 went into residential real estate in the early 1890s, and only $25 in the 1920s and about $13 in 1950.

In current prices, total annual outlays for new nonfarm residential construction during the early postwar years (1946–1953) were more than double those in the 1920–1929 decade, but when dollar values are made constant it is apparent that there was almost no change. Since there was a sizable increase in the number of dwelling units built during the later period, there was a long-run decline in the real average expenditure per unit.

Again, when prices are held constant, the startling fact emerges that the real value per dwelling declined by 37 per cent from the start of the century to the 1946–1953 period, even though average construction expenditures per dwelling more than quadrupled during that period. Because the drop in real value, shown in Chart 2, was accompanied by a decline in the average size of the household, per capita real investment changed very little. At the end of 1955, in fact, the per capita value of the nonfarm housing inventory was 7 per cent less than at the beginning of the century.

The basic unit of demand for new housing is, of course, the household. A decline in the rate of population growth, in the rate of new household formation, and in the size of households thus becomes an important underlying factor in the long-run decline in the relative importance of housing. However, the absolute number of new families has increased by 7,700,000 or 18 per cent between 1950 and 1959 and the rate of new household formation has fallen off far less than the rate of total population growth. Moreover, the size of the housing stock has increased through conversions of existing units, as well as through new construction. Population changes and conversions do not, by themselves, explain the marked downtrend in real capital per new dwelling unit.

Part of the decline in real expenditures since the 1920s can be explained by construction changes. There has been a tremendous shift of residential building to the West and South and to rural nonfarm areas where, primarily for reasons of climate, the cost per unit tends to be smaller. Other forces that operate toward a reduction of real capital per unit include the historic decline in the average size of households, the trend toward lighter materials and construction, and, especially in the last fifteen years, the

Chart **2.** Average construction cost of private nonfarm housing units started, in current and 1929 prices, 1889–1960

Sources: Current and 1929 prices, 1889–1953: Grebler, Blank, and Winnick, *Capital Formation in Residential Real Estate*, Princeton Univ. Press, 1956, chart 12, p. 107, and table J-1, p. 426. Current prices, 1954–1960: Housing and Home Finance Agency, *Housing Statistics*, March, 1961, table A-3, p. 9.

building of a larger proportion of smaller and therefore less costly houses.

Similarly, there is no single clear-cut explanation for the decreasing place of housing in total consumer expenditures. As Chart 3 shows, average consumer expenditures for housing accounted for a decreasing proportion of total expenditures, from nearly one-fourth before World War I to a low of about 10 to 12 per cent right after World War II, depending on which series of figures are used. Since then the proportion has gone up but to nowhere near the earlier ratios. Part of the reason for the decline undoubtedly is the upward change in family income over the period: as incomes rise, proportionate expenditures for housing and food tend to decrease. Another part of the reason is the great increase in housing costs since the war compared with other consumer goods. Using 1947–1949 as a

Chart 3. Housing expenditures as a percentage of total personal consumption expenditures

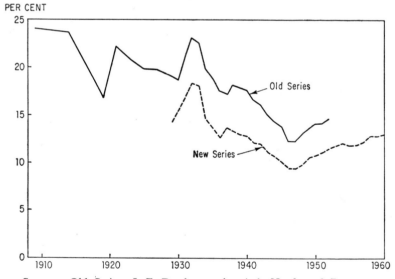

Sources: Old Series: J. F. Dewhurst, *America's Needs and Resources,* Twentieth Century Fund, 1955, table 33, pp. 102–103. New Series: Housing and Home Finance Agency, *Housing Statistics,* March, 1961, table A-42, p. 49.

base, residential construction costs have increased far more than all consumer prices; the construction cost index for dwelling units stood at an all-time high of 139.7 in 1960 compared with 126.5 for all consumer prices. Rising costs mean that consumers get less house in real terms for the same outlay. Between 1929 and 1955, the real purchasing power of consumers increased by more than 50 per cent. But, aside from some effect of mortgage credit changes, the purchasing power of the average family with respect to housing made no advance during the past generation and only a small gain over the past half century. In combination, those two facts help explain why consumers are reluctant to increase their proportionate expenditures for housing.

Future Trends

Although housing as an economic activity has failed to hold its own share of the American economy during the last three decades, several major forces suggest its steady growth in dollar output during the next two decades. Among them are the rapid population increase of the last twenty years, the rise in home-ownership in the years since World War II, and the trend toward suburban locations and densities. The first of these, population trends arising from war and postwar birth rates, implies a large absolute growth in building volume. The others may provide an opportunity for the housing industry to recapture some of its lost markets.

Beginning in 1940, the number of children born each year rose steadily—from 2.3 million in 1940 to 3.2 million in 1946, 3.7 million in 1951, and over 4 million in some of the years since 1954. This spectacular increase in the child population probably means that between 1960 and 1975 the number of young couples being married will mount steadily from about 1 million each year beginning in 1960 to over 2 million a year in the 1970s. Although the population reaching marriageable age is not the only factor that influences housing requirements, it is the most important one. It is now fixed for the next generation.

Beyond this period—by 1980—there may be more than 2 million new families entering the housing market each year. Estimates of the Bureau of the Census indicate that the population of the United States may reach 272 million by 1980, a growth of nearly 100 million in twenty-two years. In addition to the number of new families such growth implies, the expectation is that there will be more large families needing larger homes. At the other end of the scale, the extension of life expectancy combined with more ample social security and retirement systems will mean more older people in the population who will desire to maintain their own houses or apartments. The population over 65 years of age is expected to increase from about 16 million in 1960 to over 20 million by 1985.

Another factor in the future demand for housing is the growing number of one-person households or households not consisting of husband and wife; in 1960 about one-fourth of our non-farm dwellings were occupied by such households. By 1980 the rate of increase of these types of households will probably be more than double that of husband-and-wife families. Here again a change in population characteristics augurs a greatly enlarged demand for housing of certain types. These additions of single-person and aged families may continue to reduce average family size in keeping with the long-range trend even at a time when child population will be growing at unprecedented rates. More homes for larger families and more homes for smaller families, more for younger families and more for older couples, will probably raise the volume of residential building to unprecedented levels.

At the same time, some migration from rural and farm areas to cities will continue. Even conservative estimates suggest that virtually all of our population growth will continue to take place in urban areas. The growth of population in central cities is already being limited by overcrowding; in many of our older cities and in some new ones population is declining. Certainly there cannot be any great expansion of the central cities. But in the suburban areas population by 1975 may well increase by 75 per cent or more and in the rural outskirts of metropolitan areas by 150 per cent or more. Under these circumstances suburban areas will face investment requirements of unprecedented size for schools, highways, recreation and health, sewerage and water facilities.

The growth of population and household formation does not in itself assure that an equivalent effective demand for housing can be expected. The demand for new housing depends upon the level and distribution of income among families, consumer choices between housing and other expenditures, the cost, kind, and location of housing, and social and individual standards of housing adequacy.

Projections of national income and employment indicate that 86 million persons will be employed by 1975 and that per capita income will be 50 per cent higher than it was in the late 1950s. A shorter work week will be offset by higher productivity. Women will constitute a higher proportion of the labor force. If these projections are realized, the number of families with incomes over $7,500 will double and the number of families with incomes of less than $3,000 will decline. As a result, it is reasonable to expect a large increase in the effective demand for housing.

If the trend toward lower proportional expenditures for housing can be arrested or reversed, demand might exceed two million new or newly converted homes per year by the mid-1970s. The tendency for housing expenditures to decline as incomes rise may be offset by the shift in the population to higher proportions of white-collar workers who traditionally spend more, proportionally, for housing. To the extent that increased building efficiency can offset rising land and other costs, the building industry may obtain a larger share of an enormously enlarged national income.

The building industry will, at the same time, have to meet a heavy replacement demand, as our existing stock of housing grows old and deteriorates. Forecasts of housing requirements must include estimates of the number of substandard units to be replaced, the number of dwellings which deteriorate and drop out of use each year, the number which are demolished to make way for new land uses, and the number converted to nonresidential uses or lost through fire, storm, or other disaster. All of these are in addition to the estimated net total of new family formation. Defining housing requirements for the United States thus implies an estimate of the number of dwellings which are or will become so obsolete or deteriorated as to necessitate replacement or rehabilitation; and this estimate must be based on some assumption of a minimum standard of housing.

Estimates of future housing requirements made by both government and private agencies in the 1950–1960 decade vary from 1,200,000 to 1,800,000 additional new or converted units per year during the 1960s, and well over 2,000,000 units per year during the 1970s. These estimates assume that until new building and net new conversions (additional units created by conversion minus losses to other uses) exceed new family formation, the housing stock will continue to deteriorate at the rate of depreciation and other losses that occur annually. Since 1950 new building has met new family formation, but left little surplus to replace losses and deteriorating houses.

Can the gap between demand and the requirements of a rising standard of housing be closed in the years ahead? The answer depends largely upon the behavior of consumers, of the building industry, of the Federal government in its credit policies, and of communities working toward comprehensive programs of renewal and development. If the expected growth of the economy is achieved, millions of consumers will have larger incomes with which to pay for better housing; others will still require some public aid for housing improvement. Any sizable expansion of housebuilding should provide the building industry with an unprecedented opportunity to improve its efficiency and to reorganize for greater service. How well the opportunity is realized, however, rests on the extent to which the industry, government at all levels, and consumers can devise better means for organizing and expressing their common interests or for overcoming their conflicting ones.

Any dramatic increase in the effective demand for new and improved housing will depend as much on the determination of the leaders of America's urban and suburban communities to solve some of their municipal problems as it will on changes in the industry itself. The housing industry has a right to question whether by making heavy investments in new designs, building processes, research, and financing and merchandising methods, it can overcome the historical ambivalence of the consumer toward its product unless at the same time the urban environment is recast in a more livable, efficient, and satisfying form. Also, national public policy must be implemented more consistently if residential construction and rehabilitation are to go forward at a high and relatively stable rate and if the housing industry is to be encouraged to provide a better product at a lower cost.

Chapter 3

HOUSING AND THE MARKET

The most striking aspect of the housing market is the degree to which used houses outweigh new houses in importance. The vast stock of older houses constitutes 97 per cent of the supply in any year. Although the demands of new home buyers exert only a small influence on supply, they do dictate what will be available to most other later purchasers. New housing is largely limited to single-family, detached houses in suburban locations for white families of child-rearing age, middle income and popular tastes. In recent years relatively few new units have been built for rent, and few other special preferences have been served.

The stock of housing has been improved by the volume of new construction since the war, but in 1956 one of every five non-farm dwelling units was still dilapidated or lacking basic facilities, and at least 2 million others were located in slums, industrial areas, or neighborhoods with poor public services. Still others were overcrowded or obsolete, or they suffered from little maintenance. However, by 1960 further improvements reduced the number of dilapidated units in the United States to 3 million from 4.5 million in 1950.

The housing market functions crudely. The market for new houses is so narrow that the supply of older houses is chronically deficient: homes filter down so slowly that they are often dilapidated before they reach low-income families. The large supply of substandard dwellings cuts demand for better used dwellings. An improved market requires a higher volume of new construction for a broader cross section of the population, more rapid filtration of older homes, systematic demolition or rehabilitation of substandard residences, and improvement in standards of maintenance and repair.

For housing, as for other commodities, the market largely governs the quantity, quality, cost, and distribution of the product. The housing market is an elaborate interplay between investors and producers seeking profit on the one hand and consumers seeking satisfaction on the other. Presumably a well-functioning housing market guarantees the best allocation of resources and the best pattern of satisfaction of consumer wants. Its self-adjusting balance maintains an equilibrium between supply and demand.

The theory of a balanced market, however, is often at odds with the facts. For all that Americans are better housed, on the whole, than people in other countries, there are some segments of the market where the mechanism simply does not work. A closer look at the country's housing supply reveals imbalances in kind, cost, size, and location.

The Housing Inventory

The decade 1950–1960 was one of unprecedented building activity. During those ten years, the housing industry added over 12 million new units to the housing supply. Even so, too few houses were built or rehabilitated to meet the present and future requirements of the American people.

In 1950, the total stock consisted of 46 million dwelling units, most of which—39 million—constituted the nonfarm housing supply. Cities, towns, and villages in 1950 accounted for 30 million of the 39 million nonfarm homes. The remaining nine million dwellings were located in rural areas, including the outskirts of cities, but not on properties used for agriculture. At least a fifth of the total population lived in these rural nonfarm dwellings and were employed in urban rather than farm occupations. It is in this rural nonfarm fringe and the suburbs that most new homes have been added between 1950 and 1960.

By 1960, the total stock of housing units—the 1960 census definition of housing unit was slightly different from the 1950 definition of dwelling unit—reached 58 million. Of these about 10 per cent were vacant. Of the vacant units, about one-third were summer or other seasonal residences; the remainder of the vacancies were in year-round units. The proportion of units available for rent or sale increased from 1.6 per cent in April, 1950, to 3.5 per cent in the last quarter of 1960.

At the end of World War II—for the first time in the period of industrialization and urbanization beginning in 1890—the number of owners exceeded the number of renters. There were 8 million more homeowners in 1950 than in 1940, an increase of 55 per cent. In contrast, the number of renters declined slightly.

From 1950 to 1960 the number of homeowners increased from 23.6 million to 32.8 million (62 per cent of housing units). In the same period, although the proportion of renters declined from 45 per cent to 38 per cent, their absolute number increased

Chart 4. Private nonfarm dwelling units started, by type of structure, 1920–1960

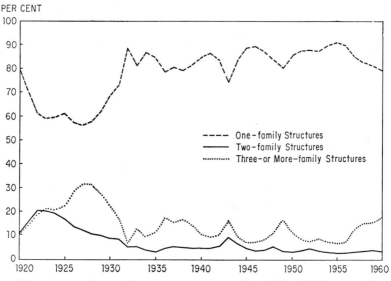

Note: 1959 and 1960 data represent a new series which includes starts in Alaska and Hawaii, among other changes.

Sources: 1920–1952: Grebler, Blank, and Winnick, *Capital Formation in Residential Real Estate*, Princeton Univ. Press, 1956, chart 4, p. 44, and table B-2, pp. 333–334. 1953–1960: Computed from Housing and Home Finance Agency, *Housing Statistics*, March, 1961, table A-9, p. 16.

slightly from 19.3 million to 20.2 million. The increase in home-ownership reflects rapid population growth, larger family incomes, and continued availability of long-term mortgage money. Also, with greater prosperity, the proportion of young (age 25 to 34) homeowners increased by 80 per cent from 1949 to 1959.

Until about 1930, structures with two or more dwelling units represented a high proportion of all new residential construction and accounted for 30 to 44 per cent of total nonfarm construction during the building boom of the 1920s. Beginning in the 1930s, however, the proportions began to alter: 227,000 new one-family houses were under construction in 1930, 485,000 in 1940, and over a million in the peak postwar building year of 1950.

A large proportion of the new dwellings were built with two or more units prior to 1930 because of the intensive growth of the central cities and their resulting high densities. After 1930, with the diminishing availability of land in central cities for new residential growth and the favorable circumstances of credit for home buyers, the bulk of new building shifted to suburban single-family houses. Indeed, only twice since 1940 (in 1943 and 1960) have single-family structures made up less than 80 per cent of the new dwelling units started in any year.

Chart 5. Percentage distribution of all dwelling units by type of structure, 1956

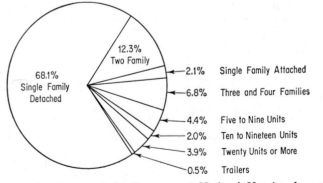

Source: U.S. Bureau of the Census, *1956 National Housing Inventory*, vol. III, part 1, 1959, table 1, p. 15.

The two-family structure, typical of an earlier period, now makes up only 5 per cent or less of all new starts. In 1950 only 45,000 two-family houses and in 1960 only 49,000 were added to the housing supply. Chart 4 shows the percentage of nonfarm residential starts according to type since 1920. Chart 5 shows the percentage of all dwelling units by type in 1956.

Condition and Equipment

It is possible for older residences to be kept in such good condition and to be so modernized and re-equipped, that they compare favorably with new ones. In fact, however, older homes are rarely well maintained unless location and design combine to justify high annual expenditures. Most of the housing stock deteriorates and becomes obsolete. The age of all dwelling units in 1956 is shown in Chart 6.

According to the preliminary reports of the 1960 Census of Housing, American housing facilities improved substantially since 1950. Occupied housing units which were not dilapidated and which contained all plumbing facilities constituted only 64 per cent of all occupied units in 1950 but 83 per cent in 1960. The number of these sound units increased from 27.7 million to 44.2 million in these ten years. In the period the number of dilapidated units was reduced from 4.5 million units to 3 million.

Owner-occupied houses improved most. In 1960 close to 90 per cent of owner-occupied houses were not dilapidated and had all plumbing facilities, compared with about 70 per cent in 1950. Over 75 per cent of renter-occupied units in 1960 were

Chart 6. Age of all dwelling units, 1956 percentage distribution

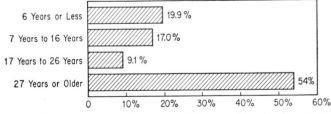

Source: U.S. Bureau of the Census, *1956 National Housing Inventory*, vol. III, part 1, 1959, table 1, p. 15.

not dilapidated and contained private toilets, baths, and hot water. In 1950 only 59 per cent reached that level of quality.

The number of occupied units that were dilapidated or lacked some or all plumbing facilities was reduced in the decade by about 40 per cent to 8.8 million in 1960. The distribution of these deficient units was uneven. Thus, while renters constituted about 38 per cent of the households in 1960, they occupied more than half of the deficient units. Similarly, the South, which had about 30 per cent of the occupied units in 1960, had about half of the housing which was dilapidated or lacked plumbing facilities. Also, among Negroes and other nonwhites, one-half of the renters and one-third of the owners lived in units that were substandard in 1960. (In the total population, one-fourth of the renters and one-ninth of the owners lived in substandard units.) Despite the significant improvement in housing, many Americans continue to live in deficient units in urban and metropolitan areas and elsewhere.

Physical substandardness is more evident in the rural nonfarm than in the urban areas. Actually in 1950 only 15 per cent of urban houses had plumbing deficiencies as against about 42 per cent of rural nonfarm houses. (The equivalent 1960 figures were not available when this book went to press.) Moreover, only 2 per cent of urban dwelling units lacked running water, but 22 per cent of rural nonfarm homes were deficient in this respect. So far as they can be measured, conditions in the areas that are approaching urbanization are worse than conditions in the cities.

Within the standard metropolitan areas of the country, one and one-half million units existing in 1950 were significantly improved in quality by 1956. In the same period, three-quarters of a million units were downgraded. Half of the upgraded units were in the central cities as against the suburbs, but most of the downgraded units were in the central cities.

Value and Rent

The median value for owner-occupied nonfarm dwellings in 1950 was $7,400 but by 1956 had reached $11,400. One-third of the owned units in 1950 were higher-priced properties worth

$10,000 or more. Another third were worth $6,000 to $10,000. The remainder were worth less than $6,000. Of these, 21 per cent had a value of less than $4,000. By 1956, the $10,000 and over category covered 59 per cent of the owner-occupied nonfarm dwelling units. Twenty-two per cent were in the $6,000 to $10,000 class and the remainder, under $6,000. The under $4,000 class had decreased from 21 per cent to 10 per cent. By January, 1959, the total market value of owner-occupied nonfarm houses was estimated at $372 billion, an increase from $183 billion in 1949.

For renter-occupied nonfarm dwelling units, the median gross monthly rent including utilities in 1950 was $42 per month. By 1956, the median rent had reached $60 per month. In this period, the units renting at $100 a month and over increased from less than 3 per cent to about 10 per cent. Those renting at $40 and under decreased from 44 per cent to 19.5 per cent. These comparisons between 1950 and 1956 values and rents are shown in Chart 7.

Chart 7. Percentage distribution of nonfarm dwelling units by value and gross monthly rent, 1950 and 1956

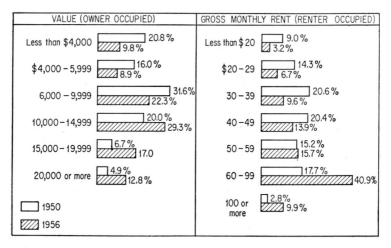

Source: U.S. Bureau of the Census, *1956 National Housing Inventory,* vol. III, part 1, 1959, table 3, pp. 20–21.

The price distribution of the housing stock reflects the fact that millions of families can afford only very modestly priced dwellings. Several millions are inhabiting dwellings valued or rented at prices so low as to suggest that they must have been substandard when created, or have suffered from lack of adequate maintenance and repair for many years. This is particularly true of the rental stock, where very low rentals manifestly cannot produce any appreciable yield to the owner and also taxes, operating costs, and maintenance and repair costs. Probably it is the last which is the first to be sacrificed.

Deteriorated Areas

Physical condition and kind of equipment are only part of the measure of housing quality. An equally important factor, but one not recognized by the Census Bureau, is location. A house may be a sound structure and have adeqate interior plumbing, but if it is surrounded by factories emitting noxious fumes or fronts on a street used twenty-four hours a day by heavy trucks, it must be considered locationally substandard. Its economic future as a dwelling is probably dim.

Locational obsolescence affects a far larger number of dwellings than those engulfed in areas of heavy industry. There are many standard dwellings in neighborhoods where most of the other dwellings are substandard by Census Bureau criteria. Though physically fit, these dwellings are locationally unfit because they rarely can withstand neighborhood blight. A large proportion of them will be cleared through private or public operations, or will fall into substandard condition during the next generation.

The Twentieth Century Fund has estimated that in 1950 two million nondilapidated units, 400,000 of which lacked running water, were substandard in this wider sense and should be either rehabilitated or replaced. The Fund based its estimate on the assumption that if more than half the units in a block were substandard (dilapidated or lacking essential plumbing facilities), then the whole block was substandard. The general validity of this estimate is confirmed by the fact that 20 per cent of the units demolished in slum clearance projects were of standard quality by the Census Bureau definition.

Too Much Space and Too Little

Whether housing is adequate in terms of space depends on the size and other characteristics of the family. Because the quantity of housing which a family can purchase depends on income, which usually rises over the life cycle, young and growing families tend to have less space than they require, while older families whose children have left home may have too much.

The median size of American dwellings in 1950 was four and one-half rooms, about the same as it had been ten years before and a little smaller than in 1956. Almost a quarter of all urban dwelling units consisted of three rooms or less, and close to another quarter of six or more. Over two-fifths had four or five rooms. But housing space is by no means evenly distributed among its users. For example, nearly 40 per cent of all households consisted of one and two persons, but only 10 per cent of the housing supply consisted of one- and two-room dwelling units. Thus, 30 per cent of the families in 1950 lived in dwellings larger than suggested by their family size. But 15 per cent of the population was overcrowded by usual housing standards: this group lived in houses in which there were more persons than rooms. Five and one-half per cent of the housing supply was seriously overcrowded by these same standards: more than one and one-half persons per room. Overcrowding—defined as anything above one person per room—was much more prevalent in tenant-occupied than in owner-occupied dwellings: the rate for the former was 20 per cent, for the latter 10 per cent.

The Market and Its Limits

The market for housing consists primarily of an existing stockpile. The one-fifth of American households who move in an average year for the most part exchange one used dwelling for another. Maintaining and altering the existing housing stock is, therefore, a major concern of the housing industry and of public policy. Not only does new residential building have to compete with the preponderant supply of older houses in design, location, and price, but the size of the new housing market is severely limited by the durability and adaptability of the older houses. Rarely are houses demolished because of physical deterioration. More often, demolition is the result of a shift of land to other uses, including streets, highways, or other public building.

Because of this relationship between new production and total supply, net additions to the housing inventory in any year have less impact on the total housing supply than would seem to be the case when housing starts average a million or more a year. The effect of new housing is limited largely to local areas, and even to distinct submarkets, in terms of price and credit terms or rent class, location, type of dwelling, and other characteristics. The entrepreneurs engaged in new building can have little direct influence on the total market. The many resulting uncertainties in demand add to the risks and contribute to the violence of fluctuations in building activity.

Any attempt to improve the functioning of the housing market must face two basic difficulties. First, the market for new homes is small and affects the bulk of the supply very slowly. Second, the existing stock in recent years has not filtered down to successively lower-income users until the dwellings were deteriorated. Reasonable progress requires an expansion of the market for new housing, radical improvements in maintenance and conversion, and equally major improvements in the filtration process.

Although the American economy provides the consumer with a choice of merchandise which is unparalleled in human history, it limits the consumer's choice in housing in a number of important respects. Only about half of all consumer families in the market are able ever to get new homes or apartments; the rest get houses or apartments vacated by earlier users. Even among the former half, real choice is limited to the single family, detached suburban home. Only if the family is white, desires to live in a suburban area of a city, does not mind a relatively long journey to work, does not mind mowing a large lawn and maintaining a large lot, wants to own and can afford to do so, is there any substantial range of choice in the new-house market. If such a family wants to live near the central part of the city, prefers to have a row house, or rent a new apartment of three or more bedrooms, its chances of finding new housing are exceedingly small in most urban market areas.

Indeed, the number of families *not* served according to their need or preference by the housing industry is larger than that served by it. The industry builds single-family, detached suburban homes for white families of upper and middle incomes and mass or popular tastes. Its production for families of other types, in other locations, and in other sizes and price ranges is limited. Most families are eliminated because their income is insufficient to buy or rent a suitable home; others, because of their race or religion. And, not least important, in most cities those who want to buy a house designed by one of America's great living architects find that builders do not build sales houses designed by them.

The home-building industry, in short, responds to its market much as Henry Ford is said to have responded in the twenties to his market: "They can have it any color they want as long as it is black."

Can Filtration Work?

Improvement in the filtration process, by which homes are successively brought within the reach of lower-income groups, is essential to a more effective market. Houses originally built for higher-income households should become available to less well-to-do families at lower costs when the houses age, and when marked changes occur in preferences for style, size, or location. Presumably the used housing would be better housing than the new occupants had previously had and thus would find a ready market.

The analogy is often made with the automobile industry and the automobile market. Most American families own an automobile. Although many cannot afford a new car, families of even very low income often buy a used car in reasonably good condition. According to the filtering concept, the housing market should operate in the same way to provide families of low income with good used houses, passed on to them at reduced prices after initial occupancy by higher-income families. But if the process is to work in the housing market as it does in the automobile market, there must be a substantial enough increase in the production of new housing to force freer circulation of essentially sound, old housing, and there must be a steady removal of substandard and blighted housing at a faster rate and in larger numbers than present renewal plans contemplate.

Because of the extreme swings from feast to famine which characterize residential building in this country, the filtering process has never worked consistently and effectively. It is true that housing built for the well-to-do families of an earlier period has come to provide a large part of the housing supply for families of much lower incomes. As the city engulfed or encroached on the good residential areas of a century ago, the original owners pulled up stakes and moved still farther out. But this was only a temporary phenomenon of filtering and even at its best did not provide satisfactory housing for the new users. By the time the houses became available to them, they were already locationally obsolete in the main. Moreover, they were unsuited, without extensive modernization or alteration, to the needs of the families who could afford their depreciated value. Without the pressure of competition from a constantly expanding supply of new housing in the upper range of prices, the mansions and large apartments of a few generations ago thus came to make up a large part of the blighted and "gray" areas of today.

There are a number of reasons why the filtration process has not worked effectively. A basic obstacle is the extreme longevity of housing. Although automobiles, for example, depreciate very rapidly, houses depreciate only gradually. Moreover, styles of houses go out of fashion slowly and a house may in fact be worth as much a generation after its construction as it was when new. Another obstacle to successful filtering is that large initial investment in houses combined with long-term inflation makes the resale of houses at substantially lower prices unlikely during the initial amortization period.

Where the process of economic depreciation takes a very long time, the houses which eventually do come on the market for lower-income families require heavy maintenance or repair. The filtering idea assumes that respectable housing will find its way to the bottom of the housing ladder without substantial change in quality; the essence of the theory actually is a decline in value which is based on a decline in desirability—something quite different from a decline in physical quality. Obviously, unless wholly substandard housing is continually being removed from the market, the end product of the filtering process is the very blight which public policy seeks to remedy.

The principal requirement for successful filtration, then, is a volume of new construction sustained for a long enough period at a high enough rate to create the surpluses which the theory assumes. But the market normally tends to prevent surpluses by a reduction in the volume of new construction. When families buy new homes and vacate old ones, the vacated dwellings depress the prices of all other existing houses and thus attract a higher proportion of buyers. New construction then continues only for those able to take large losses, the comparatively well-to-do. Home building declines until new family formation has absorbed the vacant units. Then new building resumes, but again only for the comparatively well-to-do.

In times of acute shortage, as in the period immediately following World War II, all the market forces act to inhibit filtering. The quality of used housing may then decline without a corresponding decrease in price. In fact, price inflation results in "filtering upward." When incomes and prices drop or increase together, each income group tends to maintain its previous relative position in the housing market. When housing prices rise as fast as, or faster than, average income, as they did in the mid-1950s, little effective filtration can occur. Successful filtering of the housing stock is often impeded also because racial restrictions and discriminations still segment the market at any level, but most particularly at the levels of suburban location and middle incomes.

It is clear that filtration cannot work by itself. A program to improve the filtration process must recognize and overcome the difficulties which have prevented its operation with any degree of success in the past. The key to success—and the key to the outlook of this book—is the enlargement of supply through an increased volume of new construction which will force down the prices of older dwellings. The short spurts of production in past boom years ended before they could aid the filtration process in any decisive way. If production is to be increased substantially, the new housing market must be considerably expanded, making it possible for hundreds of thousands of additional families to buy or rent new homes each year. This means changes in credit aids to bring new housing into the reach of those now out of the market, reductions in the cost of housing, and major shifts in consumer behavior, especially among the upper-income groups which would have to be persuaded to seek superior and more costly housing. At the same time vigorous public effort will be required to remove the most dilapidated part of the supply from the market.

THE CONSUMER

Chapter 4

THE ECONOMIC BEHAVIOR OF HOUSING CONSUMERS

Not all consumers want the same kind of shelter. The allocation of the consumer dollar to housing varies substantially according to income, family size, age, occupation, education and race. For example, as income increases, the proportion of income spent on housing goes down. As another example, the lowest economic groups have a surprisingly high rate of home ownership, but only because many old persons with small retirement incomes own houses for which they paid long ago. Also, within each income class, housing expenditures are higher for white-collar than for blue-collar workers.

Consumers as a whole have downgraded housing in their hierarchy of values and expenditures, thus posing a serious problem to American cities in their efforts to renew the deteriorating supply of housing and to the housing industry in its efforts to increase the supply of new housing. In order to make housing more competitive with other commodities, the industry will have to provide a demonstrably better product for the price, and appeal to a wider range of incomes. For their part, consumers will have to realize that unless their demand for housing is such as to encourage the industry to augment the supply, and local government to conserve and enhance its value, the result will be an inevitable limitation in the range of housing choices and neighborhood amenities.

49

In our economy, the consumer is presumed to be sovereign in the market place. He buys what he wants according to his ability to pay and the relative satisfaction he expects to derive from his purchase compared with other things he might buy. In the housing market, however, the consumer's choice is often limited by noneconomic factors. He may not be able to find the kind of dwelling he wants in the location he prefers; and, because of his race or ethnic origin, he may not be permitted to bid for what he wants. But despite these inequities in the market, many of the limitations on consumer choice in housing are self-imposed.

For the past half century consumers have been consistently spending smaller proportions of their incomes on housing. The trend has been so marked that Louis Winnick in a book in this series says that "if we do not have all the housing we want, the proximate cause is that the consumer is not spending enough." Statistical studies of consumer expenditures show the decline in dramatic terms by their separate listing of household equipment, for which expenditures have increased, and of basic shelter. Burnham Kelly takes issue with this method in another book in this series. He says that the line between the basic house and its equipment is fading so rapidly that economists "should go beyond the statistics on *housing* and include in their consideration expenditures on *household operation.* . . ." But even when this is done, the combined budget allocation for shelter and equipment is still less than it was earlier in the century. The relative drop in housing expenditures has been accompanied by increases in expenditures for such things as alcohol and tobacco, vacations and other kinds of recreation, and, of course, the automobile. To the extent that the automobile is a function of housing, at least in suburban locations, transportation dollars may have to substitute for housing dollars. On the whole, however, it is fair to conclude that consumers prefer to spend their money on other things than housing.

Characteristics of the Housing Consumer

The demand for housing varies with changes in household income, the size of families, and the age and other characteristics of the population. Beyond this constantly shifting pattern of demand, the housing market is influenced by a number of other factors which are described elsewhere in this book. For example, the fact that housing is immobile and has a much longer life than other consumer goods often acts as a brake on the introduction of new design both for houses and for the neighborhoods in which they stand; and the production of housing is very sensitive to the general level of economic prosperity and the availability of credit.

The market for housing is enormous because every person requires shelter. In 1960, the value of shelter services consumed by the nation reached the all-time high of $43 billion. These vast expenditures came from a market consisting of 53 million spending units in 1960, of which about 90 per cent were nonfarm. They varied greatly in incomes and requirements. Income distribution is shown in Chart 8.

A trend toward improvement in income, which started in the late 1930s, continued after World War II. Not only did average family income after taxes increase from $4,000 to $5,400 in con-

Chart 8. Percentage distribution of urban family income, 1950 and 1959

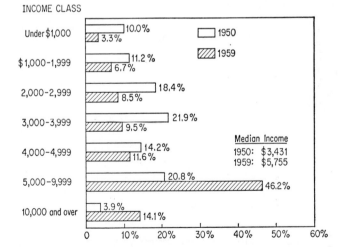

Sources: U.S. Bureau of the Census, *U.S. Census of Population: 1950,* vol II, P-B1, 1952, table 57, p. 1–104. U.S. Bureau of the Census, *Current Population Reports,* ser. P-60, no. 35, Jan. 5, 1961, table 1, p. 23.

Chart 9. Nonfarm households by size, 1956

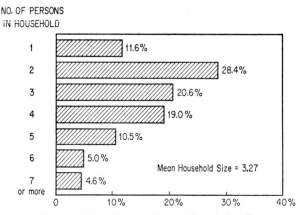

Source: U.S. Bureau of the Census, *Current Population Reports*, ser. P-20, no. 75, June 9, 1957.

stant dollars in the period between 1947 and 1959, but the proportion of families in the lowest income groups declined notably. The proportion of families with incomes under $3,000 (in 1959 dollars) declined from 34 per cent to 23 per cent, while the proportion with incomes of $5,000 or more increased from 34

Chart 10. Nonfarm households by number of children under 18, 1956

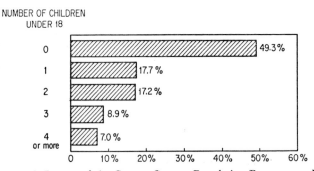

Source: U.S. Bureau of the Census, *Current Population Reports*, ser. P-20, no. 75, June 9, 1957.

per cent to 55 per cent. The total market for housing represents a collection of submarkets made up of numerous groups with different spending patterns. For example, the proportion of income spent on housing differs substantially for professional as against blue-collar families, and for aged couples as against new families who do not yet have children. The major household subgroups constituting the market are shown in Charts 9, 10, and 11, which describe the distribution of nonfarm households in 1956 according to the size of household, number and age of children, and age of household head. The important effects of these changing characteristics of the population on the consumption of housing are discussed later in this chapter. (1956 figures for household characteristics are used here to provide comparability with the *1956 National Housing Inventory* referred to in other parts of this book.)

A full understanding of the structure of housing demand can be obtained only by examining the housing expenditures made by families in each of the subgroups. Unfortunately, the most comprehensive data available for this purpose are old; they appear in the *Study of Consumer Expenditures* (SCE) a survey made in 1950 by the Bureau of Labor Statistics.

Chart 11. Age of household heads, urban and rural nonfarm, 1956

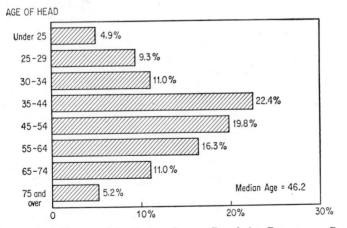

Source: U.S. Bureau of the Census, *Current Population Reports*, ser. P-20, no. 75, June 9, 1957.

The survey revealed that in 1950 urban families spent an average of almost $600 per year for housing and utilities. This sum included a very small amount for vacation cottages. Housing expenditures amounted to 15.2 per cent of average income after taxes.

The survey also showed that as family income increased, the proportion of income spent on housing fell. The proportion of income, after taxes, allocated to housing decreased from over 50 per cent for families with less than $1,000 in income to 18.0 per cent in the $2,000 to $3,000 income bracket, and only 13.5 per cent in the $5,000 to $6,000 bracket. Families with incomes of $10,000 or more devoted the smallest share—9.1 per cent—to housing.

The principal cause of the high expenditures for housing by low-income families is an income level so low that even a minimal outlay for housing absorbs a disproportionately high share of their earnings. It is also true that low-income families often under-report their incomes. Moreover, their reported income may not be a fair indication of their actual economic position because of temporary unemployment. Thus consumption may be high because economic expectations are higher than present circumstances or because accumulated assets (such as savings or inheritances or a house long since fully paid for) do not show up in current income.

The main reason for the shrinkage in the percentage of housing expenditures as incomes increase is that as families become increasingly well-to-do they appear to derive relatively greater satisfaction from luxury goods than from improvements in housing and other necessities. Thus, as the proportion spent on housing and food declines, the proportion spent on clothing and automobiles rises markedly, as shown in Chart 12.

The first and largest item in every family's budget, of course, is food and beverages. In the *Study of Consumer Expenditures,* the proportion of total consumption expenditures allocated to this category in 1950 ranged from 24.5 per cent to 36.3 per cent. As in the case of housing, however, at higher incomes a smaller share was spent for food. At incomes of $10,000 or more, food and beverages accounted for 24.5 per cent of total consumption, while at incomes between $2,000 and $3,000 the ratio rose to 34.7 per cent.

The second largest family expenditure is either housing or transportation, depending on the family's income class. With incomes under $5,000 families allocated larger shares of consumption to housing than to transportation, including the purchase price of an automobile. At the $2,000 to $3,000 level, for example, 17.6 per cent went to housing and utilities, and 10.9 per cent to transportation. At the $4,000 to $5,000 level the proportions were 14.9 per cent and 14.4 per cent. In the $7,500 to $10,-000 income class, the proportions were reversed in startling

Chart 12. Selected consumer expenditures as percentages of total consumption, by income groups, U.S. urban families, 1950

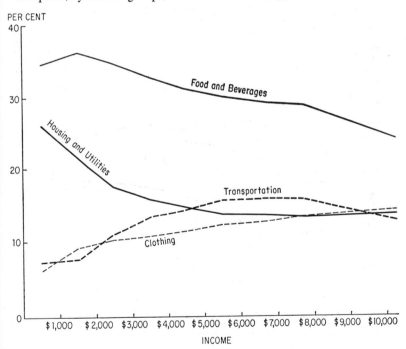

Source: U.S. Bureau of Labor Statistics and Wharton School of Business and Finance, *Survey of Consumer Expenditures,* vol. XVIII, University of Pennsylvania, 1956, table 1-2.

degree. Families in this income group allocated only 13.3 per cent of consumption dollars to housing, while the transportation share increased to 15.5 per cent.

WHO OWNS OR RENTS?

The spectacular rise in homeownership which occurred between 1940 and 1960, when the number of nonfarm homeowners far exceeded the net gain in homeownership in the preceding 150 years of American history, cannot be wholly accounted for by any single factor. Even the lowest income groups have a high rate of homeownership. In the Bureau of Labor Statistics study, however, the 42 per cent of families with less than $1,000 in annual income who owned their own homes was heavily

Chart 13. Homeownership rate, age of head, and size of family by income, U.S. urban families, 1950

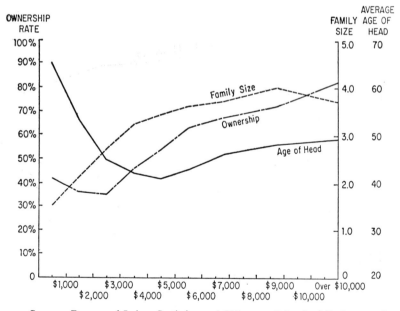

Source: Bureau of Labor Statistics and Wharton School of Business and Finance, *Study of Consumer Expenditures*, vol. XVIII, University of Pennsylvania, 1956, table 2.

weighted with older persons whose houses were bought in earlier years and were free of debt. The rate of homeownership dropped to 35 per cent for families in the $2,000 to $3,000 income group, but, as Chart 13 shows, increased in each successive income bracket.

A rise in the homeownership rate, accompanied by higher incomes, is less pronounced, however, for childless couples than for other kinds of families. Childless couples more often rent than do couples of the same age and income who have children.

The study revealed a significant change in consumption patterns when families shift from renting to homeownership. For the large middle-income group, housing outlays (including utilities) increased with home purchases from a range of 12 to 16 per cent to a range of 20 to 22 per cent of income before taxes.

Location also accounts for differences in the amounts families spend on housing. Families who lived in the suburbs of Northern cities in 1950 spent more for housing and utilities than did families in any other part of the country—$717 on the average. Families in smaller Southern cities averaged only $456 a year.

RELATIONSHIP TO SIZE OF FAMILY

Next to size of income, size of family might be expected to be the most important determinant of housing expenditure. This is not the case, however. It is true that large families occupy more space. Five-person households, for example, averaged 5.40 rooms compared with 4.39 for two-person households. But larger families also put more pressure on the family budget for food, clothing, and other necessities. Two-person families with incomes of $3,000 to $4,000 devoted 30.4 per cent of consumption expenditures to food and beverages in 1950, but five-person families with the same income spent 36.4 per cent. Inevitably, the pressure for all necessities causes large families to spend less on their housing in proportion to their incomes. A family in the $4,000 to $5,000 range devoted 15.7 per cent of consumption dollars to housing if the family was composed of two persons, 15.3 per cent if three persons, 14.5 per cent if four persons, and 13.9 per cent if five persons.

Obviously, if large families spend less on housing but still obtain more space, they must compromise with quality. The 1950 Housing Census found that nearly one out of three households with seven or more persons lived in dilapidated units compared with one out of nine for all households. Another penalty of family size is overcrowding. Of all the 1950 nonfarm households which occupied space at a ratio of more than two persons to a room, 80 per cent were households of five or more persons. (The 1960 figures will be available only after this book is published.)

The family life cycle, as the accompanying table reveals, is paralleled by a corresponding life cycle in the expenditure patterns for housing. There is also a life cycle in the mortgage indebtedness of families, but the SCE excluded mortgage amortization from housing costs, thereby systematically understating the current cash outlays for housing of younger and middle-aged families in relation to older families. Families of the same incomes but of different ages and composition had different rates of homeownership. For example, across an age span of about fifteen years (20 to 35) families with an income differential of only $826 ($3,050 to $3,876) showed ownership ratios varying from 13 per cent to 34 per cent as average family size increased from 2.5 persons to 3.3 persons. The national trend in homeownership must be constantly viewed, therefore, against changes in the nation's demographic structure as well as in income, mortgage terms, and housing prices.

The housing expenditures of older families in each income group were higher than might be expected in terms of family size. The possibility is strong that these families, whose present housing is the result of past decisions, were overspending on housing compared with other goods and services. Clearly, they had more space than their size indicated was required. One of the principal impediments to a more efficient distribution of housing space is the reluctance of older families to move to smaller quarters when their size decreases. But it is often difficult for older people to make more suitable arrangements. Credit, for example, may be hard to arrange if mortgage financing is necessary to exchange a larger unit for a smaller one. Rental units in de-

TABLE 1. CONSUMPTION EXPENDITURES BY AGE OF HEAD, U.S. URBAN FAMILIES, 1950

	Under 25		25–34		35–44		45–54		55–64		65–74		75 and over	
	Average income before taxes													
	$3,050		$3,876		$4,464		$4,500		$3,850		$2,687		$2,161	
	Amt.	%	Amt.	%	Amt.	%	Amt.	%	Amt.	%	Amt.	%	Amt.	%
Housing and utilities.........	$ 469	14.9	$ 592	15.7	$ 654	15.0	$ 644	14.8	$ 586	16.0	$ 492	19.2	$ 472	22.7
Total consumption...........	3,142	100.0	3,870	100.0	4,360	100.0	4,342	100.0	3,657	100.0	2,567	100.0	2,076	100.0
Home ownership ratio........		13.0		34.0		50.0		54.0		59.0		59.0		60.0
Average family size...........		2.5		3.3		3.6		3.1		2.6		2.1		1.9

Source: U.S. Bureau of Labor Statistics and Wharton School of Business and Finance, *Study of Consumer Expenditures*, vol. XVIII, University of Pennsylvania, 1956, table 1–2.

sired locations are often unavailable. Most important, perhaps, is the sense of security the older couple feels in retaining its own home, one that is not only comfortingly familiar but long since amortized.

OCCUPATION, EDUCATION, AND RACE

Housing expenditures vary with occupation and education within each income class.

As consumers acquire more education and move out of blue-collar occupations, they spend more for housing. In 1950, families in all income groups up to $6,000 spent more on housing if they were clerical and sales employees, salaried professionals, or self-employed than if they were skilled or unskilled wage earners. The salaried professional whose income was between $4,000 and $5,000 spent $787 for housing, while the skilled worker with the same income spent only $627. Even the salaried professional who earned only $2,000 to $3,000 spent $510 on housing, while the skilled worker with the same income spent only $474. (See table on next page.) Occupational status is so closely linked to educational attainment that much the same proportions exist when housing expenditures are compared with the number of years of education.

Finally, the SCE revealed important differences in the housing expenditures of Negroes compared with those of whites. On the whole, Negro families spent less on housing than did white families of the same size and income; this was especially true in the lower income classes and in the South. (See Chart 14.) In evaluating the study's data it is important to bear in mind that the size and quality of the housing obtained is not known. Because of discrimination, Negroes usually pay an excessive premium for successful entry into the middle-income part of the market. Moreover, the housing burden for all Negro families is higher than that for white families. Even when they spend the same amount as whites, Negroes rarely obtain the same level of quality in housing and neighborhood amenities. Because they get less for their money they appear to react by spending more on other consumer goods like food, beverages, and clothing.

TABLE 2. HOUSING EXPENDITURES AND TENURE BY OCCUPATION AND INCOME GROUPS, U.S. URBAN FAMILIES, 1950

Occupation	Under $1,000		$1,000–$1,999		$2,000–$2,999		$3,000–$3,999		$4,000–$4,999		$5,000–$5,999		$6,000–$7,499		$7,500–$9,999		$10,000 and over	
	Amount	Owners %	Amount	Owners %	Amount	Owners %	Amount	Owners %	Amount	Owners %	Amount	Owners %	Amount	Owners %	Amount	Owners %	Amount	Owners %
Self-employed............	$444	42	$436	55	$538	56	$619	58	$728	69	$745	75	$781	75	$ 959	78	$1,425	80
Salaried, professionals, etc ...	453	35	315	12	510	27	658	37	787	50	795	62	916	62	1,032	75	1,501	82
Clerical and sales workers....	449	46	424	24	531	22	589	42	663	58	805	58	875	61	943	59	1,516	80
Skilled wage earners........	535	26	354	40	474	38	552	52	627	52	696	65	786	71	814	71	858	100
Semi-skilled wage earners....	294	52	351	26	453	29	514	44	600	50	674	62	737	67	784	70	1,146	75
Unskilled wage earners.......	264	32	336	24	430	31	525	42	612	45	607	56	775	64	612	76	....	::
Not gainfully employed	331	45	425	51	494	56	616	60	678	69	781	65	808	61	1,165	69	1,802	84

Note: Housing expenditures combine expenditures for housing and fuel, light and refrigeration.
Source: U.S. Bureau of Labor Statistics and Wharton School of Business and Finance, *Study of Consumer Expenditures*, vol. XVIII, University of Pennsylvania, 1956, table 4-2.

Chart **14.** Housing expenditure by race and income for selected family sizes in urban areas, 1950

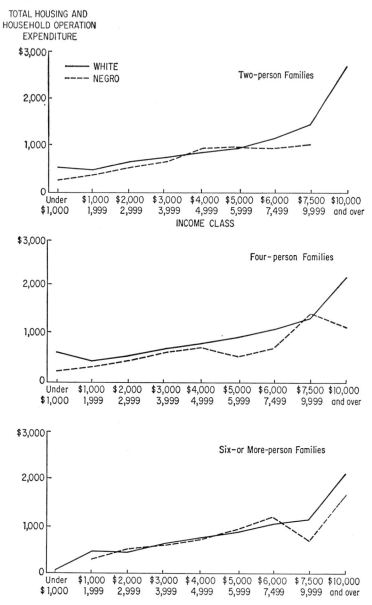

Source: U.S. Bureau of Labor Statistics and Wharton School of Business and Finance, *Study of Consumer Expenditures*, vol. XVIII, University of Pennsylvania, 1956, table 10-d.

Historical Trends in Housing Expenditures

There has been a long-term relative decline in housing expenditures. This trend toward a decreased rate of spending for housing is shown in the national income accounts: housing outlays, as a part of total consumption, dropped from 19 per cent to 13 per cent between 1909 and 1960. During the same period combined expenditures for transportation and recreation more than doubled.

The shift in national resources away from housing also shows up in the drop in the per capita value of the nonfarm housing supply. Studies by Leo Grebler for the National Bureau of Economic Research show that at the end of 1955 the value was 7 per cent less than in 1900, and 15 per cent less than after the great building boom of the 1920s. The impact of wars and depression on housing is evidently very strong. The first major decline in per capita housing wealth since records have been accurate enough to give the picture showed up right after World War I, and the second and more important sag was the result of the collapse of the construction industry during the 1930s and the restrictions on private building occasioned by military requirements as the nation entered World War II.

The per capita value of housing in 1900 was $793. (All values in this paragraph are in 1929 dollars.) Yet in spite of such temporary advances as a jump during the 1920s, when per capita value reached a peak of $870, and a slow climb after World War II, the long-run pattern of decline has been undeniable. In 1955, per capita housing value stood at about $740, or less than in 1900. This is an especially significant point of comparison in the light of the fact that 1955 was the seventh successive year in which housing starts had topped one million. But despite the recovery in per capita value which accompanied the postwar building boom, the increase in the decade was only half as great as the gain made in the ten years between the close of World War I and the onset of the Depression.

In part the decline represents the decrease in the size and real value of new dwelling units. Dwelling units built during the 1920s averaged 4.81 rooms compared with an average of 4.26

for those built between 1940 and 1950. The trend toward less floor area, a more accurate measure of size, is reflected in statistics for new FHA houses, which decreased from an average of 1,177 square feet to 983 square feet between 1935 and 1950. Since 1950, there has been some reversal of this trend, and a higher proportion of four- and five-bedroom houses is now being built. In 1960, the average new FHA home was 1,091 square feet in size and it contained 5½ rooms.

The real value per new dwelling unit, measured in constant dollars, declined about 40 per cent between 1890 and 1950, despite more mechanical and electrical equipment. In addition to the decline in number of rooms, a fact occasioned in part by the conversions of large units to small units during the 1930s and 1940s, this drop in value is also explained by regional population shifts to the South and West, where climatic conditions permit less expensive construction. The trend toward lighter and less expensive materials also reduced the value of new homes.

To what extent is the decline in the real per capita value of the housing stock explained by a shift in consumer preferences away from housing? Just how favorable is the prospect for persuading America's consumers to rank housing higher in their budget allocations? The SCE data make clear that some decline in the proportion of housing expenditures to total expenditures must be expected as real incomes rise. Louis Winnick in another book in this series says, however, that "the long-run rise in residential construction costs must . . . be placed at the very center of any explanation of why consumer demand for housing has been disproportionate to the rise in real income and why housing appears to be a continuing problem for America and indeed for every industrial country." Residential construction costs have risen steadily since the prewar housing peak in 1925 without rendering any appreciable advantage to the housing commodity as a whole. Between 1925 and 1960 (using the same base) costs have risen more than two and a half times, vastly more than the rise in wholesale prices or in the prices of consumer goods and services. The prices of building materials have risen much more rapidly than all wholesale prices, while building wage rates have increased faster than the prices of materials. If, as a result, prices of housing continue to rise at a higher rate than incomes, without any appreciable improvement in the product, the prospect for stimulating much greater relative expenditures for housing would seem to be doubtful.

A different set of accounts reinforces this view. In 1929 the per capita money income (after taxes) in the United States was $682; by 1955 it had increased to $1,629. Nevertheless, despite an increase in real purchasing power of over 50 per cent, the average consumer with a $682 income in 1929 could buy more housing than his 1955 counterpart with a money income of $1,629. Since 1955 the difference has probably been widening.

Important as they are, rising costs are not the only explanation for the low value consumers put on housing. As pointed out earlier in this chapter, the decline in housing expenditures must also be attributed to the consumer's growing preference for other commodities. But the volume of all spending by consumers is so high that a small shift in the amount that goes to housing, assuming that a runaway inflation in construction costs were avoided, could result in a much higher volume of construction and improved housing standards. Even a single percentage point rise in the share of housing expenditures would have a dramatic effect. And if consumers did in fact devote the frequently advocated 20 per cent of their budgets to housing, current housing expenditures would rise by many billions.

In the second half of the 1950-1960 decade, some new characteristics of demand appeared which strengthen the possibility that consumers might devote a larger share of their budgets to housing in the years ahead. One is the improvement in the position of minority groups, who, because of various kinds of discrimination, have been prevented heretofore from applying their gains in real income to housing. Another is an emerging shift in the hierarchy of consumer values which suggests that as consumer incomes rise, a large part of the increase might be directed to housing if the convenience and attractiveness of the product were improved.

Chapter 5

THE DISFRANCHISED CONSUMER

Low-income families, Negroes and other racial minorities are unable to compete in the housing market. Not only are large numbers of the homes of these groups substandard physically, but they are overcrowded and heavily concentrated in decaying or segregated areas. Persons who live in such areas are most likely to be displaced by slum clearance programs, urban highway programs, and municipal capital improvements of all kinds. Although Federal and state laws require relocation in "decent, safe, and sanitary" housing, such housing is not always available.

Social discrimination not only limits the housing available to Negroes and other minority groups but also restricts their job opportunities and hence their income. Low income and restricted choices of where to live are thus interlinked as the causes of so heavy a concentration of Negroes and other racial minorities in slum housing.

But racial discrimination limits the housing market even for upper-income families of minority origin. New building open to Negroes is rare, small in volume, and usually segregated; mortgage loans are often unobtainable, or differentially priced; real estate brokers often restrict offerings to segregated areas or areas in rapid transition.

Both Federal and state courts are beginning to enforce nondiscriminatory measures in the sale or rental of new housing; some builders are trying to break through traditions of local discrimination; lenders are experimenting with ways to provide more mortgage money to minority families; and the FHA and

VA are pursuing mortgage insurance and guarantee policies which recognize equality of opportunity in Federal aids. Beyond these scattered but not inconsiderable improvements, perhaps the most optimistic outlook for the future comes from the rise in the incomes of nonwhite urban families.

The rapidly growing number of aged persons and couples constitutes the second largest group of the underprivileged in housing. Their special problems are receiving increasing attention from public and private agencies.

Discrimination of various types can be further abated by court decisions, state and local laws, and changing business and public attitudes. A variety of experiments are required to devise new ways of providing housing for low-income families through public housing, rehabilitation of existing homes, and experiments with direct rent-subsidy plans linked with strong code enforcement and an expansion of the supply of new housing.

The actual operation of the housing market, as we have seen, falls far short of the ideal concept of a free market in a democratic society. Consumer sovereignty is often more fiction than fact because of the many impediments in production and marketing which limit the output and availability of the kind of housing families need and at the prices they are willing to pay. This chapter deals with the group of consumers who because of low incomes or discrimination (or both) have no effective vote in the housing market—the disfranchised consumers.

Disfranchisement in housing is not primarily a political term in the sense that, for example, citizens of the District of Columbia are disfranchised in local affairs. It refers instead to the barriers to choice imposed on some consumers in the housing market by such factors as traditional attitudes toward race, religious belief, or national origin.

Race and poverty are formidable forms of disfranchisement in the housing market. When they operate together, they virtually eliminate freedom of choice in housing. Insofar as the problem is economic, the fact that real incomes are rising at a substantial rate and tend toward less inequality is a hopeful sign. Insofar as the problem is one of racial discrimination, advances are also occurring, even though in the aggregate they are still small.

Beyond the centrally significant disfranchisements which race and low income impose are the less obvious conditions at the rim. Because of the sharp constriction of the immigration laws, the problem is no longer how and where to house masses of new and unassimilated immigrants from foreign countries. Migrants, however, as distinct from immigrants—that is, new arrivals from the South, white as well as Negro, and from Puerto Rico—are a large portion of the disadvantaged group in housing today. In quite a different but equally real sense, some of the aged likewise undergo aspects of disfranchisement; and in a steadily aging society such as ours, they represent a group which will be moving more and more toward the focus of importance.

Low-Income Consumers

Of all the disadvantaged consumers of housing, those with low incomes are the most numerous. Their position is most serious when, as is often the case, low incomes accompany handicaps of race, ethnic origin, or age.

In 1959, the median annual income of all urban families (and unrelated individuals) was $5,755. About one-fourth had incomes below $4,000, the budget needed for a minimum decent standard of living. One-tenth had incomes of less than $2,000 a year. This group consists to a considerable extent of broken families, the aged, and the minorities—particularly the new arrivals in the city from the rural South, Puerto Rico, and Mexico.

Roughly half of all low-income families in the United States occupy substandard housing. In 1956, 45 per cent of the owned units occupied by families with less than $2,000 in income were of substandard quality. Among renter families, the corresponding percentage was 57. In the next income category, $2,000 to $3,999 (which accounted for one-fifth of urban families in 1956), 25 per cent of owned units in the United States and 31 per cent of rented units were substandard.

Despite the poor quality and overcrowding of housing occupied by low-income families, housing costs exert a heavy pressure on family budgets. For example, in 1956 in standard metropolitan areas 41 per cent of renters with incomes of $2,000 or less paid more than 30 per cent of their income for rent. And among the owners with incomes of $2,000 or less, 70 per cent had homes valued at $6,000 or more or at least three times their income. Although the incomes of some families are temporarily low, and thus do not always provide an accurate correlation between size of income and value of the dwelling, it is generally true that most low-income families spend larger proportions of their incomes for rent or housing expense than they can reasonably afford. This means that their expenditures for food, clothing, education, recreation, and other essentials to a healthy and productive life are reduced below levels which enable them to maintain their full contribution to society.

Of course, few very low-income families are in the new house market, as is apparent in the accompanying table. This table shows that builders and realtors using FHA mortgage financing sold few houses in 1959 to families in the lowest 30 per

TABLE 3. INCOME OF PURCHASERS OF HOMES WITH FHA MORTGAGES, 1959

Income group	Percentage of urban families in income group	Percentage of new homes bought by income group	Percentage of existing homes bought by income group
Under $4,000	28.0	1.9	4.0
$4,000–$5,999	25.2	28.9	33.8
$6,000–$7,999	20.7	36.9	32.6
$8,000–$9,999	11.9	20.3	17.7
$10,000 and over	14.1	12.0	11.9

Sources: U.S. Department of Commerce, Bureau of the Census, *Current Population Reports*, series P-60, no. 35, Jan. 5, 1961, p. 23; and U.S. Federal Housing Administration, *26th Annual Report, 1959*, p. 74.

cent of the income distribution. Less than 2 per cent of the new housing went to these families. Even after allowance for the partial nature of the data, this is convincing evidence that the home-building industry does not serve many American families.

PUBLIC HOUSING

Historically, one of the first methods of providing better housing for low-income families was through public housing. Although Federal and state governments had experimented with public housing in earlier periods, it was not until 1937 that Congress adopted the United States Housing Act which authorized a continuing program of Federal loans and annual subsidies for low-rent public housing.

The Housing Act of 1949 extended the Federally aided low-rent housing program, and several states have subsequently authorized programs of public housing aided by the state or by its municipalities. In New York State these exceed the Federally aided housing programs. In total, however, all public housing programs represent fewer than a million and a half dwelling units, or between 2 and 3 per cent of the total housing supply in the United States. Thus they are less significant in quantity than trailers and motels, or summer cottages. In only a few cities does public housing constitute a significant portion of the housing supply. This is true even though virtually all large cities have some public housing and a duly constituted housing authority, and virtually all of the states have public housing legislation.

Public housing programs have a vastly larger significance in human terms than their size would indicate. In many cities, public housing constitutes practically the only new housing built for Negro families and also the only new housing built during the last half century which provides decent, safe, and sanitary dwellings for families of low incomes. In a few cities a substantial proportion of dilapidated, unsafe, and unsanitary dwellings has been cleared and replaced by public housing. Public housing accounts for a very large proportion of all efforts to clear slums and to replace them with sound dwellings. Public housing also provides a large part of the special housing for the aged. Thus, in March, 1961, 482 of the 829 Federally subsidized public housing units put under contract were for the aged.

Public housing has great significance for the urban renewal effort in which virtually all cities are engaged. It constitutes the only supply of housing over which public officials have effective control and which they can make available for the relocation of families displaced by urban renewal, highway construction, and related programs. Despite the strenuous efforts of local authorities to find dwellings in the existing supply for families displaced as a result of slum clearance and public works, the number of such dwellings in good condition and at low enough rents is small indeed.

FAMILY SUBSIDIES AND RENT CERTIFICATES

A possible alternative to public housing as a means of solving the housing problem of low-income families is the public provision of family subsidies. In Scandinavian countries, family subsidies provide additional income directly from the state to any family having an income lower than that considered necessary for decent living. Such subsidies typically go to very large families or to families whose principal wage earner is in an unskilled or low-paid occupation. Under the family subsidy scheme, it is possible for families even in the lowest income groups to purchase or rent a home in Scandinavian nonprofit housing cooperatives.

Welfare agencies in many states in this country do issue rent certificates to families on relief. During the depression years, millions of families received such payments. In typical postwar years five million or more "cases" received some form of public assistance, but these included both families and individuals, and recipients of categorical aids such as old age pensions and aid for the blind and general assistance or welfare. Some groups, however, have long urged a form of rent subsidy more like the Scandinavian, where the subsidy is a matter of right for any family receiving less than a certain income. In the United States, comparable rent payments are made only to families on relief who are, or may be required to be, pauperized prior to the receipt of aid.

Welfare agencies here and abroad resist the notion that families must be pauperized in order to obtain shelter assistance from the state. However, housing specialists in the United States usually oppose the broader rent certificate plan on the grounds that it would be too expensive and that it would not contribute to the expansion of the housing supply. The expenditure of several billion dollars per year for rent subsidies would evoke a corresponding improvement in the housing supply only if it could be linked to a continuing program of housing code enforcement and new building. Without this safeguard, the sum would create inflationary pressures which would raise the prices or rents on the old, substandard housing occupied by the families that would be eligible for the subsidies. Eventually, of course, the increased consumer demand arising from family subsidies might result in some increased production of new housing. But in the meantime the excessive demand relative to the fairly stable supply of housing could create large windfall gains for the owners of substandard properties and low-priced units.

In an attempt to overcome the obvious disadvantages of the rent certificate scheme, it has been proposed that rent certificates should be made available only for use in newly built dwellings. Such a plan would face difficulties: for one thing, it could easily create captive markets for certain builders.

Nevertheless, a family subsidy program can be an effective alternative to public housing if it is coupled with code enforcement and with direct aids to cooperative and other developers which would assure an additional new volume of private construction exceeding the value of the subsidy. Over a period of a decade, a general family subsidy plan might meet the needs for housing of millions of families who now lack adequate shelter and have little prospect of obtaining it in the foreseeable future.

REHABILITATION AND CODE ENFORCEMENT

Several national groups, most prominent among them the National Association of Real Estate Boards, have urged that extensive programs of rehabilitation be employed as at least a partial solution to the housing problems of low-income groups. Although not all rehabilitation programs are code enforcement programs, there is a close connection between the two. Either separately or in conjunction, they often face major obstacles in improving the condition of substandard housing without increasing rents and sales prices to a point where low-income families are priced out of the market. Chapter 11 discusses the benefits and problems of these measures in a general review of the economic feasibility of rehabilitation.

Problems of the Aging Population

Particular note must be taken of the most rapidly growing proportion of the population with low incomes. These are the aged —the persons who are over sixty-five. In 1900, there were slightly over 3 million in this age group, or 4.1 per cent of the total population. By 1960, the number had increased to over 15 million or almost 9 per cent of the total population. The Census Bureau estimates that by 1975 there will be well over 20 million persons over sixty-five.

Nearly 70 per cent of this age group lived in their own households in 1950, over two-thirds in their own houses. But over a fourth of the dwellings they owned were valued at less than $2,000. Although overcrowding is rarely a problem in the older household, the condition of the dwelling is apt to be poor.

The incomes of the aged portion of the population are low. About one-tenth of the families whose head was over sixty-five had incomes under $1,000 in 1959 and almost another one-fourth had incomes between $1,000 and $2,000. Although reported incomes are low, a few of these families may have substantial capital resources, and others receive social security or other welfare benefits or incomes from retirement plans. However, the postwar inflation has cut deeply into savings and income from pensions. And although payments under social security and other welfare plans have increased, they are still far below the level required to provide adequate housing in the absence of other resources.

Not nearly enough is known about either the real incomes of the elderly or their housing preferences and needs for housing. But each day, some one thousand persons in this country enter the over-sixty-five age bracket.

HOUSING FOR THE AGED

In recognition of the fast-growing number of older persons, the Federal government and a number of states now provide special assistance to housing designed and built specifically for the aged. For example, New York and Massachusetts give state aid to low-rent public housing for this group. Since 1956 the Federal government has broadened its program of mortgage aids to private builders of housing for the aged. It now offers three kinds of assistance to housing the elderly: FHA mortgage insurance, direct loans to nonprofit projects, and aid to local housing authorities to build public housing units for elderly individuals and couples of low income.

By the beginning of 1961, about 30,000 units of housing specifically planned for the elderly had been completed or approved for construction. About half the units were privately financed, mainly with FHA insurance. Mortgage insurance or loans totaled nearly $200 million.

Racial Discrimination in Housing

Irrespective of age and income, Negroes find the housing market's door very hard to open. Puerto Ricans and Mexicans are also subject to much of the discrimination which Negroes face. In 1960, nonwhite households constituted about 10 per cent of the housing in the United States. The South has about half the nonwhite housing units.

The incomes of nonwhite families are far lower on the average than those of white families. In 1952, white urban families of two or more persons had a median income of $4,884, whereas nonwhite families had a median income of $2,631. By 1959, the situation had improved somewhat. The median income of nonwhite urban families had increased to $3,519 compared with $5,994 for white families. Between 1952 and 1959, the ratio of nonwhite to white median income increased from 54 per cent to 59 per cent. Also, in times of economic recession, the Negro is the first to feel the pinch; in the 1957–1958 recession about 35 per cent of the unemployed were Negro. Because a large proportion of all nonwhite families have low incomes, it is understandable, then, that they should occupy a large proportion of the substandard dwellings.

But only a combination of low income and powerful discriminatory forces in the housing market could produce the dramatic difference in housing conditions which exists between whites and nonwhites. As noted in Chapter 3, half of the non-white renter-occupied units and a third of the owner-occupied ones are substandard. The proportion of Negro families that live in overcrowded conditions is several times that of white families, dramatic evidence of the failure of the accessible housing supply to keep up with the growth of Negro population. The rate of doubling (married couples living with other families) is much higher among nonwhites than it is among whites.

When housing conditions are analyzed by price or rent class, nonwhite households uniformly have poorer houses than do whites, with a higher percentage of dilapidation and a lower percentage of sanitary facilities. It is probably true, however, that the Negro who has lived for a number of years in a Northern city has improved his housing situation considerably.

As a result of rising incomes, however, the rate of home-ownership has increased rapidly among nonwhites. Despite an increase in the purchase of homes by nonwhite families, only one-third of the nonwhite families owned their own homes in 1950 as compared with 57 per cent of white families. By 1960, two-fifths of nonwhite families owned their homes compared with almost two-thirds of white families. The average value of homes owned by nonwhites is much less than that of homes owned by white families in both rural nonfarm and urban areas.

Doubtless many persons live in areas occupied predominantly by minority groups as a result of their own choice. There they can find friends of similar station, churches, stores, and other services meeting their special needs and tastes. These constitute market attractions which tend to hold groups together even in the absence of discriminatory pressures.

The line between voluntary and involuntary concentrations of population is a difficult one to follow. By and large, the market tends to reinforce all manner of pressures for the involuntary segregation of persons with similar characteristics. These can be lumped under the one word "discrimination." The newly arrived Irish or Italian laborer in the last century was told where he could live and he was not given much opportunity to live elsewhere. The same discriminatory forces operate today with respect to other groups.

The chain of market discrimination is a difficult one to break. If prejudices in the community are strong enough, a builder who desires to undertake a development for a minority group may find it difficult or impossible to acquire a tract of land for the purpose. The mortgage lender will raise questions concerning the economic soundness of the project, suggesting that it will depreciate adjoining properties, and point to the uncertain mortgage history of the prospective buyers. Even if the project is finally approved, he will be more rigorous in his examination of the employment history and credit records of prospective owners than he might otherwise be.

Real estate brokers also help to maintain these barriers. Ordinarily they will not have a house for rent or for sale to a person belonging to a prescribed group. If a Negro finds a house in an all-white neighborhood, the owner may refuse to sell or rent to him. Even if he finds a willing seller in an all-white neighborhood, the Negro will usually find that mortgage lenders are reluctant or flatly unwilling to make a loan to him for the purchase.

Most builders of new suburban residential developments also conform to the traditions of exclusion. Quite universally they will refuse to sell a house to a Negro purchaser, just as a few years ago they might have refused to sell to a person with an Italian name. Most "Nordic" buyers of a higher-priced home have had the experience of being assured by real estate brokers that the neighborhood in which they were buying contained no Catholics, no Jews, or representatives of some other prescribed group.

Several types of nonmarket forces also operate to maintain the ghetto and reinforce the slum. Of these the most powerful are physical violence and the use of the police powers of the state or the municipality. Physical violence has been used historically to prevent each migrant group in turn from invading forbidden areas. Although the use of violence against persons of European origin and of the Jewish and Catholic faiths has almost disappeared in America in recent years, there are still occasional examples of religious bigotry which find violent expression. But the use of violence to prevent Negroes from moving into white or predominantly white residential areas is not at all uncommon, particularly in Northern cities. The pathology of neighborhood organization and incitement to violence in these cases is well documented. In Southern cities the Negro challenge to white residential areas scarcely exists, but the use of violence against Negroes in connection with other problems serves as a constant threat.

Since World War II, the National Association of Home Builders has come to recognize that substantial markets for new homes are being ignored by the industry and that profitable opportunities for additional business may be lost. Some of the country's largest mortgage lenders are recognizing that they are less competitive with other classes of savings and mortgage-lending institutions solely because of their discriminatory policies.

More important, however, than lost opportunity for the housing industry is the fact that when groups are confined to ghettos, and can obtain new housing only by expanding the ghetto into adjoining areas occupied by different groups, acute social tensions produce serious disruptions in the way of life of the discriminating group.

This is most clear in the case of certain Northern cities with large Negro ghettos, whose population has increased by 50 to 100 per cent or more between 1940 and 1960. During this time almost no new homes in vacant areas have been built for Negroes. As a consequence the only possibility for additional housing for Negroes in these cities has been through the purchase or rent of housing occupied by whites. Even on the borders of the ghetto, brokers, realtors, and lenders refuse to sell or rent houses to Negroes until a block is broken by the voluntary or involuntary action of its residents. When a block is broken, every effort is then made by some persons in the real estate business to persuade the whites that they must move immediately. They circulate rumors that property values will depreciate. Mortgage lenders who normally refuse to lend to Negroes now will lend only to Negroes. Thus, purchase by white families becomes difficult or impossible. Under these circumstances the whites feel that their accustomed friendships, their neighborhood associations, their churches, their way of life is disrupted. In effect, they are forced to leave.

The use of the power of the state to enforce racial and religious segregation in housing ended in 1948 when the Supreme Court prohibited the use of state authority to enforce private restrictive covenants. Until recently, however, the Federal Housing Administration (FHA) refused to insure mortgages on nonsegregated developments. In 1958 a California court forbade such discrimination in that state by ruling that houses insured by the FHA and the Veterans Administration (VA) could not be sold if they were restricted racially. By 1960, the VA had agreed that all houses it had taken back because of default on the loan would be resold on a nondiscriminatory basis.

It has been charged that urban redevelopment powers have been used to intensify racial segregation. In actual fact slum clearance is Negro clearance in many communities; the worst and first-cleared slum areas are usually those occupied predominantly by Negroes. If such slum clearance projects were accompanied by developments on vacant land to accommodate the displaced population, the cry of discrimination might never be raised; but virtually no new houses are being built on vacant land for non-white minority groups.

Slum clearance has thus placed intense pressure upon the housing supply and has forced either a doubling up of the affected minorities or the conversion of areas occupied by other groups to occupancy by the displaced minority. Nation-wide programs for the construction of urban express highways are having similar effects. Public authorities often choose rights-of-way through densely developed urban slum areas, which usually are Negro areas also. The cumulative adverse impact of the highway program on minority groups and their housing situation may prove to be greater than that caused by renewal programs.

Public housing programs have also had the effect of intensifying segregation, although usually inadvertently. Public housing agencies, seeking to clear the worst slums first, have usually cleared areas occupied by nonwhites and other minority groups. Because public housing projects are required by law to admit new families in accordance with some standard of need, these same minorities with the lowest incomes and the poorest housing conditions are given preference in the occupancy of the projects. As a result, many public housing projects are occupied exclusively by nonwhites or other minorities.

Although these policies have doubtless reflected the relatively greater need of minority groups, they have also tended to intensify segregation, sometimes in communities where segregation had never existed prior to the development of public housing projects. Some Northern housing authorities have nondiscrimination policies aimed at producing a nonsegregated pattern. However, the concentration of nonwhites in the low-income groups is so large that the overwhelming majority of applicants for admission are nonwhites. In Southern cities the effort of public housing authorities to provide a larger proportion of public housing for Negroes than for whites, because the housing conditions of Negroes are so much worse than those of whites, has also led to new patterns of segregation.

The direct use of governmental authority to enforce segregation has been outlawed since the Supreme Court decision noted above. There are, however, numerous instances of the use of indirect government powers to maintain discriminatory housing patterns. Municipal officials may deny building permits, refuse to accept streets, disapprove subdivision plats, fail to extend water or sewage facilities, and in other ways harass builders who propose residential developments which are intended to attract members of minority groups. In these instances the administering official publicly disclaims that a racial factor has anything to do with the denial of a privilege or right that otherwise would be granted.

ANTI-DISCRIMINATION MEASURES

Discriminatory practices still occur in many localities and prevail in others but their force is shrinking under many pressures. Some of these are court actions such as the Supreme Court's outlawing of restricting covenants mentioned earlier. Others are evidenced in new legislation. By 1959, for example, fourteen states had enacted laws against racial discrimination in housing

—California, Colorado, Connecticut, Indiana, Massachusetts, Michigan, Minnesota, New Jersey, New York, Oregon, Pennsylvania, Rhode Island, Washington, and Wisconsin.

The most evident sign of progress against discriminatory practices is a shift in public attitudes. The United States Commission on Civil Rights took cognizance of this fact in its first report in 1959, although it had few positive recommendations to make beyond the extremely important one that equality of opportunity for good housing must go hand in hand with a larger supply of low-price housing for *all* lower-income families. The Commission also recommended that the President issue an executive order "stating the constitutional objective of equal opportunity in housing, directing all federal agencies to shape their policies and practices to make the maximum contribution to this goal."

In recent years there has been a marked abatement of race riots which once plagued some Northern cities. Only a year after a Negro had bought a house in Levittown, Pennsylvania, touching off a rabble-rousing demonstration, a second Negro family moved in without a ripple of disturbance. With rare exceptions, law and order are promptly enforced.

A higher level of popular understanding increasingly underlines the contradiction between discrimination and democratic objectives. A market free of racial or religious discrimination would eliminate the conditions which now cause segregation; but in most areas of the country this would not eliminate the concentration of racial and religious groups which results from normal free market choice. Many Negroes prefer to live in predominantly Negro areas where they have a wide choice of friends and religious and recreational institutions which fit their desires and tastes. In some of the older communities in the country where discrimination against Catholics in the real estate market has virtually disappeared, predominantly Catholic neighborhoods still exist. Many Jews prefer to live in neighborhoods predominantly occupied by Jews. While this pattern is not so obvious among white Protestants, nevertheless groups similar in education, religion, and income tend to live together in different areas of cities and suburbs.

In 1960, a Philadelphia study by Chester Rapkin and William Grigsby (*The Demand for Housing in Eastwick*) showed that in new residential areas with homes priced at over $12,000, not more than 1 or 2 per cent would be purchased by Negroes. This is a pattern which would probably find acceptance among prospective white purchasers. Philadelphia home builders now resist the entrance of Negroes into suburban housing developments, but, even if they did not, it would have little quantitative effect. Moreover, such a policy would eliminate the discriminations which now exclude the relatively rare representative of a minority group who has the education, the income, and the desire to live in the typical new subdivision.

Since the end of World War II, both the Federal government and some private builders have attempted to loosen the housing market for minority groups, particularly Negroes. There are now somewhere between fifty and a hundred newly built (that is, since World War II) projects specifically designated for unsegregated sale or rent. Some of the obstacles faced by builders of unsegregated housing have been mentioned above. When, however, sites have been found, building permits obtained, and financing arranged, many builders experience considerable difficulty in marketing the houses. According to the Commission on Race and Housing: "Those [Negroes] who (a) are able to pay for new housing, (b) are in the market at a particular time, and (c) interested in a particular development are likely to be only a small fraction of the whole nonwhite population in an area." Moreover, the Commission emphasizes, Negroes who are hesitant about moving far away from existing Negro communities may, in many cases, be so habituated to a comparatively low level of expenditure for housing that their need for new housing as defined by others does not constitute an effective demand for it.

The long-run solution to providing good housing for the country's disfranchised consumers is an adequate housing supply. This means a "ladder of homes" to permit families to move with small increases in housing expenditures from poor to better housing. Thus, relating the American incentive system to the housing supply requires a stock of housing, new and old, in good condition, at all price levels and locations to correspond with the requirements of consumers including racial minorities, the aged and others who have previously been disfranchised.

Chapter 6

WHAT THE CONSUMER WANTS

The housing industry has not systematically studied its market. Home builders and government lending agencies have concentrated largely on producing single-family houses. While this emphasis reflects the preference of the largest single market group, it ignores the important other preferences for a wide range of housing types, forms of tenure, locations, and neighborhoods. In America, families do not ordinarily live in any one house or type of house all their lives; on the contrary, their housing preferences pass through what may be called a "housing life cycle." During this cycle, most families will live in small central-city and suburban apartments when they are first married, will often move to larger apartments or single houses when the children are born, and may sell their large houses and move to small houses or apartments when the children grow up and leave home. The available housing supply in some of these periods may consist—for the great majority of Americans of moderate means—largely of inferior offerings.

The high mobility of American families provides evidence of shifting preferences during the family life cycle. Although 20 per cent of all Americans move every year, two-thirds of the moves are within a metropolitan area, and therefore are to serve a changed preference for space, location, dwelling type or design, or some related desire. Millions of single persons comprise a large group whose requirements are neglected in the market. The potential market opportunities are poorly understood and have evoked little producer response. A wider range of choice for housing consumers is clearly one prerequisite to greater consumer satisfaction.

One of the hopes for persuading the American consumer to value housing more highly and thus to create a higher level of effective demand for new and rehabilitated building is to offer him a product that he wants.

But what does the consumer want? Unfortunately, no one knows, at least with sufficient assurance to cause the building industry to make many drastic changes in its present practices. The purchase or rental of any dwelling represents a series of compromises by the consumer. He does not like every feature in the house he selects, nor does he dislike every feature in the house he rejects. He makes his decision by striking the best balance he can, within his means, between what he likes and what he dislikes. And, by and large, producers use this market test as an index of consumer wants. Houses and apartments which show the best current rate of sale or rent are produced in still greater number. But observed behavior can be a misleading guide to preferred behavior.

This chapter deals with consumer housing preferences as they have been revealed by attitude surveys and by the observation of actual behavior. It also considers the problem of shifts in preference as real income increases and life adapts itself to new conditions.

What Attitude Surveys Show

Government agencies, housing magazines, and research institutions have attempted over the years to find out what kind of housing different groups of consumers would like to have. Their efforts have not been very successful, partly because few of the surveys meet accepted standards of statistical sampling. In most cases, respondents are accepted on a catch-as-catch-can basis: subscribers to a given magazine or persons in attendance at a conference of potential home buyers. Another important limitation is that elicited responses do not always have a cost dimension: the stated ideal often represents a combination of preferred tenure, location, and housing type without regard to the costs involved. Moreover, no matter how skillfully a question is framed, the answer is bound to be limited by the individual respondent's level of comprehension and articulateness. Also, as Robert K.

Merton points out in his essay, "The Social Psychology of Housing" (1948), rarely can the consumer judge what his reactions will be to an environment he has not experienced.

Some part of the producer's failure to provide shelter in amounts, sizes, designs, and locations that the consumer prefers is this inability of the consumer to see himself clearly. Caught as he usually is between necessity and preference, the consumer tends to make his housing decisions on the basis of arbitrary judgments. But despite all the difficulties inherent in attitude surveys, they are an important aid to an understanding of the consumer of housing.

TENURE PREFERENCES

Surveys taken since the early thirties show that 70 per cent of the country's population desire homeownership for themselves. That 70 per cent of the population reveals itself persistently in favor of homeownership is not necessarily an indication of effective demand. The ideal of owning a piece of land and the dwelling on it is tightly woven into our whole cultural pattern. It has a pervading effect on opinion even when almost two-fifths of the population rents and a substantial portion prefers that form of tenure.

The motives for homeownership are many and closely interrelated. As long ago as 1937, a survey made by the editors of *Architectural Forum* showed that four out of five persons who preferred homeownership did so because they liked the "feeling" of ownership and liked to be able to fix up their dwellings to suit themselves. These two points accounted for half of all the expressed motives. Men stressed their pride in ownership and its attendant independence, and women, the opportunity ownership provided for change in the dwelling. The relative strength of independence as a value was greater among the older families than among the younger, higher in the middle middle class than in the lower middle class, and greater for smaller families than for larger ones. The editors concluded that "the urge to own is based more on emotional than on financial grounds; it is more concerned with satisfaction of the ego than with considerations of economy."

Janet Abu-Lughod, in a comprehensive analysis of the significant attitude surveys on housing for the volume in this series, *Housing Choices and Housing Constraints,* stresses the point that the quality of the housing in terms of its livability is the least dominant of all factors in ownership preferences. Homeownership is only partly the result of a rational, utilitarian decision; most often it stems from a combination of circumstances that include size of the family, need to provide the children with adequate play space, dislike of neighbors, changes in employment, rising income, and a desire to demonstrate personal success. The very fact of homeownership seems to give many people a larger measure of prestige and social status than they obtain through rental tenure. These persons believe that, in the eyes of the community, they become stable and dependable citizens when they become homeowners.

The degree of preference for homeownership varies markedly among income groups. In the upper-income group it runs to about 80 per cent, in the middle-income group to 75 per cent, in the low-income group to 66 per cent. Among the groups which achieve their preference for homeownership, the most numerous by far are the self-employed and managerial groups. Closely following them are the professional and semiprofessional groups.

If satisfaction with tenure is to be achieved, attempts must be made to increase the rate at which consumers who wish to can shift more easily from rented dwellings to owned ones, and to widen the opportunity for rental housing for those families which prefer to rent. In other countries intermediate forms of tenure have been devised, like the lease for the life of the tenant, which provide some of the advantages of owning along with those of renting. Cooperative ownership, prevalent in Europe, and growing in the United States, offers some of the advantages of renting along with those of owning.

DWELLING TYPE AND SIZE PREFERENCES

Every survey indicates that almost all families prefer a single-family, detached house. Yet many millions of American families live in attached houses, two- or four-family houses, or apartments. In some metropolitan areas, the proportion is half or more. Evidently millions of individuals and families, when confronted with either the economies or the locational advantages of other dwelling types, abandon their preference for the single-family, detached house. Row houses, still popular in Eastern cities, provide much of the privacy of single family houses, some private outdoor space, and locations convenient to work and shops. Apartments, too, permit locations near centers of urban activities and in addition freedom from maintenance responsibility, both tremendous advantages to many families.

No one can forecast whether the expressed preference for the single-family house will be reflected more decisively in family behavior. If it is, cities may spread out over areas perhaps five to ten times their present size. Doubtless they will continue to have high density centers but their historical character as urban places will be wholly different. Cities may well become endless expanses of low-density suburbia.

The principal criteria for satisfaction with a dwelling unit are the amount and distribution of space, physical condition, and equipment. As long as condition and equipment are well below the standards of the household, concern about space remains relatively dormant. Thus the family that lacks a bathtub usually exhibits little concern over a separate bedroom for each child. Space is a sophisticated preference, a largely self-generating luxury that accompanies a higher standard of living. In that sense, it is a concern primarily of the middle- and upper-income family.

Typically, the consumer thinks of space in terms of number of rooms rather than in terms of square feet of floor space. A six-room house will make many consumers happier than a five-room house of greater dimensions. The number of bedrooms is extremely important. In the 1930s it was usually two; in the 1950s usually three. There is a growing demand for four-bedroom houses. But even overcrowded families rank sleeping space only fourth in importance. For them, space for leisure, cooking, and eating takes precedence, and in that order. As space demands approach fulfillment, attention and complaints center on improvements in equipment and layout.

What is the modal (or mythical?) consumer's picture of his

dream house? Ideally, it is a free-standing, single-story house of "modified contemporary-traditional" style, set on a 70-foot by 100-foot lot off a curving street and surrounded by houses different from, and somewhat more pretentious than, itself. It has six rooms, three or four bedrooms, a large kitchen, one and a half or two baths with colored tile walls and separate tub and shower, a large living room, and, perhaps, a "family room." It also has a garage large enough for storage purposes, a porch, a flagstone patio, a den or guest room, and a basement.

CITY VERSUS SUBURBS

Preferences for tenure, type, and location of dwelling are often interrelated. For example, the desire for ownership usually implies a single-family dwelling, and a single-family dwelling usually means a suburban location. Since the end of World War II, with little central-city land available for development, preference for the owned, single-family house has almost automatically meant preference for the suburbs.

There is considerable debate as to whether suburban location is a specific and valid preference or merely a by-product of other preferences. Some persons believe improvements in transportation and communication merely made it possible for people to do what they had always wanted: to live in an environment with green space and air and sunshine, but to keep their chances of making a living in the great metropolitan labor market.

Others are less convinced of the validity of this position and see in the modern suburban movement a pincers action: people who want to escape some aspects of their present location and housing can find what they consider to be more desirable conditions only if they sacrifice locational convenience, time, and effort.

Undoubtedly one of the strong motivations for a family's move to the suburbs is the belief that suburban living is beneficial for children. But there are other reasons too. One is the negatively expressed desire to get away from the city, with its noise, traffic, and faster pace. Another is the desire to be near friends, relatives, or the "right sort of people." And, finally, the reason is sometimes advanced that suburban living is less expensive than city living. Obviously, the importance of this latter motive depends in part on the individual family's income and in part on costs in a particular area. It is seldom cited by middle- and upper-income families living in the built-up suburbs of the large Eastern metropolitan centers; it is most frequently cited by lower middle-income groups living in semirural fringe areas of moderate-sized urban communities.

One of the most important deductions that can be made from the evidence on city versus suburban location is that if central-city renewal programs are to be successful in either holding the middle-income family in the city or attracting it back from the suburbs, more drastic changes must be planned in the types, densities, and forms of tenure of central-city housing than have been anticipated. And, considering the importance of neighborhood and schools to suburban parents, the scale of change will have to be larger than is usually assumed by proponents of rehabilitation.

HOW IMPORTANT IS THE NEIGHBORHOOD?

There is another aspect of locational preference which is perhaps even more important than the broad choice between the city and the suburbs. That is the satisfaction a family finds with the neighborhood in which it lives.

Studies seem to indicate that few housing consumers are motivated to change their residences primarily because of inadequacies in the physical condition of their neighborhoods. Nor are they particularly concerned about distance from place of work or shopping and entertainment facilities. But some families will change neighborhoods, despite satisfaction with their dwellings, if the social characteristics of their neighbors become obviously different from their own. In general, the higher the socioeconomic status of the individual, the more likely he is to be content with the characteristics of his neighbors. Also if the family regards its dwelling as a temporary one, the social characteristics of the neighborhood are relatively meaningless.

In the decade which followed World War II, rising family incomes and liberal mortgage terms combined to make it possible for many families to satisfy the desire for a better neighborhood along with the desire for permanent tenure.

MOBILITY

The willingness of the American family to change location with changing circumstances is without parallel. About 20 per cent of all persons move during any given year. For example, between March, 1958, and March, 1959, the Bureau of the Census reports that 32.8 million persons—almost one out of every five—moved from one dwelling to another. Two-thirds of the movers stayed in the same county, however. A large proportion of those who moved were young adults. Of the group between the ages of 20 and 24, two out of five changed their residences between 1958 and 1959.

If past behavior is an accurate gauge of future trends, it is reasonable to suppose that within one year 20 to 25 per cent of all families will have moved at least once; that within two years, 30 to 33 per cent will have moved; that within five years, 50 to 57 per cent will have moved; that within ten years, about 75 per cent will have moved; and that within twenty years, no more than 10 per cent will be living in dwellings they occupy today.

Apparently not more than half the people who move do so because of dissatisfaction with house or neighborhood. The relationship between mobility and dissatisfaction with a dwelling may stand unbalanced, however. A shortage of dwelling units can depress the mobility rate even when dissatisfaction is high. Also, less than half of the persons who say they are dissatisfied with their housing actually translate their desire to move into action.

In the past twenty-five years, the discrepancy between the mobility rates of renters and owners has decreased steadily; that is, renters have become more stable in their market behavior and owners more mobile. However the mobility rate of homeowners is still less than half as great as that of renters. In 1956, 57 per cent of renters had occupied their present unit for two to three years, but about half of the owner group had been in their homes six years or more. Mobility is generally highest near the central core of the city and at the fast-growing periphery of the city or its suburban ring. Between these two polar regions are large areas where both dwelling unit turnover and interneighborhood mobility are quite low.

In sum:

1. Mobility rates are inflated by multiple or frequent movers who constitute a small percentage of the population and yet account for a large proportion of the moves made.

2. Out of the 20 per cent who do move each year, about 7 per cent move for "economic" reasons having nothing to do with satisfactions or dissatisfactions with their housing.

3. An additional 2 or 3 per cent are involuntary movers, moving not out of a desire to increase their housing satisfactions, but because their dwellings have been taken away from them through fire, demolition, sale, or eviction.

4. Still another 1 per cent or more have moved for the very good reason that a new family desiring an independent household has been formed.

5. Out of the 20 per cent who move each year, perhaps only 8 per cent actually move to obtain housing more suitable to their needs. Of these, somewhat under half buy houses.

6. A considerable proportion of moves within metropolitan areas result from upgrading, the process of moving to progressively better neighborhoods as families improve their income and status.

THE CITY DWELLER

There is a vast amount of documentation on why people move to the suburbs. We know almost nothing, however, about why people do not move to the suburbs or, if they have lived in the suburbs and now live in the city, why they changed their minds. In 1957, *Fortune* magazine and ACTION collaborated in a survey of a selected sample of central-city residents in New York, Philadelphia, and Chicago to try to find out what kind of people live in certain types of central-city housing, where they come from, and why. The housing types covered by the survey, which was conducted by Janet Abu-Lughod, were new luxury apartments, older apartment buildings, and rehabilitated town houses.

It is by no means true that all Americans prefer the suburbs over the city, or that the present residents of our large urban centers are all unwilling captives. For many persons, the positive advantages of urban life make the city, with all its discomforts, an unmatched location. "They *like* the city," William H. Whyte, Jr., observes in *The Exploding Metropolis* on the basis of the *Fortune*—ACTION survey, "They like the privacy; they like the specialization, and the hundreds of one-of-a-kind shops; they like the excitement . . . the heterogeneity, the contrasts, the mixture of odd people. . . . 'No matter what goes on,' says a Chicago man, 'it goes on *here.*' "

The types of consumers who find merit in central locations are younger individuals, both married and unmarried, older couples with grown children, widows, and unattached older persons. These groups account for perhaps half of all American households and are growing in number. However, if town houses and other central-city dwellings are to attract families with children, there must be a satisfactory public solution to the school problem. Presently, families with high incomes in the large cities of the Northeast rely almost exclusively upon private schools.

Almost half of the respondents in the *Fortune*–ACTION survey had moved in from peripheral and suburban areas, or anticipated moving out to the suburbs in the future. The survey showed that the suburban and the in-town housing markets feed and support each other, with many consumers shifting from one market to the other over their lifetimes. The hope that the central city can continue to attract even greater numbers of suburbanites is not unfounded. The chances of its doing so depend on whether high-quality housing can be made available in desirable central locations at costs competitive with suburban ones. They also depend on the ability of the central city to rid itself of racial ghettos and crime and to provide a higher level of services.

The advantages which attract or hold people in the central city are chiefly ones of convenience. Central-city residents like being close to their work and downtown shopping. Being close to work is particularly important, for in-town residents appear to be more wedded to their jobs than their friends in the suburbs.

Although the survey found that central-city residents tend to lead active lives and to lead them in a center-directed way, it also established the fact that many leisure-time interests do not require downtown living. This was particularly true for families in the rehabilitated houses who preferred sedentary home activities or visiting with neighbors to the more central commercial forms of entertainment. Despite the evidence that few central-city residents have recreational interests that require downtown location, the fact of easy access to central recreational facilities such as theaters, museums, restaurants, and concert halls was a decided advantage which they appreciated. This psychic satisfaction seems to derive from the knowledge that, if one wants to, one can take advantage of these offerings. One of the major conclusions of the survey is that central-city residents are keenly aware of how the central city can satisfy housing and other needs at different periods in their lives.

The main question in analyzing the survey is whether the central city will reassert itself as a good place to live. William H. Whyte, Jr., says:

One thing is clear. The cities have a magnificent opportunity. There are definite signs of a small but significant move back from suburbia. There is also evidence that many people who will be moving to suburbia would prefer to stay in the city—and it would not take too much more in amenities and space to make them stay. . . . The next few years will be critical. The fact that the potential market will be increasing won't mean anything unless there is a great deal more—and much better—housing to attract the market.

Nevertheless, migration back to the city remains only a small fraction of the migration to the suburbs.

The Life Cycle and Family Types

Studies of housing attitudes, preferences, and behavior can be extremely misleading unless they are related to an understanding of the number and types of "families" in the housing market and the life cycle of the housing consumer.

Only about half of the "families" that occupy the American housing supply are husband-wife-child families. The other half consists, at any time, of single persons, households of two or more unrelated persons, married couples, and widowed, divorced, or separated persons with or without children. Most studies of housing preferences deal only with the first of these categories. They therefore ignore the incomes, dwelling preferences, and locational preferences of millions of housing consumers. The overwhelming preference for single-family, detached houses expressed in consumer surveys refers to preferences of only a fraction of the market. The concentration of home building on single-family houses largely ignores this fact. Indeed it has been estimated that the largest potential housing market of the future consists of 13 million "families" *not* consisting of husband-wife-child, who now live with others.

The life cycle of the "normal" housing consumer takes him through some, but rarely all, of those other classes of household. Thus the "typical" housing consumer may occupy a small apartment as a single person from the age of 20 to 22. He may move to an apartment with a friend for two years. At age 24 he marries and moves to another apartment with his wife, living there for a year or so when their first child is born. At that time the young family moves to a larger apartment which they occupy for the next three years. At the age of 29 a second child arrives. The first one is now three years old and needs outdoor play space; the second child needs a bedroom.

The family would like to buy a home, but still lacks the down payment or income. They rent an older home near the edge of the city for two years. In their early thirties, with the third child on the way, they purchase a small new suburban house with three bedrooms. It is too small but it is the best they can afford, and the family occupies it usually until the husband is in his mid-forties. Then, if the husband's income has increased substantially, they sell their house for enough to get the down payment on a larger house, one with four bedrooms and a den-guest room to accommodate visiting parents and friends.

Here the "typical" family plans to stay "for the rest of our lives." But in fact, if their income goes up, they may move again to a still better home or a better neighborhood. The likelihood is that the family will remain in the second owned home for twelve to fifteen years. Then all of the children will be graduated from high school and will be employed, away at college, or possibly married and living in their own homes. Some families at this stage of the family cycle move to the greater convenience of an apartment or a smaller house. Others may move to a more pretentious home. But most will continue to occupy their "permanent" home.

After the death of one partner, usually the husband in his mid-sixties, the remaining partner may move to a smaller apartment or into the home of a married child.

The "typical" family has occupied six apartments, one rented house, and two or three owned houses during its life cycle, a total of ten dwellings. Its longest period of tenure was between ten and fifteen years, in later middle age. A change of job to another city, a war, a depression, a divorce, an early death—any of these contingencies of life might have produced a larger total number of dwellings and other types or locations. Of the fifty or more years of adult history, a scant twenty were years in which the family was composed of husband-wife-young children, yet this is the only family for which the housing industry provides a significant supply of new dwellings, and it is this type of family that receives major attention in most surveys of consumer preference.

How Will Consumer Wants Change?

Nelson Foote, who in *Housing Choices and Housing Constraints* in this series, explored many of the demographic, social, and economic forces which are molding new patterns of behavior in American family life, believes that Americans are becoming more discriminating and articulate about the way they like to live. He points out that a fast-growing proportion of families have already started to differentiate their styles of life instead of merely upgrading them. In the process of upgrading, people consciously seek to achieve a standard of living shared by a majority of the population. In the process of differentiating they seek, somewhat less consciously, to set themselves apart from others by their style of living. They may do so by shifting their spending from television sets to high-fidelity sound equipment, by developing leisure-time activities which the whole family shares, by centering family life almost wholly within the dwelling, by serving the community in a purposeful fashion. Whatever the new style of life may be, it starts at the point when some level of upgrading has been achieved and then branches out horizontally from that norm.

The principal expression of this new behavior pattern is in the use of leisure time. Since the turn of the century, the work week in this country has dropped from sixty hours to less than forty for most workers. The number of paid holidays has increased and the paid vacation has lengthened. Such facts led the Twentieth Century Fund to conclude that

to a lessening degree is a man's job the central focus of his concern. Work no longer appears to him as the only road to virtue and salvation. Outside the job lies the world of family and cultural pursuits. And attainment of satisfaction in such areas seems hardly less significant than advancement along the straight and narrow path of the career.

Inevitably, such "attainment of satisfaction" will have an increasing impact on the house—its site, its design, and its equipment for family living. Not everyone can indulge his taste. Millions of families must take what they can get or hold on to what they already have.

When a family achieves sufficient status to give it a large number of options on where to live, its choice of location tends to be based primarily on what it wants out of life. The family that wants space more than it wants a wall-oven may start looking at old houses in unfashionable neighborhoods, if that is the only way it can get the space or differentiation it needs. The family that wants access to theaters and museums or jazz establishments more than it wants a garden or a barbecue pit may look for an apartment near the downtown area of the central city, even if it means going back to public transportation.

It may be significant that by the 1960s some industries had begun to play down the theme of "keeping up with the Joneses" in their campaigns to market consumer goods. Instead, they were appealing to the consumer to dare to be different. They were beginning to realize that there is no single-faced, single-purpose consumer for any commodity—even for housing. There probably never was, but the fiction was preserved for a long time by many groups, including the producers of housing.

THE PRODUCER

Chapter 7

HOUSING PRODUCTION:
ACTORS AND ACTIONS

Management responsibility in the housing industry is divided among many poorly coordinated elements. In addition to various types of builders, the industry is made up of materials manufacturers and suppliers, general contractors, subcontractors, labor unions, several types of investors, realtors, various classes of mortgage lenders, subdividers, and land developers, and many Federal, state, and local government agencies. There is little effective communication among these groups or between them and the consumer of the product.

Among the many deterrents to the rationalization of the building industry is localism. Because the ultimate product of the industry is constructed on a specific piece of land in a specific locality, restrictive local practices and regulations are a major barrier to improvements in housing construction.

The two major lines of development in the production of houses since World War II are off-site and on-site factory assembly. Prefabrication of whole house packages has progressed slowly. Prefabrication of parts or components has become widespread. Similar methods underlie the on-site factory assembly techniques that are employed more and more by large merchant builders. Both production methods help reduce construction costs and permit other management controls that lead to economies of bulk purchasing, materials simplification, regularized employment, and savings normal to other industries.

Further progress toward more efficient production will require additional capital investment in the industry and better communication among its participants. Most important, however, is the extension of technical research by appropriate private and public groups on the assembly of the whole house, on problems of land acquisition and development, and on the financing and installation of community facilities and utility services for housing.

Home building is one of America's industrial frontiers. Though one of the largest industries, it has only recently been influenced by modern business management and technology. Its great productive achievements are still those of a scattered army of materials and equipment producers, builders, land developers, and brokers, large and small, efficient and inefficient, operating full blast one year and coasting the next. Rationalization, the prime achievement of the American economic system, has yet to bring most of its economies of scale, entrepreneurial expertise, and technological innovation to bear on the business of producing and marketing an ample supply of housing. Despite impressive advances in the last decades, most of the business of home building is carried on by a vast congeries of disparate operators who not only are poorly organized among themselves but often work in virtual isolation from each other. Home building hardly justifies the term of "housing industry."

Home building is initiated by many different organizations and individuals: custom builders, merchant builders, land developers, cooperatives, other groups and institutions, public agencies, various classes of investors. These initiators are supported by building materials suppliers, prefabricators, contractors, subcontractors, labor, and lending institutions. The commitment of many of the participants in home building is partial; their principal activity is in the larger construction industry. This transient character of their relationship to home building is a major weakness of the industry. There are other serious weaknesses, however. Diffuse location and regulatory structure discourage the heavy capital investment needed to advance organization, technology, and marketing. The industry is wholly lacking in centralized management responsibility. Responsibility is divided among a score of relatively autonomous elements, each seeking to protect itself against the fluctuations and insecurities of the business. There is a lack of technological research and development on a scale comparable to that of other industries. And, finally, the industry does not engage in market research and the development of merchandising techniques of the sort which support the fast growth of competing industries.

These weaknesses result from a variety of conditions, some of which are inherent in the industry or beyond its control. Four deserve special emphasis, since they must be changed as a prelude to decisive industrial progress. These are the problems of cyclical instability, land, government regulation, and the market effects of the existing supply of housing.

The notoriously unstable character of home building, its susceptibility to wide fluctuations in the business cycle, its extreme dependence upon externally supplied credit, and, in recent years, its dependence on unstable credit terms, have evidently deterred large-scale capital investment in the industry. An ample supply of well-located and well-serviced sites is essential to the housing industry, but the difficulties of assembling land under our system of land ownership and the industry's dependence upon local governments for utilities and other services prevent an effective site assembly process. Housing is also subject to a host of regulations by governments, regulations which prevent many evils but which can also cripple innovation and experiment. Lastly, the home-building industry is impeded by competition with the huge existing supply of housing. In the light of these difficulties, the weaknesses of the industry become understandable and, conceivably, remediable.

The great technological advances engendered by World War II did a good deal to limber up the housing industry, and there has been considerable improvement in home building methods in the years since 1940. But there are still great opportunities for further improvement.

Case History of Confusion

Two major categories of producers, the custom builder and the merchant builder, occupy crucial positions; they account for about three-quarters of all home building. Confronting them and dealing with them are a much greater number of entrepreneurs, who have in common the fact that they too either initiate or must collaborate in home building. The list includes Federal agencies, municipal bodies, investors, investor-builders, realtors, life insurance companies, savings and loan associations, savings bankers, commercial bankers, mortgage brokers, rehabilitators, subdividers, general contractors, subcontractors, labor, and, of course, suppliers, ranging from the local lumber yard to General Electric.

The costly interactions of the housing industry's considerable body of actors, which are examined in this chapter, can be suggested by a description of how most houses get built. Typically, the builder in the housebuilding field starts with blueprints taken from a published book of plans and accommodates them to facts of topography, local preferences and restrictions, and his own experience and ideas. Only a small number of houses benefit from the services of a professional architect.

Next the builder finds a piece of land or scattered lots which he believes to be suitable for the house or houses proposed. Often he uses the services of a real estate broker. With his land cost fixed, the builder estimates construction costs, dealing in the process with subcontractors and suppliers, computing social security costs, adding in the costs of his own labor force and the amount of his profit. One or more building permits are secured, often aided by friendly acquaintance with the local building inspector. Meanwhile, a loan is negotiated that will become a mortgage when the house is completed to the satisfaction of the local bank or savings and loan association and of the Federal Housing Administration or the Veterans Administration, if they insure or guarantee the mortgage.

Perhaps the most distinguishing characteristic of the industry is the universal use of subcontractors who supply special materials, install them, and supervise their own share of the job. Even among large-scale operative builders, subcontractors account for 30 per cent of the cost of a house. In many speculative developments the entire construction job, involving 60 to 80 per cent of the final cost, may be subcontracted. Subcontractors typically engage in both residential and nonresidential work, in new building, and in repair and maintenance. They are vendors and installers, so that their attention is divided among several interests and activities. Albert G. H. Dietz, of the Massachusetts Institute of Technology, in work he did for this series, described the traditional process this way:

The typical builder expects to do some of the work with his own force and to subcontract the balance. Usually he retains carpentry because this trade carries through the entire job. The work progresses in a number of separate operations. Subcontractor number one enters, after the house is laid out on the lot, and with his bulldozer, power shovel, and other equipment strips the topsoil and excavates for the foundation. He also digs any necessary trenches. He is followed by subcontractor number two (masonry), who erects the sectional forms for a poured concrete foundation, for which dealer number one provides the ready-mixed concrete. The forms may, of course, be custom-built by the contractor, utilizing lumber which will later be reused in the superstructure; and the foundation may be concrete blocks or other masonry supplied by dealer number one and erected by subcontractor number two.

The contractor, drawing on his first construction loan from the bank (if he plans to use one), brings in his carpenters and erects the framing for floors, walls, partitions, and roof with material procured from dealer number two. Subcontractor number three (the plumber) begins to install the rough plumbing, including sewer and water connections to the street. Subcontractor number two erects the chimney. While the roofing is being applied by the contractor or by subcontractor number four (the roofer and sheet metal man), subcontractor number five (the electrician) and subcontractor number six (the heating man) install their rough lines and make necessary connections to street utilities. In the meantime, windows and exterior doors are being hung. These are obtained from dealer number two (lumber) or dealer number three (millwork).

At least one payment has by this time been made by the owner, so the builder is in a financial position to meet some of his obligations and to proceed with subcontractor number seven (the plasterer). However, the building inspector, the plumbing inspector, the wiring inspector, and possibly the heating inspector must approve the construction to this point. An FHA or VA inspector may also have to pass on the construction. [Closing in parts of the structure may be delayed for days until all inspections have been completed.]

With the insulation installed, and lath and plaster applied, millwork and flooring arrive from dealers two and three and are erected by the contractor's own crew, or the flooring may be installed by subcontractor number eight (the floor layer). Eventually, the time comes for subcontractors three (plumber), five (electrician), and six (heating) to install fixtures and appliances either supplied by themselves or purchased by them from dealers four, five, and six—or by the contractor or in some instances by the owner. In the meantime, subcontractor two (masonry) is finishing the fireplace and subcontractor four (sheet metal) is installing the hood over the kitchen range.

Subcontractor number nine (the painter), who has already applied at least one coat of paint outdoors, arrives and applies paint and whatever other finishes are called for at the same time that he hangs wallpaper purchased from dealer number seven, from whom he may also purchase his paint if he does not obtain it directly from the paint manufacturer or from a wholesaler.

Finally, the contractor installs the finish hardware purchased from dealer number eight. He also grades the yard and he may plant it with grass seed purchased from dealer number nine, the nurseryman; on the other hand, the owner may elect to save a little money and undertake to do the final grading and seeding himself.

After the last bit of haggling over extras has been completed, the contractor has furnished proof that all bills have been paid, and the inspectors have made their last inspections, the owner with considerable misgiving makes the final payments, which the contractor hopes will provide a profit after he pays off his last bank loan.

The difficulty with this somewhat intricate process is not simply its complexity. One of the largest developers, the Levitt firm, for instance, relies heavily on a large number of subcontractors and yet keeps costs low. Firms in other industries deal with many suppliers—General Motors has some 18,000 of them—without adverse effects on production efficiency. The basic problem is management. Too many sorts of people are in on too many of the basic acts of housebuilding for the producer to plan his operation with any precision. He cannot, for example, set up exact supply-in supply-out schedules of the sort common in most industries. He cannot establish a firm work schedule, since the start of one trade is dependent upon the completion of the work of another, and each trade is working on its own under a contract which it is trying to make profitable.

The housing industry, in other words, is not a clear-cut entity like steel-making or textile manufacturing, in which the operations of any single firm are under continuous management control. It is, in fact, a heterogeneous aggregation of more or less related industries, government bodies, financial institutions, and labor unions. This structure was well suited to the day when the objective was to provide single units of any design, material, and size at any time anywhere. Under modern conditions of demand, the wonder is that it works so well.

THE BUILDERS

A 1948 survey by the Bureau of Labor Statistics revealed that about 250,000, or nearly one-fifth, of the houses built in that year were put up by "firms" which built only one house. Half of all builders erected fewer than ten houses a year, and 89 per cent built fewer than 25. The remaining 11 per cent of the builders produced 47 per cent of the houses. Thus "builders" is a category that ranges from amateur one-house builders to large businesses producing several thousand homes a year.

An analysis of the membership of the National Association of Home Builders revealed that in 1959, 10 per cent of the members built 59 per cent of the houses built by members. Only 1.5 per cent of the members built 500 or more houses in that year. Fifty-eight per cent built 25 or fewer.

The one-house builder may be a part-time contractor who works on other jobs and builds a house on the side, or he may be a prospective owner building his own home with his own labor or through subcontractors. Whether he engages in building on a full-time or part-time basis, and whether as a business or for his own use, such a builder buys materials, lets subcontracts, and employs labor on a retail basis—one house at a time.

The custom builder, a businessman who builds houses to the specifications of individual buyers, operates in much the same way. He may build several or even many houses each year, but each house built involves separate purchases, subcontracts, permits, and employment. The custom builder's organization is the same regardless of size: minimal office organization and overhead, and a system of materials supply and subcontracting that prevents him from exercising more than loose control over his operation but does not prevent his taking—or seeking to take—a profit on the profits already taken by the suppliers and the sub-contractors.

The large-scale builder is growing in number and size. He may be an operative builder (or merchant builder, as he prefers to be called), land subdivider, or general contractor. Operative builders are responsible for more than half of all building. They build speculatively for sale to consumers rather than by contract with a particular customer. Compared with custom builders, operative builders may have tighter controls over their organizations and operations. Their approach to the production of houses differs considerably from that of other builders.

The operative builder acquires land for the erection of houses, arranges the financing of the project, subdivides land and determines building design, undertakes the carpentry work, and oversees the performance of the other work that is subcontracted. He may even maintain a sales force to sell properties when they are completed. Since he produces groups of houses from similar or identical plans at one location during a single undertaking, he is in a position to obtain important economies in the purchase of land, the mass construction of structures, the purchase of supplies, and the scheduling of labor and equipment. The scale of his operation may vary from five to ten properties to thousands, with economies of operation usually increasing with the size of a project. The factor common to each such project, however, is improved management control.

Some of the largest builders, like the Centex Construction Company of Dallas, William J. Levitt, the Mackle Brothers of Miami, and John F. Lang of Phoenix, produce one or more thousands of dwellings a year. Because of the large volume of sales required for their operations, the mass builders concentrate in the fastest growing portions of urban America: the Southwest, Florida, Texas, and the New York, Washington, and Chicago areas.

Many of the largest builders gained their experience in mass construction during the war when the government bore the risk. Some, like Centex, have become national firms, working in widely separated areas. A firm such as Levitt's has so sound a balance sheet (unlike that of the usual small builder) that it can get regular commercial loans rather than the more restrictive construction loans for its full-size residential communities. In 1959, Levitt and Sons, Inc., for the first time, offered stock in the company to the public.

Subdividers and general contractors work together to accomplish much the same result. The subdivider options a piece of land, arranges for its subdivision, obtains financing, secures local government permits and Federal insurance commitments, and provides house plans. Thereafter he "buys the job"; that is, he purchases the rest of the work from general contractors and subcontractors, sharing to greater or lesser extent with the general contractor the function of management, and leaving the sale of the finished properties in the hands of real estate brokers.

General contracting is a fairly sizable operation, but it includes organizations that work on heavy projects like road work or utility construction. Moreover, contractors for residential building usually engage in commercial and industrial building as well. But, as a group, they often have sufficient economic weight and sufficient management experience with sizable building projects to bargain effectively with other groups, including building unions.

Public authorities, cooperatives, nonprofit associations, labor organizations, and welfare and civic groups initiate 3 per cent to 5 per cent of new dwelling units. Investors in rental housing initiate 8 or 10 per cent to 15 per cent. They may include individuals, syndicates, or lending institutions. These groups often have substantial funds of their own or access to other funds. Their ability to secure financing sometimes gives them an economic weight greater than that of other producers on particular developments, and they employ different production methods. Usually they are dependent upon the building services of others: architectural firms, general contractors, and the like.

SUBCONTRACTORS AND SUPPLIERS

Subcontracting is characteristic of all building operations, regardless of size or sponsorship. It accounts for most of the dollar volume of residential building, apparently increasing in proportion on larger projects. There are more than sixty types of sub-contracting, the most common being excavation, masonry, carpentry, plumbing and heating, electrical, plastering, and painting. Flooring, roofing, glazing, tile setting, and cabinetwork come next. These and other subcontracts are found in even single house projects. Subcontracts usually, but not invariably, require the subcontractor to supply the materials and install them in the building. Thus the subcontractor is both purchasing agent and employer of specialized workmen. On large developments, however, the merchant builder may do the purchasing himself and subcontract only installation work.

Subcontracting flourishes not only because of the need for special skills and special materials, but also because no single building effort can offer steady employment for all of the skills required. The subcontractor can keep his plumbers busy on a mixture of new building and maintenance and repair on old buildings, residential and nonresidential. The same continuity of business provides him with a volume of purchases sufficient to justify normal trade discounts. Subcontractors vary widely in size and some are large and stable enough to constitute very large business firms, but the larger the business the more diverse the locations and jobs. Hence the largest subcontractors may be large materials dealers, or even producers who also install.

Behind the subcontractor or the builder lies a broad system for producing and distributing building materials. Both subcontractors and builders obtain materials from wholesalers, jobbers, regional sales offices and warehouses which exist to stock, sell, and supply the wide range of building materials and equipment of varying sizes and qualities that go into building. This system must supply the retail needs of house repair and maintenance, the wholesale needs of large builders, and the equally large requirements of nonresidential buildings. It is perhaps for this reason that the ubiquitous lumber yard—supplying lumber, builders' hardware, millwork, and usually credit—remains a major feature of the industry, providing much of the additional capacity needed in times of building booms. Actually, many suppliers do a bigger business each year in the modernization, maintenance, and repair of the 58 million existing dwellings than they do in the erection of the million or so new dwellings. Replacement of roofing, linoleum, and flooring, together with modernization of bathrooms, kitchens, plumbing, and heating equipment is a substantial business, typically carried on by manufacturer's dealers who not only sell but install the various products.

MANUFACTURERS

Manufacturers of building materials are stronger than any other group involved in housing, but not strong enough to bring to housing the much needed rationalization that is characteristic of their own operations. There are large companies in the fields traditionally associated with housing—plumbing fixtures, cement, plaster, lumber, glass, heating equipment, and stock millwork—and also in the raw materials industries and appliance fields which also supply to housing. These firms are aggressive in merchandising, research, and development, but only part of their sales are directed to housing. The 1959 gross sales of a few of them, shown in the accompanying table, indicate their size.

TABLE 4. VOLUME OF BUSINESS FOR SELECTED CORPORATIONS

Industry	Company	1959 sales
Cement.....................	Lone Star	$ 88,731,000
Equipment..................	General Electric	4,349,509,000
Glass......................	Pittsburgh Plate Glass	606,947,000
Lumber and plywood..........	Weyerhaeuser	458,339,000
Paints.....................	National Lead	530,551,000
Plumbing and heating........	American Standard	517,413,000
Metals.....................	United States Steel	3,643,040,000
Wallboard, roofing and tile.....	Johns Manville	377,562,000

Source: "The Fortune Directory—The 500 Largest Industrial Corporations," *Fortune,* July, 1960.

There are also many small manufacturers who produce for local markets, such as those for bricks and cement block. And finally, there are companies which install as well as manufacture material, thus serving both as subcontractors and as suppliers.

Large suppliers and some manufacturers allow discounts for the quantity orders of large-scale merchant builders, some of whom are said to buy more consumer durable goods than any retail outlet. But even so, there is little "factory-to-factory" selling in the housing industry.

ARCHITECTS AND BROKERS

Architects, landscape architects, engineers, lawyers, and real estate brokers also play a significant role in housing. Because of their professional status architects rarely initiate business; in fact they are not consulted for most housing. The smaller producers tend to use plans developed from their own experience or to copy and modify stock plans appearing in trade journals, popular magazines, and the like. Merchant builders, however, are turning more and more to professional architects; some of the large-scale builders have full-time architectural staffs of their own, as do the prefabricators of packaged houses. A few architects have developed large practices on a royalty basis with large builders. The consequence of these practices is a wide gap between the architectural quality of the best built larger developments and the product of the smaller speculators. The materials manufacturers and trade associations who hold national design competitions and seek to popularize the system of fixed fee plus royalty for architects are helping to narrow the gap.

In comparison with architects, real estate brokers are omnipresent. Some brokers initiate building projects. Most of them serve as intermediaries at the beginning of the housebuilding process by assembling a site and negotiating its sale to an individual or a merchant builder, and at the end of the process, by servicing the market for the sale of houses to consumers. The consumer depends upon the broker for information about the characteristics of a dwelling, its relative value, the soundness of its construction, its conformity to codes and ordinances, the characteristics of the neighborhood in which it is located, and even the sources of funds by which it can be financed. Real estate brokers often engage in buying and selling for their own accounts and they manage properties, serve as mortgage brokers, and act as rental agents.

The typical brokerage is a one- or two-man operation. Rarely is it as large as five. Large-scale developers typically bypass brokers and sell their houses through salesman employed on a salary basis. Other merchant builders retain brokers on a fee basis—usually less than the standard 5 per cent.

Who Is in Charge Here?

The modern concept of managerial responsibility hardly operates within the home-building industry which, on the whole, functions like a complex of medieval guilds, each guild accepting limited duties and responsibilities, each guild protecting its own interests. The builder, the subcontractor, the materials supplier, the broker, the subdivider, the manufacturer of raw or finished materials, each has a part to play; as do the Federal government and the mortgage lender, discussed in detail elsewhere in this volume; and the local government with its regulations for building, land subdivision, and land use. The lenders provide most of the funds for building and for home purchase, but their rightful concern for the security of the depositors' money leads them to extremes of caution—and dependence upon the initiative of others. The regulations of local government may prevent bad building, but they cannot assure good or adequate buildings. Each participant in the home-building process is important; each depends on the other. But no one is in charge.

Many forces work to perpetuate confusion of management in the housing industry. The industry must provide a wide variety of house prices and dwelling types under sundry financial arrangements at numerous locations spread over a vast continent. The uniquely complex process of putting up a structure requires the processing of land as well as of equipment and material, the approval of the community as well as of the owner. Construction takes place on a specific plot of land in a specific locality. The business of building and the profession of design, the system of mortgage finance, the code of community standards, and the union-unit bylaws are all based on the notion that houses will continue to be built as they always have been. A host of persons, ranging from the local lumber yard owner and the local banker to the FHA inspectors and the producers of building materials, have a vested interest in the traditional house production system. Most of these forces and the conventions which surround them are imbedded in local practice. Indeed, local habits are so taken for granted in home building that they operate practically with the force of fixed rules. Thus localism stands out as a strong inherent impediment to improved housing at lower prices.

Localism is both a cause and an effect of the small scope of the average builder. His output is too small to give him enough economic weight to act as an efficient manager. He finds it difficult to maintain exact accounts, he cannot control his financing, nor can he obtain the best bargains in dealing with other interests that make up the housing industry. It is easy for him to get into building; all he has to do is declare himself a contractor and then call on the services of subcontractors and building materials suppliers. It is also easy for him to get out of the industry; only rarely does he have any permanent investment in it.

If no one is in charge in the home-building industry and if localism seems to defeat aggressive leadership at most points, the large merchant builders and contractors are in a better position than most other participants to effect important changes. They can benefit from certain controls over cost that are not available to small builders, and they can economize by the use of mass-construction techniques that are possible only in quantity production. Quantity production permits the large builder to schedule work systematically, to obtain package delivery of precut materials to each house site, reducing the idle and lost time that comes from moving crews from building to building, and to make connections with utilities and road systems on a wholesale basis. Furthermore, quantity production stimulates the development of specialized work crews, sales staffs, and experts in municipal controls and Federal regulations. But only a few of the largest scale merchant builders are yet at the point where they can exercise decisive influence upon the costs of materials, subcontracts, labor, and land, or upon government regulations and private landing policies.

The relative strength of the various parts of the industry may be weighed in terms of their relative contribution to the sum total of housing costs. Builders typically allocate costs according to a fourfold division of land, labor, subcontracts, and materials. Usually on-site labor accounts for 30 to 40 per cent of construction costs, building materials account for another 40 per cent of construction costs, and land, fees, other services, and profit account for the rest. This division tends to obscure the basic contributions of other parts of the industry. The builder knows what he pays for the labor directly employed by him, but not what labor costs are in the bids of his subcontractors. He knows the price tags on building materials which he purchases directly, but he does not know the price tags on the materials provided by subcontractors. Only the big merchant builders are in a position to exercise any decisive influence over the largest costs in their own operations.

There are no systematic studies of the relative efficiency of the different elements of the building industry. From time to time, there have been intensive studies of building labor, materials distribution processes, or other single parts of the housing industry, but most of them reveal nothing about relative efficiency. Perhaps the best study in this field is Sherman Maisel's analysis of the relative efficiency of different-sized operative builders in the San Francisco Bay area, which showed that costs decreased from $9,500 to $8,750 as the size of the builder increased, while overhead and profits rose from $741 to $1,608.

Will Prefabrication Help?

The manufacture of houses or of their component parts before they reach the site on which they are to be erected is, variously, a system of providing builders with supplies, a method of creating and merchandizing an almost complete house package, and a philosophy of production. The philosophy expresses itself in the hope that prefabrication will eventually provide for housing the economies and efficiencies that characterize large vertically organized industries. Despite significant progress during the postwar period, both in the development and in the marketing of prefabricated houses, the hope has not yet been realized.

The completeness of the prefabricated package varies from about 25 per cent to 90 per cent of the material comprising the house. Some prefabricators offer a house complete except for its site connections, but most prefabricators supply merely the shell materials for the superstructure, leaving to local contractors the provision and installation of plumbing and heating, foundations, final finish, and many fixtures. Another variation is the manufacture by local lumber dealers of wall panels, cabinets, and millwork of standard dimensions and of varying completeness. The erection of a house from such materials clearly effects certain economies, but it does not change the fundamental process by which most houses are built. In all but the first of these circumstances, most of the total cost of a prefabricated house is incurred on the site rather than in the factory. Even when a near-complete house is delivered, land must be cleared, the site graded, and utilities and foundations installed.

Prefabricated housing still accounts for less than one-tenth of all residential building, and no single firm produces the large number of units characteristic of large firms in other industries. The largest prefabricator (including its subsidiaries) in the United States produced about 45,000 units in 1959, or about 3.5 per cent of all single-family nonfarm homes produced. (Its production dropped to about 30,000 dwelling units in 1960.) The total output of the prefabricators in 1959 was estimated at from 90,000 units to as many as 140,000 units, depending on the definition of prefabrication. The level of industrialization possible with this volume of production is obviously different from the level of industrialization in some other industries where several large manufacturers may each be responsible for 10 per cent or more of production.

Moreover, manufacturers of most other consumer goods have control of their products up to the time they are finished and sold to a wholesaler, sometimes even up to the time they are sold to the customer. The prefabricator has no such control, for he is dependent upon a builder-dealer in the field who will arrange for the acquisition of the land, the installation of foundations and utilities, the erection of the house, and in most cases the final mortgage and sale. The prefabricator, in short, has little effective control over his builder-dealer and for all his manufacturing efficiency falls victim to the inefficiencies of localism. The best example of an exception to these generalizations is

National Homes, which now, through its dealers, carries its package process through land acquisition, manufacture, and mortgage financing. The market prices of finished prefabricated homes usually are set to compete with prices of houses built by conventional construction. Thus their potential economies will benefit consumers only if competition forces all prices down.

Viewed not as the producer of a finished product but as a supplier of packages of materials, the prefabricator still serves to help rationalize the building industry. This view recognizes that the diversity of building types, sizes, prices, and locations imposes limitations on the degree of standardization possible in home building. It recognizes also that prefabrication makes possible for houses on scattered sites some of the economies of merchant building. Seen in this way, progress in prefabrication is to be measured not only in terms of the number of complete prefabricated packages sold, but in terms of the influence of prefabrication on the suppliers of conventional builders: lumber yards, cabinet manufacturers, and manufacturers of other house components. Actually, there has been steady progress since World War II both in the production of more or less completely prefabricated packages and in the production of prefabricated components. Both types of production have undoubtedly served to increase the efficiency of the home-building industry.

Meanwhile housing of a fully prefabricated, industrialized sort is being provided in dramatically increasing numbers by the trailer manufacturers, who operate wholly outside the housing industry. The market for mobile homes is made up principally of persons in mobile or semi-mobile occupations, retired persons, and couples without adolescent children, but it continues to grow at a fast rate. In 1959 there were 3.5 million persons living in 1.2 million mobile homes. The 148,600 trailers sold that year equaled more than 10 per cent of all housing starts and exceeded the number of prefabricated house sales. Sales of mobile homes and travel trailers totaled $691 million in 1959; output, however, decreased in 1960.

The growth in the trailer industry results not from increased recreational use of trailers but from increased residential use. The mobile home is mobile in the sense that it *can* be moved, even though it rarely is. The usual trailer is now so wide and so long that its owner may move without moving the trailer, selling the old one and buying a new one at the new location. The trailer is, in effect, a highly compact, highly efficient, easily exchanged dwelling that requires minimum maintenance and minimum financial involvement—f.o.b. prices for a 40-foot model running as low as $5,000. However, the square foot cost is still higher than that of efficiently produced development houses.

Trailers are produced, distributed, and financed the way automobiles are. Indeed, the trailer business is essentially an appendage of the automobile and truck industry from whose already rationalized operations it benefits. Furthermore, it is freed from all the production complexities associated with erecting a piece of local real property. No one envisages a nation of homes on wheels; but the trailer dramatizes the efficiency of an industrialized dwelling and the acceptance of such a dwelling by a part of the market.

Outlook for the Future

The diffusion of responsibility for home building among a dozen or more types of businesses means that no one single element in the industry is strong enough to exercise unifying leadership for the industry as a whole. Because the industry is made up of so many relatively small operating units, no one exerts the economic influence necessary to convert it into a more effective structure. Incentives for improved efficiency are lacking, particularly in those parts of the industry that account for a significant proportion of costs; and a division of attention by many producers between residential and other types of building impedes consolidation or simplification. Because more and more of the housing dollar is going into their products, the appliance or equipment manufacturers conceivably might supply the unifying force; but in each case they deal in markets vastly larger and more remunerative than home building.

Experience in the period from 1950 to 1960 points to the large merchant builder as the most hopeful element in achieving rationalization of the industry. He has already produced economies in building and begun to analyze cost components. His volume puts him in an effective position to bargain with mortgage lenders, labor, subcontractors, materials suppliers, and local government. His economies of scale bring him a kind of fiscal stability denied the small builder and hence a readier access to investment funds. Large orders for materials mean that he can ask for and get specialized designs and product research from basic suppliers. A closer control over on-site labor means the opportunity to schedule operations to avoid seasonal swings in production.

Only within a large, tight-knit, efficiently managed organization is it possible to strengthen or eliminate most of the weak links in the long chain of actions that keep the majority of builders inefficient and insecure. Two organizational prototypes for the future obviously are Levitt and National Homes, one using on-site factory assembly, the other off-site factory manufacture. Both have concentrated on managerial improvements and innovations and, as their volume of production has risen year by year, each has employed real advances in design and technology. Each, however, faces the problem of land and sites. In 1959 one large builder estimated that 40 per cent of his costs were attributable to planning, finding, and assembling land and dealing with local controls. The remainder divided itself evenly between the cost of underground utilities and community facilities and the house itself.

Not many builders can afford to operate as large-scale land developers. The economic opportunities in land development are so attractive to certain types of investors, however, that they are setting up special organizations in many parts of the country to buy and develop large acreages for residential building. But until communities develop urban land policies whose effect will be to reserve and service an adequate supply of suitably located land for residential development, the full potential of industrialized housing is unlikely to emerge.

Large-volume factory and on-site production does not mean that the day of the small builder is over; there will continue to be a market for his custom-built product. But they do offer a hopeful beginning toward the kind of rationalization in building that should ultimately provide the consumer with an improved product in a steadier volume.

Chapter 8

LABOR'S ROLE IN HOME BUILDING

The labor force for residential building has been as large as 1,375,000 in some years since the end of War World II. Shortages throughout the construction force from which residential labor is drawn appear probable as a result of changes in the population and in the labor force, and shifts in education and hours of work. Such shortages will intensify pressures toward greater industrialization.

Labor stands to make substantial gains in home building. The demand for its services will be maintained as the housing industry responds to the requirements of expected increases in family formation. Moreover, the trend to either on-site or off-site factory assembly will lessen seasonal unemployment and reduce job mobility. Both working conditions and collateral benefits are likely to improve under greater industrialization and, probably, wider unionization. At present not more than half of residential labor is unionized.

Leaders in the building trades unions are seeking ways to cut any artificial restraints on labor's productivity and to iron out differences between craft and industrial unions. Since local building trades unions are influential in specifying the content of building codes, their participation is essential in the updating of building codes to eliminate wasteful use of materials and labor, to substitute performance standards for materials and structural specification, to permit adoption of standard codes by reference, and to encourage standardization in the manufacture of building components. The industry and the building trades unions must jointly expand training courses to increase the supply of workers

118

skilled both in new techniques of residential construction and in rehabilitation.

Many persons in and out of the housing industry view labor as the unturned key to greater productivity in the home-building field and, in the long run, to lower costs to the consumer. This opinion is not new. For thirty years public investigations of the housing industry have been seeking the facts of labor's relationship to housing productivity. Just how widespread are restrictive practices? Are building wages too high? Does the residential labor force receive a fair share of the construction industry's gain in productivity? How much are builders penalized in their efforts to introduce new materials and methods into the building operation by labor's jurisdictional strikes and work limitation? How seriously does labor suffer from job insecurity because of seasonal layoffs and the varying demand for its services from one year to another and from one part of the country to another? Does a persistence in handicraft methods operate to the disadvantage of technological innovation?

After dozens of surveys and thousands of printed pages, these and many other questions about labor's industrial relations and practices are still unanswered to everyone's satisfaction. But the general conclusion that comes through time and again is reasonably clear: the organizational structure and operating practices of labor in the residential building trades show steady improvement. William Haber and Harold M. Levinson in *Labor Relations and Productivity in the Building Trades* emphasize that although "available data fail to justify the confidence of easy solutions to the [building] industry's problems . . . the pessimism and discouragement often expressed by the industry's many critics [are unjustified]. On the contrary, the forces promoting progress are vigorous, and there is justified assurance in the capacity of the industry to increase its control over the problems which have led to high costs in the past." Frederick Gutheim, in *Building, USA*, makes much the same point when he concludes that under the rules of the game, as both management and labor play it, "labor is doing its part. These are the tranquil, strikefree years—

on the surface. Capable and objective surveys of building labor's famous faults have returned a relatively clean bill of health in such specific charges as technological obstruction, excessive jurisdictionalism, obsolescent hiring and training practices. Further progress, however, cannot be made by perfecting the old model."

Before examining the old model to see what changes in it might contribute to a higher level of industrialization in the housing industry, at the same time that they might enhance the welfare of the worker, it will be useful to pin down some of the facts of labor costs in relation to construction costs. Throughout the following discussion it must be remembered that construction and home building are by no means synonymous terms. The labor force in home building is only part of the total labor force in the construction industry.

Labor Costs as a Factor in Production

In the seventy years since 1890, construction costs have increased more than twice as fast as the general price level and have been paralleled by the rise in the price of shelter. The cost of labor as a part of total construction cost is a variable item, but over a period of time it appears to stay within a fairly narrow range. According to the Bureau of Labor Statistics, the labor-to-construction-cost ratio between 1931 and 1946 fluctuated from 32 per cent to 37.5 per cent. Even in postwar New York City, where the volume of building was exceptionally large and generated strong competition for labor's services, the residential labor-to-construction-cost ratio rose only slightly. The New York City Housing Authority's detailed accounts of prewar and postwar building costs for its projects show that the cost of field labor in relationship to all costs increased only from 39 per cent to 41 per cent in a period of nearly twenty years.

But wages for building labor have been rising both absolutely and relatively during most of this century. Haber and Levinson set the percentage increase in real hourly wages between 1913 and 1952 at 108. The principal gainers in the secular rise of labor costs are helpers and laborers as distinguished from journeymen. Between 1913 and 1952, real hourly wages for the first group increased 182 per cent, but for the second group, the skilled laborers, 98 per cent. Average annual earnings in the building trades increased less than wages in manufacturing or in mining and transportation between 1929 and 1952. (See accompanying table.) Wages in the building trades are higher than wages other

TABLE 5. AVERAGE ANNUAL EARNINGS PER FULL-TIME EMPLOYEE,
SELECTED INDUSTRIES

Year	Contract construc- tion	Mining	Manu- facturing	Trans- portation	Commu- nication	All private industry
1929	$1,674	$1,526	$1,543	$1,642	$1,474	$1,408
1947	2,828	3,113	2,793	3,147	2,792	2,603
1952	4,007	4,078	3,833	4,242	3,801	3,465
Increase 1929–1952	139%	167%	148%	158%	158%	146%

Source: W. Haber and H. M. Levinson, *Labor Relations and Productivity in the Building Trades,* University of Michigan, 1956, table XXI, p. 217, se lected years.

industries pay workers for doing fairly similar kinds of tasks, and, as Chart 15 shows, are increasing faster than the prices of building materials. Average hourly wages in contract building construction rose steadily from 96 cents an hour in 1940 to $3.22 in 1959.

The differences in wages paid to unionized labor and wages paid to nonunionized labor are greater on paper than in fact and, therefore, have slight effect on differences in labor-to-construction-cost ratios. When building labor is in short supply, as it has been most of the time since the end of World War II, non-union rates tend to be as high as union rates or higher.

The Labor Force in Home Building

The size of the labor force in home building expands or contracts with the number of houses built. In 1953, it totaled 1,300,-000 on-site workers. In other years since the war, it has been as high as 1,375,000 and never under one million. These million-odd workers come from the construction industry's much larger labor pool of nearly three million workers, where few sharp lines are drawn between those who build houses and those who build office buildings, public buildings, and all manner of other structures and facilities. Indeed, many workers cross back and forth from one sector to another according to opportunities for employment and levels of compensation. This means that the supply of labor available to residential construction is determined by the level of general construction activity as well as by the level of home building.

Like construction workers generally, residential building

Chart **15**. Comparative increases in construction costs, wages, materials costs and consumer prices, 1926–1957. 1926 = 100

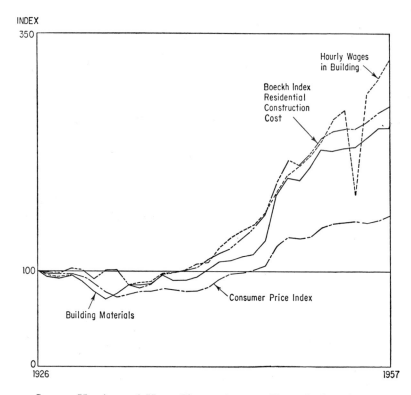

Source: Housing and Home Finance Agency, *Eleventh Annual Report.* 1957. (Computations made to convert data to 1926 index.)

workers are mobile in their locations and fairly flexible in their skills. They are rarely attached to a single employer for a longer period than is required to complete a specific job. Often they shift back and forth between being an employee and being an employer, since it is easy for them to act as subcontractors of labor in many areas. Only about half of them are members of building trades unions. Those who are work under highly localized standards of craft performance.

For the most part building workers are better paid, even in residential work, than are their counterparts in other industries and work fewer hours per week than do workers in manufacturing. However, their work is more hazardous: accidents among them occur three times as often and occasion almost three times as much lost time as in manufacturing. Only a fraction work under conditions which allow them paid vacations or benefits under health, welfare, and pension plans. During four months of each year in most parts of the country their rate of unemployment runs between 15 and 20 per cent. Even apart from conditions of weather and traditions about starting times for building operations, their employment is the most sensitive of all workers to cyclical fluctuations in the economy.

Skilled building workers outnumber unskilled workers by about two to one and tend to specialize in one craft. More than 40 per cent are carpenters, 13 per cent are bricklayers or plasterers, 10 per cent are plumbers and steamfitters, 8 per cent are painters and glaziers, 7 per cent are operating engineers, and 6 per cent are electricians. The remainder include lathers, roofers, elevator constructors, and the like. Those who concentrate most in residential building are the carpenters, bricklayers, electricians, and painters, but their skills are also the most readily transferable between housebuilding and other construction activities. To their number is added a large percentage of the unskilled laborers and helpers.

John Dunlop, in the book in this series, *Design and the Production of Houses*, emphasizes that the nature of on-site work in residential building and the extensiveness of the contractor system make the residential labor force unique compared with the total construction force. Because the typical builder maintains only a small force of his own as a rule, subcontracting the balance according to his need, residential labor is continually in the process of being organized into a succession of work crews. This means that not only do the workers shift frequently from job to job and locality to locality, but their ties are weak to particular employers and work groups.

Residential labor divides itself among three principal kinds of building operations: (1) the small-scale operation which involves intimate associations with contractors and subcontractors; (2) the large-scale building program, most characterized by apartment house construction, although to an increasing extent by operative builders whose year-round crews construct hundreds of dwellings a year; and (3) prefabrication.

SMALL-SCALE OPERATIONS

As Chapter 7 points out, the typical builder erects fewer than twenty-five houses a year. Often he acts as his own contractor. When he does, he maintains only a small staff of his own, one which is composed principally of carpenters and masons. But whether he acts as his own contractor or works through a general contractor, the bulk of the labor he employs comes to him through a system of subcontracting. The subcontractor, who may also be an independent contractor for his own services, has greater control over the labor force than does the contractor, moving himself or his pool of journeymen from one job to another as the occasion demands.

Subcontracted labor is often criticized for being inefficient labor. Work jobs are hard to coordinate and responsibility for them is divided among many persons rather than centralized under a single contracting agent. Nonetheless, the system provides an economical deployment of labor that can have real advantages to the builder as well as to the worker. It enables the builder to operate without permanent staff, and it provides the skilled worker with more steady employment, for a subcontractor shifts his workers from job to job as need arises.

As against these advantages, the small builder, the subcontractor, and the worker face problems of lost time. If the work of the preceding trade is not finished, the subcontractor cannot begin. Union rules often prevent the journeyman from working in another skill to complete a day's employment. Where these rules are not enforced, productivity in terms of the total job may be higher.

A single industrial union for the building trades, or a cooperative agreement to reduce jurisdictional problems among craft unions, probably could strengthen labor's long-run position in the residential sector. In their absence, large operative builders seem to be adapting themselves more successfully to the existing situation than are small builders, at the same time that they are providing more attractive benefits to the workers. By holding strictly to conventional craft lines, organized labor may be pricing itself out of the small-builder market.

LARGE-SCALE OPERATIONS

In any type of large-scale housebuilding, the skilled worker does not work on his own initiative or in a variety of jobs as he does in smaller operations. Some workers do nothing but hammer nails into studs or joists all day. Others install windows and doors; still others apply finishes. The separate operations are systematically scheduled and closely coordinated, usually by a foreman. Here the incentive system works extremely well. In effect, the old subcontracting system has turned into a means for putting foremen on an incentive basis.

William Levitt has been highly successful in increasing output among his workers at the same time that he has avoided jurisdictional strikes on his projects. But, whereas he has done so by insulating himself against, rather than coming to terms with, the problems of organized labor, the Mackle Company, a large-scale builder in Florida, obtains similar results under union contract.

Another characteristic of large-scale building which has important implications for labor is the increasing tendency toward year-round building operations. Most of the large operative builders now utilize a high percentage of off-site labor in the construction of structural and mechanical components. When assemblies are made on the site, they are usually put together in sheds and delivered to the house lots in packages for rapid, routine assembly. If the development is a large one, this means that once the foundations are laid down, the rest of the labor force will be gainfully occupied throughout most of the remaining months of the year in the actual building and finishing process. Particularly on the West Coast, large operative builders are deliberately breaking away from the tradition of starting building operations only in the spring months in an effort to schedule their operations evenly throughout the year. Not only does labor receive what approximates an annual wage under this arrangement, but the builder profits from the economies of a permanent, well-trained, and integrated work force.

PREFABRICATION

John Dunlop points out that although other factors than labor costs and industrial relations encourage prefabrication of building parts, "the growth in the differential expressed in dollars and cents between factory wages and construction wages has added incentive to this development." He compares the average hourly earnings in construction and durable goods manufacturing from 1939 and 1956 to show that construction labor earned 23 cents an hour more than manufacturing labor in 1939 (93 cents as against 70 cents) and 70 cents more in 1956 ($2.80 as against $2.10), and concludes that "although the percentage rise in hourly earnings in the two sectors was almost identical, the increasing dollar differential provides a strong incentive for the housing industry to experiment with ways of transferring work operations from the job site to the factory."

With minor exceptions unions do not appear to fear a shift of operations away from the site. At least they seem to be making little effort to prevent it. William Haber and H. M. Levinson are less sanguine about this than John Dunlop. They see the shift from on-site to off-site labor as a potential threat to the building trades unions, since their greatest strength traditionally is among on-site workers. Moreover, they point out that as prefabrication widens the competitive market, it brings pressure on wages and other standards which heretofore have been pretty much outside competition. And because the skills required for prefabrication are of a lower order than those required by traditional methods of construction, the whole structure of the building crafts is threatened. "In all trades affected, the unions have made strong efforts to control the new techniques by organizing the workers in the prefabricating operations" or "have followed more aggressive policies of obstruction." They would not discount the view that Dunlop advances, however, that if builders are too hard pressed by the unions, they can bypass many of the crafts by designing elements out of the structure; for instance, they can replace wet plaster walls with plywood.

As a result of new requirements for employment in prefabrication plants, trade unions are beginning to accept different wage rates in different employment situations even where the same kind of work is performed, recognizing real improvements in working conditions and job stability. Incentives and bonus plans are more readily allowed by unions which traditionally oppose them, and the regular employment pattern which prefabrication makes possible is setting precedents for paid vacations, health insurance, and retirement plans.

Trade Unions in Home Building

Twenty-two trade unions with some two million members are represented in construction work in this country. By far the largest number of them belong to AFL–CIO unions. Although only about half of all new residential building is done by union workers, union organization in home building has increased since 1950, particularly in large cities. The National Association of Home Builders questioned its member associations on this point in 1955. At that time, associations in eighteen of the thirty largest cities were producing 77 per cent of the units built in their areas under agreements with building trades unions. Almost without exception, apartment house construction is highly unionized.

As a rule, only the mechanical and structural trades are consistently well organized. Most of the unions in the finishing trades, like the painters' union, are less effectively organized. Both regionally and locally, union strength in the building trades is greatest in the North, the East, and the Far West.

Collective bargaining in home building is erratic in its coverage and difficult to achieve. Actually, most agreements on wages and working conditions are worked out in heavy construction.

RECRUITMENT AND TRAINING

From the smallest scale operation to the largest, the average worker in residential construction is less skilled than his counterpart of a generation ago. Contemporary design does not require the same degree of craftsmanship that went into the ornamental building of other periods. And the skilled core of today's labor force is an aging one; not only is it often incapable of acquiring new techniques, it is not being replaced in adequate numbers by graduates of apprenticeship and training programs.

Traditionally, building's skilled craftsmen come out of apprenticeship programs. So long as the number of apprentices is roughly equal to the number of skilled workers about to retire from the labor force, these programs provide a steady flow of replacements. However, the proportion of beginners in most trades has been dwindling for years. It may sometimes equal the replacement rate, but it rarely exceeds it. Thus, in times of heavy demand for building labor, the supply of some skilled workers is bound to be inadequate.

There were 103,612 registered apprentices in the building trades in 1956. They comprised about 60 per cent of the registered apprentices in all occupations, but were heavily concentrated in carpentry, plumbing and steamfitting, electrical and trowel work. Some of the trades are training enough replacements to make up for attrition—the bricklayers, for example, and the electricians, roofers, and plumbers. Carpenters and painters lag way behind, with eight apprentice carpenters for eighteen retired journeymen and six apprentice painters for eighteen retired painters.

This is a serious situation for the home-building industry; poor training and allocation of skilled laborers result in low efficiency and high costs. Yet home builders do not participate in formal apprenticeship programs, nor do they usually make any other effort to train workers for skilled jobs. One reason is that training is expensive and home-building jobs are of short duration.

Another is that trained labor is easily bid away by competitors and a fast rate of turnover in labor trained at the builder's expense can cut down his profit margin quickly.

Except in time of labor shortages, home builders do not concern themselves greatly with the allocation of labor between projects or among contractors. John Dunlop suggests that as home builders increase the size of their operations, and as home-building associations are better represented in labor negotiations, they "will show a greater interest in the further development of a skilled labor force and might share in the costs of apprenticeship in proportion to man-hours of work. . . ."

LABOR AND INNOVATION

When critics charge labor unions with being a negative force in the rationalization of the housing industry, they usually point to occasions when labor resists working with new materials and equipment and is unwilling to employ new methods of production. Most of the classic instances of labor's resistance to technological advance go back to the depression years when a principal objective of trade unions in the construction field was to keep their members productively employed and for as long a period each year as possible. If power machinery, spray guns, and drywall construction cut down on the number of workers or the hours they worked, the unions were ready and able to resist their introduction into the building operation.

As soon as the demand for building labor began to exceed the supply, however, unions relaxed their rules on the use of new materials and equipment and deliberate slowdowns in production became relatively rare. Although it is still possible to find examples of labor's refusing to work with plastic pipes, for example, or with prefinished panels or preglazed windows, Frederick Gutheim says that "except for objections on grounds of health (paint spray), or during a period of introduction when the bugs were being ironed out (stud gun), it is almost impossible to point to any substantial resistance to new building methods on labor's part." Moreover, in the context of a changing building technology, design can very easily bypass entire trades with specifications that eliminate the participation of a particularly troublesome segment of the building force. The accompanying table lists examples of how this is done.

TABLE 6.   SOME COMPETITIVE FACTORS IN BUILDING TECHNOLOGY

Trade	Technical innovation	Countering development	Prefabrication
Bricklaying........	Improved bricks; power saws	Curtain wall	Chimneys
Tile and glazing....	Adhesives	None	Factory sash
Plastering..........	Power mixers; plaster gun	Dry wall; plasterboard	Plasterboard
Carpentry.........	Power tools	Plywood	Precut and preassembled millwork
Painting...........	Spray gun; roller	Surfaces needing no paint	Factory prime coating
Plumbing..........	Power cutting and threading	None	Preassembly; utility core
Sheet metal work...	Power tools	Radiant and perimeter heating	Preformed ducts

Source: Editors of *Architectural Forum, Building, U.S.A.*, McGraw-Hill, New York, 1957, p. 56.

A greater drag on productivity than mere resistance to change can be a deliberate limitation of output. This is the most difficult charge of all to prove or disprove. Some builders insist that work limitation is a deliberate policy of scarcity-minded union leadership. But if this were true, there should be a higher productivity rate for nonunion labor than for union labor and this apparently is not the case. If, on the other hand, work limitation results mostly from low morale caused by feelings of job insecurity, its cure may lie in some form of incentive payments. Up to the present, however, building trades in this country have opposed incentive payments on the ground that speed-up practices lead in the end to unemployment or poor workmanship.

The most unyielding forces against technological innovation are not union rules but building codes. But it is important to point out here that the building trades unions play a stronger hand than any other organized group in setting the content and specifications of the codes. Moreover, they still resist the idea that codes should regulate performance of materials instead of the materials themselves.

JURISDICTIONAL DISPUTES

Jurisdictional disputes are common in the broad construction industry. Fortunately for the housing consumer, however, few of them affect home-building labor. Of the ones reported to the National Joint Board, established in 1948 by the contractors and the AFL building trades, most were between carpenters and roofers over the application of composition or asphalt shingles, between carpenters and cement finishers over screeds or forms, and between carpenters and plumbers over the placing of wood-backing for plumbing fixtures.

Labor attributes the great increase in jurisdictional conflicts to the Taft-Hartley regulations of 1947 which permit contractors to make work assignments without review of their decisions by union authorities. Certain of the building trades unions have long controlled the listing and hiring of available workmen in union-organized areas, and have insisted that work assignments are their prerogative alone. The National Joint Board has been a fairly effective instrument in rationalizing management-labor problems of this kind. The most difficult disputes it will have to arbitrate in the future may be those which arise from one trade being favored over another solely because of the design of the structure. Prefabrication plants find it easier, as a rule, to avoid interunion disagreements than do contractors engaged in on-site building.

The Outlook for Housing Labor

The building trades have always been the mavericks of labor. Since their employment is particularly at the mercy of weather, multiple employers, and cyclical changes in the national economy, it is hardly surprising that they look for means to stabilize their position. For years, the annual increase in productivity for that part of the construction industry that produces houses has been estimated at about 1.5 per cent. This is below the annual

rate of increase for the economy as a whole. The building industry and its labor force is going to have to face the question of
whether this rate is high enough. It is important to recognize,
however, that the problem of productivity does not rest only
with labor. A lack of technological progress will by itself mean
lower productivity.

Some experts in the construction industry are forecasting that
by 1975 a trillion of today's dollars will have been spent on construction in urban areas in this country—a trillion dollars for
highways, bridges, port facilities, schools, roads, sewer and
water facilities, hospitals, and so on. The labor to build them will
be drawn from the same supply that engages in home building.
Beginning in the middle 1960s, the demand for housing probably will be much greater than it was during the decade 1950–
1960. Indeed, by 1975 twenty million new families in metropolitan areas alone may require $300 billion worth or more of new
housing.

But meantime the work week is steadily shortening, young
men are staying in school longer, and the population as a whole
will contain proportionately fewer men in the normal range of
working years. These men will tend to avoid the discomfort and
instability of traditional site work. If the housing industry is to
get enough hands, it is going to have to find ways to compete
more successfully for labor's skills against a multitude of other
demands; and if labor is to benefit from this competition, it must
find ways to increase its productivity beyond current levels.

John Dunlop forecasts five kinds of changes in the labor factor
of home building: (1) A smaller proportion of the total man-
hours that go into residential construction will be spent on the
site. The larger proportion, which will be spent in factory fabrication of larger units and more completely finished pre-
assemblies, will carry a lower hourly wage rate. (2) The home-
building industry will become much more organized on a
union basis if the trend toward large-scale building of communities like the Levittowns increases. The principal unorganized
segments of building labor will be outside metropolitan areas.
(3) The craft structure of building labor will hold, but it will
provide a better balance between specialists and broadly trained

workers. (4) Home-builders' associations will grow in importance, finally breeching the contractors' fortifications against their participation in negotiations with labor on wages and area-wide collective bargaining agreements. Labor will draw together, if present trends continue, with its national unions coming together to provide a new mechanism for coordinating labor's policy on home-building problems. (5) As building operations become standardized and more frequently performed off the site, wage incentives in the form of piece rates and "lumping" will become more acceptable to labor as well as to management. On the whole, however, wage rates will be about the same as wage rates in other sectors of the construction industry, rising with them as all construction labor is brought under substantially the same kind of fringe benefits or industrial relations practices.

These are significant changes, but they will not occur automatically. They certainly will not come about without endless haggling and disruption to the production process unless the housing industry establishes a procedure by which its labor-management problems can be systematically and jointly reviewed by the labor unions and the home builders. The first step to obtain such a procedure was taken in 1959 with the establishment of the Construction Industry Joint Conference, at which leaders of labor unions meet regularly with leaders of the National Association of Home Builders and national contracting groups in construction. In February, 1961, it consisted of seven national contractor associations and eighteen unions.

Better labor practices and industrial relations will not by themselves drastically cut the cost of housing to the consumer. Present conditions in the housing industry which encourage low levels of research and investment are holding back development of essential time- and cost-saving new building methods, methods which organized labor already demonstrates considerable willingness to accept.

Chapter 9

INDUSTRIALIZING THE HOUSING INDUSTRY: DESIGN, MATERIALS, AND METHODS

The housing industry still relies heavily on the materials, production methods, and designs of the past. Housing has been able to survive this technological lag only through government aids that bulwark its production and consumption. Despite the failure of the home-building industry to take full advantage of the innovations available to it, the house of today is considerably different from the house of twenty-five years ago. Production methods are changing, particularly because of the evolving mass-building techniques of large merchant builders. And technological and design innovations are being stimulated by consumer dissatisfaction, by increases in family formation, and by higher costs for materials, land, and labor.

The trend is toward more factory production, whether on or off the site. Wall panels and other components are already in wide use, although their best potentials will not be realized until they are dimensionally standardized. New materials are in use, many of them the product of chemical research. Yet, on the whole, builders have not made a major effort to adapt the design of the house to new technological opportunities. Part of the problem is a shortage of designers and architects who understand both the limitations and the potentials of the industrialized process. Another part is the failure of labor, builders, and local governments to revise building practices and building codes. Mortgage lenders often exercise a restraining influence on innovations in both structures and project design.

If technological advance in home building is to be furthered, there will have to be a more experimental approach on the part of builders, labor, government, and lenders. The Federal Housing Administration, which on the whole has restrained innovation, should foster experiments in materials, methods, and design. Experiments in land development are also needed. The housing industry might stimulate consumer expectations and acceptance through wider use of competitive demonstration projects.

The technology of the housing industry has often been compared unfavorably with that of other industries. The Temporary National Economic Committee's investigations, published in 1940, illustrate the view that if the mass-production techniques used in the manufacture of automobiles were applied to the manufacture of houses, the housing "problem" would be solved almost immediately by the resulting increase in supply and decrease in cost. Critics point out how, because of its tight-knit structure, the automobile industry is able to take maximum advantage of technological advances and design innovations. They point, too, to its superior system of distribution and marketing, and to its financing mechanisms which encourage rapid turnover of the existing supply. Because all of these circumstances are lacking in the housing industry, the argument provides a recurrent and wistful hope.

There is also a widespread conviction that the housing industry could be more readily rationalized for continuous and economic production if the Federal government were to use its system of credit aids to encourage reorganization and to speed innovation. Others hold that initiative is being stifled by too many controls and by constantly shifting Federal housing policies which make it impossible for the industry to restructure its organization with confidence. In any event, the larger body of controls over housing are exercised by thousands of local building codes which impede both innovation and standardization.

The question of governmental requirements and controls is a particularly sensitive one, for design, materials, and methods of construction are at stake as well as cyclical stability and a free flow of credit. At the Federal level, FHA and VA requirements and regulations tend to keep home building in a strait jacket of conventional design, single-family houses, and suburban locations. At the local level, government perpetuates handicraft methods of construction and discourages functional design through building codes that prohibit the use of many new materials with superior qualities. Building codes that do not employ performance standards for materials and equipment rob both the builder and the consumer of many of the advantages of new technology and design. Moreover, the waste from inefficient building techniques stemming from inflexible code requirements and the lack of uniformity among codes in a single area have a measurable effect on cost. Industry spokesmen say that many present building code requirements add as much as a thousand dollars to the price of the small house without making it any safer structurally.

Although the housing industry suffers almost as much from limitations imposed upon it from outside as it does from its own disorganization, the most immediate opportunity for unchaining the "puny giant" lies in the industry itself, where managerial reform is long overdue. Improved, more centralized management not only can achieve important economies of scale, but can, if the industry responds fully to the forces that are moving it slowly toward factory production, provide a freedom for innovation on a scale that does not now exist.

This chapter deals with some of the innovations in materials, building systems, designs, equipment, and land development that are already available to the industry and suggests how the impediments to their widespread employment may be removed or mitigated. New design and technology alone will not rationalize the housing industry, nor will the rationalization of the industry remove inequities in the utilization of housing or necessarily reduce the cost of housing. The principal benefit of industrially produced housing can be an improvement in the quality of the house and its neighborhood and in the consequent opportunity for consumers to have a more satisfying residential environment.

Design and Technology

Good design is an essential factor in mass production for most products. Unfortunately, in the minds of consumers and builders alike, design is usually equated with style, but style has little to do with the essential livability of a dwelling. In designers' terms, design is a creative process leading to new forms—on the basis of understanding the way of life of those who are to live in the houses and comprehending the process of producing houses. The test of good design is over-all efficiency and economic value combined with a high level of amenity and aesthetic quality.

Although the basic character of the house has changed considerably in the last twenty-five years, the changes have come about slowly. Most improvements take place within the conventional framework and, if the National Association of Home Builders assesses its own future correctly, will continue to be less in shape, size, and basic design than in the techniques and materials builders employ. Individual houses demonstrate changing design precepts, but there are almost no examples of innovation on a large scale.

In 1960, a citizen group in Pittsburgh, Action-Housing, Inc., made plans to demonstrate in the building of a whole neighborhood how the industry can free itself—and be freed as well—for innovation. With restrictions and controls reduced to the minimum required for safety of the public and health of the residents, the East Hills project will count on the market place to decide whether the experiment provides a serviceable prototype for the industry to follow in its search for rationalization as well as in its attempt to provide housing of a demonstrably superior quality.

As a testing ground for design innovation, the market place is often disappointing: the consumer is notoriously reluctant to accept new forms for his dwelling. He does not want his house to look precisely like other houses in the neighborhood, but neither does he want it to look markedly different from them. Caught in this dilemma, it is not surprising that most builders are content to rely on minor variations of style to sell their houses. Even the large merchant builder seems unwilling to break very much with tradition—except for the two innovations of recent years, the split-level house and the family room—preferring instead to force new materials into old patterns, sometimes even at the sacrifice of cost and livability.

But builders say their biggest handicap in introducing new designs is not just consumer resistance. They point to the fact that today's houses are filled with products whose design is a sharp break with precedent. Appliances are the most obvious examples. The problem is to find designers and architects who understand equally well the limitations and potentials of the industrial process and the design requirements for contemporary living. Only if builders and manufacturers enter the housing industry on a larger scale and on a more sustained basis will they be in a position to invest in the recruitment and training of teams of architects and designers with experience across the board in housing production.

At some point, however, all products reshape themselves according to their technological and functional requirements. One might say that the industrialized house is in much the same position today as gas stoves, automobiles, and electric lights were in the early days of their development. Because each in turn superseded an already established commodity and drew on earlier methods of fabrication, manufacturers at first made them look like the familiar and long-accepted product. The gas stove was made out of the heavy black iron that went into wood-burning stoves, electric lights were modeled on gas brackets or candles, and the automobile was a buggy with an engine. When the traditional image could no longer express the new function, design caught up with technology. Many persons in and out of the industry would say that housing is now at this point, for traditional building practices are not providing homes that reflect either the new technology or the new ways of living.

In the last fifty years there has been a steady outpouring of serious effort on the part of designers to cut through traditionalism and provide a house that, however radical its design might be, would be better geared to contemporary life styles than the usual product of the home-building industry. The Robie house in Chicago, which Frank Lloyd Wright designed in 1909, is an ancestor of today's open-plan house. A central mast for utilities, a not uncommon feature of new office buildings and apartment houses, appeared in Buckminster Fuller's first Dymaxion house in 1928. The idea of a house cast in a single form, a method employed by the International Basic Economy Corporation for low-cost housing in Puerto Rico and elsewhere, goes back at least to Thomas Edison's experiments with reinforced concrete. The load-bearing steel panels which Howard Fisher prefabricated for his General Homes in 1932 had their antecedents in experiments shortly after the turn of the century by the Suspension Steel Company and others.

These and others like them were isolated experiments, however, and rarely touched the main stream of building even though some of their features became standard practice in more conventional forms. One reason is that the attention of the designer is too often centered on the potentialities of one product, one process, or one structural form. Walter Gropius offered the fabric of a solution when, in his days in Germany at the Bauhaus school in the 1920s, he counseled the importance, even the necessity, of making the manufacturer a participant in the design process.

The merchant building firm of William Levitt is a current, though not radical, example of how this can be done in some interior features. Because the scale of Levitt's operations is so great, companies that normally market the larger part of their product outside the home-building field are more than ready to work with his staff of architects and engineers to develop new or more efficient materials and components. Among the Levitt firsts is the hot-water heater and oil burner contained within a counter-high kitchen cabinet and backed against the living room fireplace, thus providing an economical and striking means of packaging the heating plant. Levitt is also primarily responsible for Plextone, a sprayed-on paint that uses coagulated separate colors to provide a finish which protects the base and conceals surface flaws. And in cooperation with Johns-Manville and the Celotex Corporation, he helped to develop various types of asbestos siding.

Levitt would be the first to say that such improvements in the kind, use, and assembling of materials that he and other large builders have pioneered are relatively insignificant compared with those which might result under different sets of circumstances. Someday there is bound to be a widespread emergence and use of standardized components for all principal parts of the structure as well as for its major items of equipment. At the point where Gropius' injunction becomes fully operative, today's house will be as obsolete in its basic design, and hence in its utility and satisfaction to the user, as it will be in the methods of its production.

Materials and Technology

Until the twentieth century practically all buildings, particularly residential ones, were made of wood, brick, or stone. In the past fifty years or so, however, a wide range of substitutes has been slowly developing. The first alternative to traditional building materials was the discovery that steel and other high-strength materials could be used in tension as well as in compression. In recent years there has been a rapid advance in the use of reinforced concrete, plywood, aluminum, wood fiber, plastics, and the like. Striking evidences of the melding of new materials and design are all around us—in bridges, public buildings, and industrial plants. In home building, however, they are still exceptional.

The line between traditional materials and new materials is rarely a sharp one. Often so-called new materials are modifications of old materials or simply combinations of old and new materials. Moreover, authentically new materials are rarely used without regard to the traditional antecedents of the materials they replace. It is possible, although it is not economically practicable, to construct an entire house out of plastic materials. But the greatest utility of plastics so far is in combination with other materials, as structural sandwiches, as occasional parts—pipes and hardware components—or as surface coverings, finishes, and adhesives.

Even within these areas of use, however, plastics appear to provide such extraordinary opportunities for new methods of construction that their manufacturers are concentrating more and more on modifications and variations that will make them increasingly applicable to the building process. Sandwich construction can serve as an example of this process of development.

Sandwich panels—two thin skins of surfacing material bonded to the sides of a structural core—have been used widely by the aircraft and trailer industries for a number of years. Since World War II, the building industry has been adapting them in many sizes and materials for use in the interiors of residential structures where they encounter relatively little opposition from builders or local code officials. These are nonstructural panels, however. Different attitudes prevail when it comes to sandwiches designed to bear loads. Structural sandwiches, like their non-load-bearing counterparts, can be made out of a wide range of materials. Some of the most promising experiments utilize plastics for the skin covers and paper for the honeycomb cores or polyester-glass-fiber for the skins and styrene or phenolic-foamed plastics for the rigid cores. The continuous lightweight core stabilizes the surfaces against buckling under compression, develops shear strength, and provides insulation.

Where sandwiches have been used for the entire structure of the house, they bear loads at the same time that they serve as the enclosing envelope, walls, floors, and roof. Houses built of such advanced types of structural sandwiches as these might avoid the kind of functional obsolescence which makes many houses built with traditional materials uncompetitive in the market after twenty or thirty years. In addition to improving quality, sandwich construction may eventually lower unit cost. The panels must be factory-fabricated and potentially provide considerable savings in site labor, one of the most costly aspects of construction with traditional materials and by conventional methods.

Any new material faces problems of cost, performance standards, and design. Again sandwich materials may be used to illustrate these problems. Most of the firms engaged in the development of sandwiches are small. As a result, there is an insufficient volume of production to put costs in a competitive position with costs of materials used in traditional construction methods. Until large manufacturers have developed the products' uses on a large scale it will be difficult to judge whether sandwich construction will be cheaper, or merely better than conventional. As the use of the new product expands it may replace more than one former component. If so, it may prove economical even at higher costs than the original single component; for example, a sandwich floor that sustains its weight without supporting beams.

Another serious deterrent, and one which holds true for most new building materials, is the problem of performance testing. While testing procedures can examine a wide range of qualities with considerable accuracy, building code officials are reluctant to accept test results for some qualities, especially where the product is not available for conventional field observation. It should not be necessary, however, for materials and assemblies that have been approved under all reasonable circumstances to be subjected to separate local inspections. When this additional procedure is required, adoption of the novel is slow and costly. Traditional field inspections are meaningless anyway when a factory-made product must be taken apart at the site and reassembled before it can be put in place. The act of disassembly is destructive when it is performed on a component that is welded or sealed to withstand the very possibility of its parts being separated. Some way must be found to set a level for over-all performance under circumstances of time and testing that will not retard the introduction of desirable innovations and yet will protect the public welfare. It should be possible for the manufacturer to present his product for a single series of official tests after which builders can use it throughout a metropolitan area, a state, or even the nation.

There are many design problems involved in the use of new materials, and once more sandwich panels can illustrate. One of these is the incorporation of utility lines in the panel without making them wholly inaccessible. One of the most irrational aspects of conventional building methods is the way pipes and wires for plumbing and electricity are threaded through a structure. Hard to get at, they are difficult and costly to repair. Manufacturers are just beginning to experiment with designs which will permit utility lines to be economically packaged in units built into the structure and still be susceptible of removal as a whole. Not only would this solve the repair problem neatly, but it would make it possible for the homeowner to replace obsolete equipment without having to break open the basic structure of the dwelling.

Structural sandwiches are merely illustrative of the innovations that can be expected. Among others, the contrasting elements of clear window or solid wall which are basic elements of design today may change to walls and roofs that can filter light and be adjusted from opaque to transparent. Climate-control systems, which can change with the weather and mood of the residents, may bring an ever-changing appearance to the house. Even fixed façade compositions may give way to constantly varying designs.

Management and Technology

The main way a new product, a new method, or a new design can become successful is for management to allocate both time and money—often in large amounts—to development, experimentation, and application. The effort must continue past what may be many setbacks. Few companies will gamble this heavily unless they foresee a large and distinct market as the culmination of their investment. The laboratories of chemical companies are working on dozens of new products today, many of which could produce radical changes in home building if they were adapted specifically for the housing industry. This is not likely to occur, however, unless the industry demonstrates a capacity for using the new products.

The increasing use of aluminum in residential building is often cited as an example of successful new-product development for housing. Aluminum is used mostly as a straight substitution for traditional materials. Its use has engendered little real design innovation. But it does exemplify the kind of long-range investment and control by management that is necessary if traditional building materials and designs are to give way eventually to the extent necessary to take full advantage of our technological potential.

The Aluminum Company of America has long been energetic in seeking out new uses for its product. The idea of an aluminum house first occurred to the company in the mid-1920s. The company thereupon began to weigh the value of the idea, the possibility of realizing it in the future, the means of taking step-by-step decisions to that end, together with the difficulties that would be imposed by the persistence of conventional building practices, building codes, and consumer habits. Alcoa pursued the idea over a period of twenty years through laboratory and market research, product development, and eventually production and sales.

From 1947 on, Alcoa worked with National Homes to tool up for production of the Viking houses. The materials needed for them could readily be produced by now-standard machinery turning out sheets and extruded forms. In early 1958 National Homes decided to go ahead. Research had long since settled most of the usual problems of standards and specifications. Announcements began to appear in the newspapers in September, 1958, and model homes were opened in localities throughout the country in 1959. Alcoa's sustained management policy was rewarded. National Homes' new line accounted for about half of its output in 1959.

This case illustrates the long time periods that frequently are necessary to see a new product or material through from conception to reality. Alcoa's long-range management program of research and product development produced no revolution. It and similar efforts will do so only when new products take new forms to perform new functions. Then new methods of factory production, based on a new technology, may be feasible. They may well be based on quite different organizations and management methods.

One approach to the industrialization of housing is to utilize highly mechanized forms of on-site assembly. The other principal approach is prefabrication of the entire house in a shop. Although the two approaches are competitive, they are by no means mutually exclusive. "Both are based largely on the same premises," Burnham Kelly says in *Design and the Production of Houses*, "but one uses a high degree of organization at a particular site whereas the other relies on organization at a central shop and minimizes activity at many sites. These approaches can be and are combined whenever it proves to be advantageous."

Whether the systems are employed separately or in combination, they utilize two kinds of technical innovation. The first involves a whole range of adaptations to conventional methods of building; the second utilizes assemblies put together in a shop instead of in the field and installed by means of connections that require a minimum of site labor.

The plaster gun is an excellent example of technical advance in traditional building practice. It permits a crew to apply twice the amount of plaster in a day that was possible by former methods. The extensive use of power is another improvement in site operations. With power-driven hoisting machinery, both conventional materials and larger assemblies can be put into place in a shorter time with a smaller crew. Whenever electrical or air-driven tools can reduce the fatigue of the worker, time and costs are saved. Moreover, the new tools operate with a much higher degree of accuracy than hand operations can produce.

But important as such improvements are to conventional building methods, the most significant trend is in the increased use of assemblies, for it is assemblies that are moving home building fastest to a new form of industrialization. Assemblies can be divided into four main types: structural assemblies, nonstructural assemblies, mechanical units, and accessories. Illustrations are prefabricated walls and roof trusses, kitchen cabinets and storage units, packaged heating and hot-water units, garbage grinders and recessed fixtures. By cutting the amount of time required for on-site installation or finishing, the skillful use of assemblies reduces field labor. More important, they provide a better product, produced under factory-controlled conditions, than can be produced by the diminishing number of skilled craftsmen in the field.

The use of assemblies raises many problems, however, that the mere adaptations of conventional systems do not. Obviously, there cannot be an endless variety of shapes, sizes, and finishes for every assembly. Standardization is essential at least to the degree that all major components must be dimensionally coordinated. Unlike the traditional wood-based technology, building by assemblies leaves little leeway for squeezing, cutting, and trimming of parts to make them fit. Sizes must be standardized and materials must have known properties. Manufacturing industry has wide experience with dimensional standardization and with testing procedures and standards which permit steady improvement in performance characteristics like durability, impact resistance, aging properties, and weather resistance. However, excessive standardization may freeze materials and products in existing forms and at existing levels of performance.

Design and the Community

The dwindling supply and the increasing cost of land are among the biggest problems most builders face. Land is still available on the fringes of cities but, by and large, only at increasing distances from urban centers and in scattered locations that lack essential utilities and are progressively less suited to housing development. Within cities the situation is even more difficult: vacant land is disappearing; only scattered or small sites remain. As a result, big builders must look for land in the fairly remote rural fringe of the metropolitan area or seek building opportunities in central-city renewal areas.

In the 1930s, the war years, and the early postwar years, land commonly accounted for 10 to 12 per cent of ultimate housing costs. Under pressure of residential expansion into agricultural areas after World War II, the per acre price of farm land jumped by 44 per cent in the eight years following 1947. The average market price of the building lot for FHA-insured houses has gone up from $1,035 in 1950 to $2,470 in 1960. Whereas in 1950 it represented 12 per cent of the property value, in 1960 it amounted to 16.6 per cent.

Cost and availability of land, then, combine to concentrate major building operations farther and farther out in the countryside. Moreover, by moving outside the limits of municipalities, builders often can avoid the restricting effects of subdivision, zoning, and building regulations or of other regulations imposed by many suburban communities to exclude houses that are less expensive or of a different design from those already in the community or to curtail additional growth.

The legal intent of most local regulations on land and buildings is to preserve health and safety. Many builders feel that it has been stretched in recent years beyond a justifiable point; but few of them have been willing, or have had the resources, to engage in court action to determine the validity of the most excessive of these local practices. The result is that restrictive regulations have often forced the average small builder out of the community or pushed up his costs and, in turn, his prices to the consumer.

There will be little ultimate advantage from industrializing the housing industry unless the larger result is a more balanced, efficiently organized, and aesthetically satisfying community for living. Technological innovation and new design forms are needed in neighborhood and land planning as much as in structures.

More and more the home buyer is buying the community at least as much as he is buying the house. If the housing industry is to meet the requirements and opportunities that lie ahead of it, it must develop the means to operate efficiently throughout the entire process of providing shelter, not just in isolated parts of the process. Greater mass production of housing can never be achieved unless developed land is produced on some equivalently large scale.

Land can be mass-produced in the sense that every large-scale developer converts farm land to tract housing, but it cannot readily be mass-assembled. There are the problems of assembling a large tract of land at a reasonable price. Much money can be tied up in land investments if sites are to be assembled in advance for several years' production. After assembly the builder often finds the local community imposing additional restrictive regulations, sometimes with the aim of killing the development.

Possible solutions to some of these problems are better land-planning design, new land assembly and investment techniques, and new legal attitudes toward land ownership. Until urban planners and designers can produce designs which avoid the monotony of much recent land planning, community and market resistance is likely to continue. The provision of more community open space, and simultaneous construction of community facilities and housing are essential elements of better land development.

During the postwar period there have been a number of large-scale land development operations sponsored by groups of builders, investors, or lenders. These firms find and assemble land, service it, and sell it to the builder who takes over construction operations. This scheme produces important economies in land planning and development. Moreover, it enables several builders to develop a single large tract, thus producing a variety of homes even on the same block front, without sacrifice of building efficiency.

In the postwar period several investment trusts have gone into the development of land for industrial parks. These same groups may develop residential land in the future.

Unchaining the "Puny Giant"

There will be no rapid revolution in the housing industry. No one of the complex, thinly related units of activity that comprise the industry has yet generated sufficient force for that. But already the kind of advances described in this chapter have brought significant changes in both the methods and the product of the industry. If they are not truly revolutionary in character, they do mark a steady evolution in the process of rationalizing the production of housing in this country. The process is slow, often intermittent, and subject to mutations caused by innovations in other industries, government, and changing market trends.

Within the slow progression of an evolutionary trend, there is always a point when a show of change becomes remarkable. This point may be at hand in the housing industry. The forces for change are so compelling that, as Burnham Kelly puts it: "There must soon come the time when the degree and character of change have reached that subtle, indefinable point at which the strength of conventional resistance suddenly fades away and there is a 'snap-over' to an entirely new industrial situation in which stereotypes are abandoned and standards undergo rapid and radical transformation."

The forces impelling change are readily identifiable. Many of them have been discussed in this and other chapters: the dissatisfaction of the consumer with the product that is presently available to him, and his increasing discrimination about the kind of housing and community environment that will best complement his new patterns of living; the prospect of a tremendous increase in the demand for housing in the 1960s and 1970s; the efficiency and economy of providing new housing in large numbers, whether they are located on raw land in the metropolitan fringe of the city or on cleared land in central-city redevelopment areas; the trend toward large home-building organizations whose very size is encouraging the use of new materials and systems of construction and a more economical utilization of labor and land; the growing tendency of the smaller builders to overcome the delays and costs inherent in on-site production by turning to off-site assembly and finishing operations; the growing influence on housing design of the large manufacturers of materials and equipment.

Before major advances can be made the localism that shackles the housing industry to the remnants of handicraft technology must be overcome.

At this point, the challenge is largely management's. If imaginative and aggressive companies in or on the edges of the housing industry are encouraged by a more substantial flow of investment money to concentrate on production for housing, the industry will undoubtedly achieve significant coordination among its separate entities, rationalization of its operating method, and, very likely, a new combination of purposes. To the consumer this will bring, if not always or at first a cheaper product, at the least a better and more functional one.

THE INVESTOR

Chapter 10

RESIDENTIAL FINANCE

The housing industry is faced with the necessity of finding new sources of money if it is to finance the enlargement and improvement of the housing supply required by the probable changes in the population and the economy during the 1960s and 1970s. Most housing is financed through long-term mortgages. The money for them comes from two principal sources: individual savings in life insurance reserves, government bonds, commercial and mutual banks, and savings and loan institutions; and from monthly payments on mortgage debt and repayments. When the economy is expanding generally, and shorter-run investment outlets offer more attractive choices to lenders, housing is likely to do badly in the competition for funds from both these sources. Because the cost of money constitutes a large share of monthly or annual housing expense, the builder and the consumer are particularly vulnerable to increases in the cost of money and shifts in its geographic or cyclical flow.

Several opportunities present themselves for enlarging the pool of investment money for housing. Local development foundations with funds from industry, business, labor, and public subscription can limber up local markets by providing equity money. Pension funds with multi-billion-dollar annual accretions to their reserves constitute a savings supply that is only beginning to be attracted to housing. Government-guaranteed mortgage debentures or a new form of mortgage investment trust may be means to tap these funds. State-chartering of mortgage corporations through which lending institutions can share risks is needed. There should be a review of existing systems of savings and mortgage-lending institutions in suburban and rural nonfarm areas to determine the extent to which the require-

ments for mortgage money are being met and to suggest addi-
tional institutions or branch systems to serve money-starved
areas.

Most home-building is financed through long-term mortgages.
Residential mortgage debt is, therefore, the largest single component in private debt as well as the largest single outlet for
long-term savings. These relationships are briefly described below as an introduction to the specific problems of housing
finance.

Raymond Goldsmith estimated total national wealth in 1958
at $1,682.1 billion. The largest part (23.3 per cent) of the total
was for nonfarm residential structures, valued at $391.4 billion. If
residential land had been included, the estimated value of the
nonfarm housing supply would have been an even larger proportion of national wealth. (See Chart 16.)

Against these tangible assets the United States in 1958 had a total

Chart **16.** National wealth, 1958, by type of asset in current dollars
and percentage

PER CENT	ASSETS	BILLIONS
23.3	Nonfarm Residential Structures	$391.4
10.7	Nonfarm Commercial and Industrial Structures	179.3
15.6	Mining, Farming, Institutional and Government Structures	262.3
11.9	Producer Durable Equipment	199.9
10.6	Consumer Durable Equipment	178.8
17.2	Land	290.9
10.7	Inventories and Other	179.5
100.0	Total	$1,682.1

Source: Raymond W. Goldsmith, preliminary estimates, National Bureau
of Economic Research, *Statistical Abstract of the United States,* 1960, Bureau
of the Census, computed from table 429, p. 326.

private net debt of $499.9 billion (increased to $581.9 billion in 1960), 44 per cent of which represented short-term borrowings of individuals and business. Long-term debt in nonfarm mortgages—$144.6 billion—comprised the largest single category in 1958. By 1960 the nonfarm mortgage figure had reached $173.9 billion. Thus mortgage debt is a major outlet for investment and savings in our economy.

A third of the savings supporting total debt are corporate savings. The remainder is drawn from the long-term savings of individuals who deposit funds in various classes of savings institutions and purchase life insurance. The total of such savings at the end of 1959 was $295.5 billion and the preliminary total for 1960, $313.5 billion. As Chart 17 shows, life insurance reserves, United States bonds, deposits in commercial and mutual savings banks, and shares in savings and loan associations are the major forms taken by individual savings. Net savings during 1956, as shown in the table amounted to $14.5 billion. It is from this

Chart **17.** Long-term savings of individuals, 1959 (1960), by type of institution, in billions of dollars

1959		BILLIONS 1959	1960(P)
18.5%	Savings and Loan Associations	$54.6	$62.2
11.8%	Mutual Savings Banks	34.9	36.3
21.3%	Commercial Banks	63.0	67.5
0.4%	Postal Savings	1.0	0.8
1.5%	Credit Unions	4.4	4.9
15.5%	U.S. Savings Bonds	45.9	45.7
31.0%	Life Insurance Reserves	91.7	96.1
100%	Total	$295.5	$313.5

Note: (P) 1960 figures are preliminary.

Source: Housing and Home Finance Agency, *Housing Statistics,* March, 1961, table A-64, p. 75.

stream of savings that the funds must be drawn to provide the mortgage capital which sustains current construction and sales of new homes, construction of new rental housing, and the re-sale of that part of the total housing supply which changes hands each year. The flow of savings into and out of residential mortgages exercises a decisive influence on the ownership of the housing stock, the rate of residential building, the ease of family movement from area to area, the level of employment in the construction industry, and the condition of our housing supply.

TABLE 7.   INDIVIDUAL LONG-TERM SAVINGS DURING 1956
(in billions of dollars)

Private insurance and pension reserves	$7.7
Government insurance and pension reserves.	3.7
U.S., state and local government bonds	3.6
Corporate and other bonds	3.5
Savings and loan associations	5.1
Currency and deposits	4.5
Total	$28.1
Less increase in debt	13.6
Net savings	$14.5

Source: U.S. Securities and Exchange Commission, *Statistical Bulletin*, May 1957, p. 19.

Credit Requirements for Housing

Residential building accounts for roughly a quarter of all new private investments. While the proportion has varied in recent years from as little as 20 per cent to nearly 50 per cent of total private investments, the volume of funds necessary to maintain nonfarm residential investment has increased steadily from roughly $3 billion per year in the prewar years to over $18 billion per year in the late 1950s. In addition to this level of capital investment and reinvestment expenditures, many billions of dollars a year are spent on the maintenance and rehabilitation of residential properties.

The housing industry finds funds readily available for new mortgage lending, for residential construction and improvement of the housing supply, if the capital requirements for government, manufacturing industry, commerce and business inventories are low, and if savings are relatively high. But when the capital requirements for manufacturing, business inventories, or utility construction are booming, housing must compete with these other outlets for funds drawn from the national savings pool. When this happens mortgage funds are tight.

The housing industry is at a comparative disadvantage in the competition for funds for several reasons. Investments in other industries are usually of shorter duration than housing investments and can be accommodated more readily to changes in the price of money. In some industries capital requirements exercise relatively little influence on the ultimate price of products to the consumer. The cost of capital in these industries is only a fraction of ultimate price. Some capital users—private utilities, local governments, and state governments—may find that they are compelled by the nature of their operations to borrow money regardless of the cost. In housing, however, the cost or availability of money exercises a decisive influence on the volume of residential building and upon consumer costs. The cost of money borrowed to buy a house, spread over ten to thirty years, will amount to one-third to three-fourths of the total housing cost, and, in extreme cases, may double the cumulative cost to the owner.

Housing finance also differs from other capital investment in the sources of its funds. Capital for long-term industrial and other investments is drawn in large part directly from corporate income in the form of reinvested earnings. Much of the capital invested in corporate bonds is institutionally owned or managed. But more than half of all residential mortgage funds comes from the relatively small savings of individuals who have share accounts in savings and loan associations or deposits in savings banks. These individual savings are obviously subject to varying economic and institutional pressures which influence both the volume of savings and the rate of yield.

The volume of mortgage loans required by the market varies from year to year not only because of fluctuations in the volume of new residential construction but also because of changes in the rate of resale of existing housing, general changes in housing prices which may affect mortgage amounts, and changes in equity payments by purchasers of homes. The volume of resale of existing homes requiring new financing may be as much as twice the volume of new residential construction. In a typical postwar year, two-thirds of all mortgage loans were issued for the purchase of existing homes.

Mortgage fund requirements are also influenced in a decisive way by repayments on outstanding mortgage debt. The reduction in this debt each year varies from 20 to 30 per cent of the outstanding mortgage indebtedness. A large part is repayment in full for purposes of sale, but a substantial proportion results from regular amortization payments. Together they provide lenders with a substantial volume of lendable funds in any year irrespective of the volume of new savings. Since the mid-1930s repayment funds have accounted for some 50 to 75 per cent of all home mortgage loan funds. During this period new savings had to provide for only a quarter to a half of the funds required each year to sustain mortgage-lending activity, including the purchase of existing homes and the construction and purchase of new homes.

To the extent that repayments and regular amortization payments flow into institutions which put very large proportions of their funds into residential mortgages, residential real estate benefits from a stable flow of funds. However, to the extent that repayments and monthly amortization payments flow into institutions which invest high proportions of their funds in other fields, residential real estate must compete on a current basis with other investment outlets. Mortgage payment funds will be re-loaned to new residential mortgages rather than to other types of mortgages, government securities, private bonds or other securities according to the competitive advantage of residential mortgage interest rates as opposed to other interest and dividend rates.

The volume of equity funds flowing into residential construction varies widely. Although they seem to have declined secularly, they accounted for as much as 40 per cent of all new funds required for residential construction in the mid-1920s, and as much as 27 per cent during the postwar building boom. Equity funds have contributed enormously to the financing of new residential construction, with amounts ranging from $1 billion a year in the depression years to over $5 billion at the postwar peak.

Builders' equity capital provides an unknown portion of this total. In times when speculative rental construction has been high, as in the late 1920s, it has been a large proportion. But a continuing problem of the home-building industry is a lack of equity capital even for short-term building, a circumstance that makes builders heavily dependent for construction loans upon suppliers, contractors, and lending institutions.

Sources of Funds

Mortgage funds are derived from several major classes of lending institutions, from individual holders of mortgages, and from the government. The proportion of the mortgage debt held by institutions has grown steadily in the last half century. At the turn of the century, only about half of all mortgage loans were held by lending institutions. By 1950 the proportion exceeded 80 per cent and by 1960 it was 83 per cent. The accompanying table shows the mortgage holdings of the major classes of mortgage lenders in recent years.

TABLE 8. NONFARM RESIDENTIAL MORTGAGE HOLDINGS OF MAJOR CLASSES OF LENDING INSTITUTIONS, 1946, 1950, 1960 (in billions of dollars)

Institution	1946	1950	1960	Per cent of increase 1946–1960
Savings and loan associations...	$7.0	$13.4	$58.9	741
Life insurance companies.......	4.0	11.1	28.9	623
Mutual savings banks..........	3.6	7.1	24.4	578
Commercial banks.............	5.1	10.4	20.5	302
Federal agencies..............	0.7	1.5	7.9	1030
Individuals and others.........	7.7	10.1	20.0	160
Total....................	$28.1	$53.6	$160.6	471

Source: Housing and Home Finance Agency, *Housing Statistics*, March, 1961, table A-49, pp. 58–59.

Savings and Loan Institutions

The largest single class of mortgage-loan holders is savings and loan associations, which since the mid-1950s have held more than a third of all mortgage loans. This proportion is lower, however, than at the peak of the building boom in 1925, when it was 51 per cent.

Savings and loan institutions are small, numerous, and highly local in character. The 4,700 members of the Federal Home Loan Bank System, which accounts for almost all of the resources of the savings and loan industry, had assets of $70 billion at the end of 1960. Another 1,600 savings and loan associations, not members of the Home Loan Bank System, had average assets of about $1 million. Only a few institutions, with assets of over $50 million each, approach the size of mutual savings or commercial banks. The typical association draws on savings from a relatively small geographic area and makes mortgage loans within the immediate vicinity of the institution. Most of its share deposits in residential mortgage loans (typically 80 to 90 per cent of assets) must be invested within fifty miles of the home office.

From 1932 to 1934, when most of the 12,000 associations of the country were in serious financial difficulties, the Federal government established a central reserve facility, deposit insurance, and national chartering and supervision for savings and loan associations. The effect of these aids has been to strengthen the industry, enforce numerous consolidations, encourage a steady flow of savings, and enable the industry to expand rapidly until it now provides the largest single stable source of funds available to the home-building industry.

Deposits in savings and loan institutions are, strictly speaking, shares in the institution. The depositor is not entitled to immediate withdrawal, as is the case with deposits in commercial and mutual savings banks. In times of money shortage the institution may limit withdrawal to a fixed percentage of the deposit. As a consequence of this corporate structure, savings and loan associations theoretically hold only long-term deposits, a large portion of which may be invested in long-term investments.

Savings and loan institutions are not required to maintain the large liquid reserves characteristic of other types of banking institutions. With a large proportion of assets invested in relatively high interest rate mortgages and a small proportion invested in low interest, short-term bonds or in cash, savings and loan associations can pay a higher dividend (or interest) rate than other classes of mortgage lenders.

Savings and loan institutions pioneered in the regularly amortized mortgage. Because these institutions confine their lending to amortized mortgages, they have a fairly large and steady flow of monthly repayments. These repayments provide a stable source of funds for new mortgage loans or for withdrawals even in periods when savings decline. Savings and loan institutions tend to make loans on smaller and cheaper houses. They loan more frequently on older properties and they typically charge slightly higher interest rates than other classes of institutions. Particularly because of their willingness to make fairly high ratio loans on older properties, savings and loan institutions are a very important source of funds for the neighborhood improvement programs of the type involved in urban renewal activity.

Savings and loan institutions have not participated heavily in the FHA program of mortgage insurance. The limitations on interest rates and mortgage ratios plus rigorous FHA supervisory and procedural requirements have not been attractive to smaller institutions. On the other hand, they have participated very heavily in the VA mortgage guarantee system.

Life Insurance Companies

Life insurance companies had combined assets of $113.6 billion in 1959. Only 24 per cent of these assets were invested in residential mortgages. This proportion, however, accounted in 1959 and 1960 for 18 per cent of all nonfarm residential mortgage debt. Life insurance companies have doubled their proportional holdings of mortgage loans since about 1935.

Life insurance companies attract savings as premiums on insurance contracts. By their nature these premiums are long-term savings. As a consequence, life insurance companies do not have to meet the withdrawal problems faced by most other classes of lending institutions and can invest very large proportions of their total assets in long-term obligations. Charter and supervisory limitations require companies to invest premiums in only the best classes of securities and on a widely diversified basis. Large proportions of their assets are invested in prime corporate, public utility and government bonds. The ease of making investments in these types of loans and the comparative difficulty of making large-volume investments in residential mortgages have tended to confine life insurance companies to comparatively low proportions of residential mortgage loans.

Because of their very large size, life insurance companies lend on a national basis, using regional offices or mortgage brokers for mortgage placement and servicing. They also tend to lend only on the best security, principally new residences in the best locations.

The adoption of the FHA system of insurance greatly facilitated the national mortgage-lending operations of life insurance companies. With FHA the companies are able to purchase mortgage loans of standard quality on a nation-wide basis. As a consequence, life insurance companies are the largest single holders of FHA-insured loans, accounting for approximately 28 per cent of all FHA mortgages as of December 31, 1959. Insurance companies are also large purchasers of mortgages from other classes of lending institutions, particularly mortgage brokers.

Commercial Banks

The 13,500 commercial banks had assets of almost $250 billion in the first quarter of 1960. Commercial banks are depositories for both short- and long-term savings. Although traditionally they receive chiefly short-term deposits, their savings deposits have exceeded those of savings and loan institutions. Because they are the primary sources for commercial and industrial credit, they are required by state and national supervisory authorities to maintain a high degree of liquidity at all times. This accounts for the fact that in recent years commercial banks have invested only 7 per cent of their assets in residential mortgages; however, this percentage represents 17 per cent of all residential mortgage holdings.

Commercial banks are both the largest single available pool

of credit in the country and one of the least stable of the sources of funds in the residential mortgage market. In times of high demand for commercial and industrial credit, commercial banks understandably put large proportions of their resources into loans of this type and may hold their residential mortgage portfolios constant or even reduce them. Relatively minor changes in portfolio policy by commercial banks exercise a very powerful influence on the total volume of new funds flowing into residential mortgages. If commercial banks are buying residential mortgages, credit is far more readily available. If commercial banks are selling or holding their portfolios constant, the tightening of the market for residential mortgage money will be felt throughout the home-building industry.

In other respects, the home-mortgage-lending operations of commercial banks are similar to those of savings and loan associations and life insurance companies. The smaller commercial banks often engage in mortgage lending on a local and customer basis. The larger banks operate on a national basis through mortgage brokers who may originate or sell and service mortgage loans for them. This tends to make commercial bank mortgage lending extremely selective and forces the companies to concentrate their mortgage lending in FHA-insured and VA-guaranteed loans. These loans have special advantages to commercial banks since they may be sold to other portfolio lenders at times when commercial and industrial credit demands are high.

Commercial banks also provide support to the mortgage market by extending loans to savings and loan institutions, based on the security of their mortgage portfolios, which enable those institutions to make residential mortgage loans in anticipation of deposits or repayments.

Mutual Savings Banks

The mutual savings banks are largely confined to the Northeastern part of the United States. There they perform some of the functions performed by savings and loan institutions or by commercial banks in other parts of the country. The 500 mutual savings banks had assets in 1960 of $41 billion, much less than the assets of the savings and loan institutions.

Mutual savings banks accept only savings deposits. Their deposits are genuine deposits, unlike the share purchases of savings and loan associations, and the depositor is entitled to receive cash payment on demand. While mutual savings banks invest the largest share of their long-term deposits in residential and other mortgages, they are required to maintain higher liquidity ratios than savings and loan associations and they are permitted to invest larger proportions of their assets in nonresidential mortgages and in selected corporate and other securities. This gives mutual savings banks a little more freedom to service other community banking needs, and gives depositors slightly greater protection than that offered by savings and loan associations in terms of withdrawal privileges.

In 1959 the mortgage holdings of mutual savings banks amounted to approximately two-thirds of their savings accounts, and mutual savings banks held 15.2 per cent of all outstanding mortgage debt in that year and in 1960. Large savings banks are national lenders and operate through agents and brokers, as do commercial banks and insurance companies. In recent years mutual savings bank purchases of nonfarm mortgages of the single-family type have been fairly constant at 6 or 7 per cent of all purchases.

Mortgage Bankers and Brokers

Mortgage bankers and brokers are a class of non-deposit mortgage-lending institution. They are corporations financed with private equity capital and bank loans that make residential and other mortgage loans for resale to deposit type institutions. Their income is derived primarily from fees connected with the placement of mortgages and the service charges paid when the ultimate purchaser is a national lender in a remote location. The larger firms have modest investment portfolios which in the aggregate account for 1 to 2 per cent of mortgage holdings. In a sense, many individual real estate brokers who make and sell mortgage loans might be considered mortgage bankers. As used here, however, the term is limited to the firms whose principal business is the making, selling, and servicing of loans.

Although the mortgage companies have relatively little capital compared with deposit types of institutions, they play an important part in the origination and servicing of mortgages and are an essential part of the system of mortgage-lending institutions. In 1959, mortgage companies were responsible for originating 48.1 per cent of all FHA-insured home mortgages. However, they held only 6.7 per cent of the outstanding amount of such insured mortgages, selling to other lenders virtually all the mortgages which they originated. Insurance companies, which originated less than 5 per cent of all FHA-insured mortgages in 1959, held 31 per cent of such mortgages; obviously they had purchased the bulk of their mortgage holdings from mortgage companies and others. The dependence of mortgage brokers upon deposit types of institutions, particularly life insurance companies and banks, makes them peculiarly vulnerable to changes in the money market. In times of credit stringency mortgage companies have no large resources of deposits or repayments to draw upon for new mortgage lending. They are dependent upon the credit resources of others. By the same token, when credit eases they become the institutions through which the growing flow of funds is directed to home building.

Other Mortgage Holders

Various Federal agencies are now substantial holders of mortgages bought under the terms of special congressional acts and authorizations. For example, the Federal National Mortgage Association's holdings at the end of 1960 were over $6 billion, an all-time high.

Individuals also comprise a large class of mortgage holders. Although declining in relative importance during the postwar years, in 1960 mortgage holdings of individuals and others were estimated to amount to approximately $20 billion. A portion of this total includes the mortgage holdings of assorted institutions like colleges, universities, estates, and trusts. The remainder consists of mortgages held by individual persons for their own account. For either trust or individual investment purposes, a mortgage is a relatively attractive form of investment, offering a substantial degree of security and a fairly high yield.

Credit Companies

Credit for home modernization and repair is drawn from many of the same sources which supply funds for home mortgages. Home modernization loans are usually made for comparatively short terms of 12 to 36 months and in amounts ranging from $200 to $2,000 or $3,000. Usually the interest charge on modernization loans is discounted in advance, with effective interest rates of 6 to 10 per cent. Commercial banks are the largest single source of this type of credit, with credit and finance companies second.

There are many relatively small credit companies, but only a few large companies which finance the consumer credit requirements of retail outlets in all parts of the country. Commercial banks hold 80 per cent of FHA-insured home modernization loans, credit companies 10 per cent, and savings institutions 10 per cent. Credit companies probably service substantially larger proportions of non-FHA home repair loans and may account for a third to a half of such loans. Credit and finance companies are not deposit institutions. They usually draw their funds from commercial loans at commercial interest rates, lending it at substantially higher rates.

Problems in the Flow of Funds

Taken together, all these sources of credit serve many of our national housing requirements admirably. Over the years, they have financed the development of our present housing supply and now provide funds to meet the mortgage requirements of higher-income families, particularly in the suburban parts of our metropolitan areas, and to accommodate the purchase of existing homes of a wide range of quality and location. The governmental aids discussed in following chapters help serve a still larger need. Despite these significant accomplishments, our system of residential finance fails to meet many home-financing needs and presents some major problems to the housing industry. These problems are briefly enumerated below, together with some of the suggestions for improvement which seem to be within the competence of private institutions.

Perhaps the most important problem is that of stabilizing the flow of mortgage funds into residential construction. At present, and despite governmental aids, this flow varies widely from year to year, creating periods during which funds are adequate and periods of acute shortage, and thus contributes to the instability of the housing industry and the economy generally. Moreover, although mortgage funds are more equitably distributed throughout the country than formerly, many central-city areas, most rural nonfarm areas, and many of the most rapidly developing parts of the country suffer from relative shortages of mortgage funds. Private institutions, obliged to balance the security of investment against the rate of return, are extremely cautious about assuming the risks involved in loans in new areas, loans on new types of construction, loans to groups which have not had a long borrowing history, loans in blighted areas undergoing renewal, and loans of longer term or higher ratio than have been traditional in the industry.

The varying characteristics of the several classes of mortgage lenders directly affect the character of their mortgage-lending activities and the volume and the stability of the funds flowing into mortgage loans. Because savings and loan associations engage almost exclusively in residential lending they are a stable source of mortgage funds. Mutual savings banks and life insurance companies are only relatively stable, and commercial banks are highly volatile. At times, when other outlets for investments are relatively more advantageous, commercial banks will withdraw almost entirely from the mortgage market. On the other hand, when competing investment opportunities are not so advantageous they will move heavily into the mortgage-lending field, and also into loans to, and warehousing arrangements with, other classes of mortgage lenders.

Residential mortgage lending is highly susceptible to changes in the demand for money, as was demonstrated with particular severity during 1957 when restrictive Federal credit policies and rising demands for industrial and commercial loans created an intense credit shortage. The interest rates paid by commercial and industrial lenders rose sharply, demands for commercial and industrial loans usurped almost all commercial bank funds, and

insurance companies and savings banks shifted marginal investment funds from residential to other types of loans. Within a period of twenty-four months the new funds flowing into residential construction dropped by approximately 30 per cent.

Under these conditions classical economists argue that residential mortgage interest rates should rise to levels competitive
with other rates; then, although credit would be tight in all fields,
no industry would suffer discrimination. Unfortunately, conventional mortgage rates move rather slowly and are subject to numerous institutional restraints. There is little competition over
rates locally and in the short run. The "going rate" tends to be
accepted by all institutions for the various types of loans they
make. The rates on FHA and VA loans are set by law within
narrow limits, and within these limits are subject to considerable
political pressure. The consumer can adapt his budget to the few
cents extra that a doubling of short-term money costs adds to
the cost of a suit or the three or four dollars a month that higher
interest rates add to the cost of his car, but he cannot so easily
make the adjustment to the same interest rate rise that increases
his housing cost by $10 or $20 a month for the next twenty years.
This inequity has forced a general recognition that changes in
credit terms often discriminate heavily against the home-building
industry, and that these discriminatory effects arise in some degree
from the institutional structure of home mortgage lending.

Debtor and Creditor Areas

Credit shortages appear first in debtor regions which do not
normally provide enough savings to meet their own needs. Interest rates are normally higher in developing areas than in
older, more static areas. In time of credit shortage debtor regions
may suffer from an acute lack of residential mortgage funds and
higher interest rates, even when funds are fairly readily available elsewhere. The combined effects of credit shortages and
higher interest rates have been abated in part by Federal intervention in home mortgage lending. FHA and VA mortgage insurance and guarantees have tended to stabilize interest rates and
to reduce the sharp differentials which formerly existed between the East and the South and West. During periods of credit

shortage, however, the inflexibility of the Federally insured and guaranteed mortgage interest rates has led to sharp curtailments of funds in debtor areas as funds shifted from interest-controlled, Federally aided mortgages to interest-free conventionals.

Much remains to be done before all market areas are adequately served with lending institutions to meet their mortgage needs. This problem is particularly acute in smaller cities and towns and in the rural nonfarm areas of the country. As improving transportation makes possible an even greater spread of urban areas, and as declining agricultural populations enlarge the proportion of the total population which is engaged in urban or nonfarm activity, the needs of developing areas will doubtless expand. State banking authorities and Federal banking and savings and loan authorities and mortgage lenders have failed to recognize the mortgage needs in such areas. Conflicts between different classes of lending institutions and traditional objections to branch banking have paralyzed public regulatory action.

As a consequence, Congress has authorized the Federal National Mortgage Association and the Veterans Administration to make direct loans in these areas. Although the dollar volume of this direct lending activity has been relatively insignificant, it is an excellent illustration of the failure of state government and of private business to take advantage of opportunities for additional service to the American public and the resulting tendency of the Federal government to intervene in areas where private action might be entirely feasible. A systematic examination of the availability of mortgage-lending and mortgage-servicing institutions in areas remote from metropolitan centers would be helpful both to government and to private business in revealing community needs and opportunities for business expansion. Perhaps such an examination would reveal the need or desirability for an expansion of the kind of chartering activity carried on by the Home Loan Bank System in the mid-1930s when the Federal government aided the establishment of new savings and loan associations in areas needing them. Perhaps such an examination would lead to the national chartering of mutual savings banks, thus providing an opportunity for this type of institution to expand in regions it does not now serve. Or perhaps such an examination would merely reveal new business opportunities for branch banks or branch service offices of mortgage brokers. It would certainly focus attention on the impediments to mortgage credit in expanding areas.

Revising the Mortgage Instrument

Legally and economically, the mortgage instrument is an antiquated device handed down to us from preceding centuries and encumbered with a host of medieval paraphernalia having little relevance to the conditions of modern urban life. The whole business of title and mortgage recording and transfer is bogged down in legal rituals and weighted with burdensome costs which prevent mortgages from competing effectively with stocks and bonds as an investment outlet. Stocks and bonds have always been a convenient instrument for investment purposes, and they are now being made even more accessible to a wider range of markets through trustee depositaries, ownership certificates, and investment trusts. A corresponding evolution has scarcely begun for the mortgage instrument.

There have been numerous suggestions in the past twenty-five years or so to modernize mortgage and title instruments or develop a debenture device which would provide evidence of ownership and permit the ready purchase and sale of interests in mortgages. The Torrens system (first used in Australia in 1858) for simplifying registration of title is an example; another is a method for incorporating ownership and using stock certificates as evidence of title. The development of some device as a substitute for, or evidence of title and interest in, the mortgage would make mortgages a more attractive form of investment and open up to mortgage investment large sources of funds, like pension funds, which now tend to avoid mortgage lending.

A new form of mortgage instrument is the so-called open-end mortgage. Strictly speaking, it has been used occasionally for many years; its real development did not occur, however, until the mid-1950s when savings and loan institutions began to provide this type of instrument in volume. Essentially, it is a device to enable the mortgagor to borrow additional amounts for home improvement on his existing mortgage, either to the extent of the initial mortgage before amortization or to some other fixed amount, and to repay the additional loan over the remaining amortization period. Substantial savings either in interest rates (as contrasted to short-term loans) or in title costs (as contrasted with a new mortgage) are realized from the open-end mortgage. Lenders find it helps to maintain customer loyalty and business. In the long run it may become an important means to finance systematic renewal programs for large-scale rehabilitation.

Construction Loans

Construction financing is often as great a problem in home building as mortgage financing. It is not unusual for home builders to borrow construction money on short-term loans from commercial banks without obtaining commitments for permanent mortgage financing. This is an obviously hazardous practice since a decline in the market for houses or a tightening of the mortgage market might leave the builder with a house for sale on which permanent mortgage financing would be unavailable. To avoid this possibility, most builders try to obtain a permanent mortgage commitment to finance the ultimate sale of the house in advance of construction. Then they get a short-term construction loan from the same or other sources and repay it with the proceeds of the permanent mortgage when the house is sold.

Construction loans are expensive to lenders because they must supervise the construction and schedule loan payments in accordance with the amount of work put into place. Most lenders withhold 25 to 30 per cent of the construction loan until completion of the building. Builders contend that this practice requires them to have more working capital than they think is necessary and that it limits the volume of building they can undertake. These problems are intensified when the construction lender is not the same institution as the ultimate mortgage lender; then the builder has to pay additional interest and other charges on the construction loan, sometimes duplicating charges on the ultimate long-term loan. If the ultimate lender is a bank or other lender who also engages in construction lending, the procedures are considerably simplified. FHA and VA commitments ordinarily provide simultaneous security for a construction loan. The number of lenders who will advance money during construction for a mortgage loan is increasing steadily, but there remain additional possibilities for consolidating construction and mortgage loans into a more smoothly working and more economical process.

Second Mortgages

Prior to the development of the FHA and VA mortgage loan systems, second mortgages and even third mortgages were not uncommon. Since first mortgage lenders could rarely exceed a mortgage ratio of 70 per cent by charter or regulatory limitations, any home buyer desiring to purchase a house and lacking a 30 per cent down payment was compelled to borrow through a second mortgage the difference between his equity and his first mortgage. Second mortgages may be risky and therefore they are typically written for shorter terms, 1 to 5 years, and at substantially higher interest rates, 6 to 10 per cent, than first mortgage loans. The widespread mortgage foreclosures early in the Depression were often credited to the prevalence of the second and third mortgage.

The adoption of the FHA and VA systems made it possible for fiduciary institutions to make high ratio loans of 90 or 100 per cent and virtually eliminated second mortgage financing for many years. But the practice revived during the postwar boom years, when there were intermittent credit shortages and the government-aided sector of the mortgage market fell off sharply. In areas where government-aided mortgages are not readily available, and on projects which are too high priced, too poorly located, or too poorly built to obtain FHA insurance, the low ratios of conventional mortgage loans still create temptations for second mortgage borrowing.

Savings and loan associations, as a result, propose the establishment of a third system of government insurance of residential mortgage loans to permit them to make higher ratio "conventional" loans. The proposal has been strongly criticized on the grounds that it means a wholly new system of government insurance when two workable systems already exist, that the new system would advance the interests of one class of mortgage lender without offering comparable advantages to others, and that it would provide none of the protections on interest rate, construction quality, and appraisals that are already a part of government mortgage guarantee and insurance programs. To the extent that it would provide insurance of low standard loans, the proposal can be fairly criticized. But demands for a new type of government insurance arise in some degree precisely because small lenders are unable to cope with the elaborate procedural requirements of existing government-aid programs. Some simplification of these requirements might ease legitimate demands for new types of insurance. More direct means to prevent widespread second mortgage lending would be inconsistent with the freedom of choice required by the American economy.

Unlocking New Sources of Funds

The largest and newest untapped source of savings for mortgage purposes are pension funds, which are estimated to have assets amounting to over $40 billion and growing at the rate of several billion dollars each year. At the end of 1958, only 2 per cent of state and local retirement funds and only 3 per cent of corporate pension funds were invested in real estate mortgages. So far these funds have been deterred from doing so in any volume because of institutional conservatism and the traditional difficulties of engaging in mortgage lending. To make this new source of savings available to the home-building industry will probably require a number of changes in mortgage practices and perhaps new mortgage instruments. A revival of the mortgage bond device, the development of a government-guaranteed debenture with mortgage backing, or the opening of this market by mortgage bankers, would serve to tap this vast new source of potential mortgage funds.

Another approach to the same problem is authorization of the establishment of mortgage investment trusts which would be free of corporate income tax liability and would be able to pass on their full income to the owners of shares in or debentures of such trusts. They would serve to attract funds into mortgage-lending and real property which otherwise would be invested in other corporate stocks and bonds.

The establishment of mortgage corporations under Federal supervision was authorized in the National Housing Act of 1934 to provide a similar type of investment. The legislation was implemented only to the extent of chartering the Federal National Mortgage Association—at that time a wholly government-owned corporation. If housing is to compete with other investment outlets for the savings of individuals and other classes of investors, an instrumentality must be developed which will permit the purchase and sale of some form of certificate or share on a basis that is comparable in security, marketability, and yield to other debt or equity instrumentalities. Presumably the mortgage corporation is the device through which funds of this type might be attracted to residential financing while preserving some of the liquidity features presented by the stock and bond markets. Federal supervision and chartering of mortgage corporations is probably necessary if investors are to be assured that the past speculative history of this type of institution will not be repeated.

A third avenue for exploration is suggested by the analogy of credit companies which provide loan funds for automobiles and other consumer durable goods purchases. Although credit companies account for a significant proportion of FHA-insured Title I home improvement loans, the arrangements under which they operate are subject to several criticisms. First, loans are based upon the credit rating of the individual borrower or cosigner without adequate recognition of the security of the improvement involved. Second, they are often a vehicle for irresponsible merchants to misrepresent the value, cost, or terms of the transaction or to engage in fraudulent selling practices. Finally, credit companies appear unable to provide financing for comprehensive residential modernization where the effort involves not merely the sale of a single consumer durable good and its installation but also the systematic modernization of the building itself. Existing arrangements, for example, permit the installation of aluminum storm windows but leave the stairs in a dilapidated condition and the heating and plumbing facilities inadequate.

Instead, such loans should be available for the systematic rehabilitation of structures throughout a neighborhood. To be sound, they will require judgment about the economic feasibility of the modernization and some assurance that all or most of the structures in the area will be rehabilitated so as to upgrade the whole neighborhood. Existing short-term, note-lending devices are not equipped to make an appraisal of the property risk as opposed to the individual risk. They are based on interest rates, repayment periods, and loan service costs which permit the advance of credit with little review of the credit risks of the individual and none of the property involved in the loan. The interest rates are high on short-term notes, averaging 9 per cent a year on declining balances. The administrative costs are low, on the presumption that the individual credit is the only criterion involved and repayment periods are necessarily short.

New York State has sought to meet some of these problems by the establishment of the state-chartered New York Mortgage Facilities Corporation. A number of lending institutions subscribed the required capital to underwrite a substantial volume of home improvement and other loans in an effort to meet the needs of urban renewal. If this experience proves successful, it may be a prototype for credit corporations organized on a community basis to provide the short- and long-term credit needed for comprehensive urban renewal activities. Private lending institutions can serve this same purpose in local areas only if they acquire lending officers familiar with urban renewal procedures and processes and if they are able to make an area commitment in support of an urban renewal program.

Another possibility, subject to some administrative complications it is true, would be the development of FHA-insured Title I local area programs under which package loans and notes would be allowed for individual structures where the improvements involved corresponded with those proposed by the renewal program. Charles Haar, in *Federal Credit and Private Housing*, has suggested that the FHA home modernization program might be administered on an area basis so that with the adoption of a renewal plan for a neighborhood FHA insurance would be readily available to borrowers and lenders in the area.

Reorganizing. Our Systems of Mortgage Lending Institutions

The distribution and the relative importance of each class of lender in the mortgage market—mutual savings banks, savings and loan institutions, mortgage banking corporations, life insurance companies, and commercial banks—vary widely from region to region. It is not unreasonable to ask whether these lending arrangements, derived in considerable degree from the nineteenth and early twentieth centuries, are appropriate and adequate for the expanding economy of the United States. Savings and loan associations in particular labor under a number of handicaps. They are small, restricted as to withdrawals and types of investment, and lack the prestige and flexibility of mutual savings banks. It is noteworthy that the effect of Federal chartering and supervision has been to enlarge their average size and to provide them with a professional level of management so that they have become comparable to savings banks in some respects, although they do not have some of the supervisory and charter restraints which are required for the latter. Meantime, the savings banks, which have been the backbone of mortgage lending and saving in the Northeastern part of the United States and which have an enviable reputation as savings institutions, have been reviewing the possibilities for geographic expansion and have taken cognizance of the need for a savings bank type of institution in other parts of the country. A committee of the New York Association of Savings Banks has recommended the development of legislation looking toward the Federal chartering of savings banks so that they can expand their services on a national basis.

Trends like these suggest the timeliness of an investigation of the adequacy of savings institutions and mortgage-lending institutions. A reorganization of our national system of savings and loan institutions might well allow them to perform the functions of savings banks. At the same time, a national chartering of savings banks might bring to other areas of the country some of the advantages of institutional responsibility, deposit safety, liquidity and ability to attract savings, offered in the Northeast by the mutual savings bank system. Both are local savings institutions which place their funds primarily in local investment outlets. Relatively minor changes in their charters, financial policies, deposit insurance and investment practices might result in the kind of nation-wide system of savings and mortgage-lending institutions that the housing industry requires if it is to meet the demands for new and rehabilitated houses and apartments.

Chapter 11

REHABILITATING THE HOUSING STOCK

Conserving and improving the salvageable housing stock to assure its maximum usefulness is an essential adjunct to the enlarged production of new dwellings, and systematic demolition or removal of obsolete buildings. It might be expected that rehabilitated older houses at appropriately depreciated prices would meet the needs of most families who cannot afford new sale or rental dwellings at acceptable quality levels.

But to date, most successful rehabilitation has been designed for the high-income market: a product of good location and a reviving demand for central-city residences. Rehabilitation for this prestige market has been able to overcome financing difficulties because of its inherent profitability. Rehabilitation for the middle-income market has been sporadic and dependent upon fortuitous market conditions. Specially favorable terms for FHA loans, authorized by the Housing Act of 1954, have failed to generate any large volume of business. The cooperation and support of local public agencies, required for general success, have often been lacking.

Rehabilitation for low-income families has rarely been successful. In a few cases, sharply rising incomes have permitted code enforcement campaigns which have provided substantial improvements in housing quality without hardship. In other cases rehabilitation has merely raised costs beyond the means of occupants, resulting in displacement. If accelerated filtration could produce lower property acquisition costs, such rehabilitation might become more widely feasible. Financing and community

178

facility programs would be required to backstop code enforcement.

Reorganized code enforcement, reinforced by planned community improvements and spot demolition, offers the promise of substantial improvements in housing quality. Broad public and private programs are necessary to encourage better maintenance and rehabilitation at standards far above those enforceable under the police power. Widespread rehabilitation and conservation will require the development of new types of firms specializing in this type of business and with sufficient financial resources.

The existing stock of housing in American communities represents an investment whose protection and enhancement is a central concern of the owner, the mortgagor, the community, the government, and the housing industry. "From its bearing on the general welfare, in terms of the health, safety, comfort, and happiness of the people," Miles Colean points out in *Residential Rehabilitation: Private Profits and Public Purposes*, "its meaning is not surpassed by any of our other assets. In terms of the business generated through real estate and financing transactions and property repair and improvement, its importance is hardly less. It provides a large source of local tax revenue. It is at once the glory and the despair of our cities."

The postwar years have demonstrated the remarkable elasticity in our stock of housing. Under conditions of high demand it has accommodated several million more families than new construction could have provided. As demand shifts from larger to smaller units, or vice versa, the stock changes to meet new requirements. Much of this change results from rehabilitation of existing dwellings, the repairs, alterations, modernizations, and equipment replacements that are essential to adapt a relatively fixed supply of structures to the changing needs of our population.

In 1960, property-owners spent more than $13 billion on maintenance, remodeling, and repairs to all kinds of housing. Rehabilitation of owner-occupied single-family houses which accounted for about $8 billion of this total has been primarily the result of the individual homeowner's desire to improve the appearance and livability of his own dwelling. About 3 of every 10 dollars spent by owner-occupants were for "do-it-yourself" improvements.

Two principal questions underlie any discussion of rehabilitation. First, is it an essential activity in the improvement of American communities? Second, is it, or can it be, an economic operation for those who invest in it? Because an affirmative answer to the first question does not insure a favorable response to the second, the corollary question arises of whether public policy should provide incentives to private rehabilitation and, if so, what form the incentives should take.

As Miles Colean observes:

> In a market economy, the test of feasibility is profitability. If we find that the tasks of maintaining and improving the existing housing supply and of adapting it to altered environmental conditions can make for good business and satisfactory investment, then we may point the way both to an important economic opportunity and to a means for reducing governmental burdens. Or, if we find that the business opportunities are unexploited, then we may seek the reasons, and undertake to suggest remedies. Out of this exploration, we may in the end hope to find a rational basis for public policies aimed on the one hand at improving the economic potentials of rehabilitation and on the other at defining the areas in which the community may determine that private effort must be supplemented by public action.

More often than not the rehabilitation process is looked at almost wholly from the point of view of supply. How many units are there that require rehabilitation? What is their condition? How much will they cost to rehabilitate? These are significant questions and accurate answers to them are essential. But merely answering them does little to widen the scope of rehabilitation operations or to assure the individual investor in rehabilitation that his activities will bring him a proper level of economic return. However, in a private economy such as ours, the key to successful production is effective demand. Who wants what? When will he want it? Where will he want it? How much will he pay for it?

Since the end of World War II, rehabilitation has emerged as a recognizable form of business activity which is engaged in by two general classes of private entrepreneurs: contract remodelers and operative remodelers. The contract remodeler, acting on an owner's orders, arranges for the repairs or remodeling the owner decides to undertake. He usually subcontracts part of the work—the wiring, say, or the plumbing—but he supervises the entire job and submits to the owner a single bill for his "home modernizing service."

After a bad start at the end of World War II, when contract remodeling was widely typified by the sharp practices of firms which sell elaborate construction jobs at excessive prices to unwary homeowners, the business has developed into an important and more reputable service to homeowners, particularly to those in the middle-income range. After careful consultation with an owner about what he wants and can afford, the contract remodeler handles the entire job and, in addition, often helps the owner obtain the loan to pay for it.

Most contract remodelers work on a cost-plus contract. Their success lies in aggressive selling techniques, a sense of popular taste, precise cost estimating, and broad contacts with reliable financing institutions many of which are savings and loan associations. On the whole, theirs is basically a risk-free operation. Unlike operative remodelers, contract remodelers do not have to invest their own funds in the properties they rehabilitate. Homeowners make the investment instead, financing the cost of the improvements by personal loans, open-end or new mortgages, or FHA Title I loans.

Contract work for residential rehabilitation has increased from about $1 billion in 1950 to $6 billion in 1960. By early 1961, the country's biggest rehabilitator had an annual gross of over $4 million.

The operative remodeler is often, but not always, a person with experience in real estate or home building. He buys property, repairs or remodels it, and then sells it. Some rehabilitators retain the properties they remodel as income-producing investments on a rental basis.

A realistic estimate of the potentialities of investment in rehabilitation requires a searching look at its submarkets. The New

York Temporary State Housing Rent Commission published in 1960 an investigation of the prospects for rehabilitating various kinds of properties in Morningside Heights, a fifty-year-old neighborhood of New York City ("Prospects for Rehabilitation," directed by Morton J. Schussheim). Converting thirty-four rooming houses into less crowded use was considered a prerequisite to area-wide rehabilitation, but no other changes were anticipated in community facilities, land use, or other features of the environment. The study is predominantly a market analysis of the costs of bringing fireproof elevator buildings, nonfireproof elevator buildings, and walk-up buildings to various levels of rehabilitation, under different financing schemes, and under the same or new owners. In almost no situation was it practical for rehabilitation to be undertaken under conventional loans. With state loans at 3½ per cent interest rates, or FHA loans under Section 220 of the Housing Act of 1954, rehabilitation or modernization was feasible for a large majority of the buildings, although in many cases modernization would cause rent increases that would be burdensome to the tenants.

In *Residential Rehabilitation*, a book in this series, William W. Nash concentrates on three rehabilitation submarkets: the upper-income market represented by families with incomes in excess of $7,500; the middle-income market represented by families with incomes between $3,500 and $7,500; and the low-income market represented by families with incomes below $3,500. Admittedly, these are gross distinctions. Between the first two categories in particular, effective demand shifts back and forth, with a whole range of individual factors, some tangible like family size, others intangible like social status. Moreover, demand for rehabilitated dwellings in these submarkets is more heavily influenced by the location of the units than is the case with existing housing which has not yet reached the point of requiring rehabilitation.

Prestige Rehabilitation

The phrase "prestige rehabilitation" describes the kind of rehabilitation that has the greatest appeal to persons of high income and that is frankly geared to their ability to pay a premium for convenient location and social distinction. With few exceptions, one of which is described below, prestige rehabilitation takes place in or near the areas of a city which once housed the well-to-do. The character of the population will have changed, property values will have declined, and individual structures will have deteriorated or become obsolete by modern standards of design and equipment. Yet the area will have certain intrinsic values that make it particularly attractive to many business and professional people.

A strong attraction is architectural style. In one city it may be of the Federal period, in another it may be fully adorned Victorian. Another attraction is proximity to cultural and entertainment facilities and to the important business and financial complex of the city. The longer the commuting distance is between the downtown area of the city and the upper-income suburbs outside the city, the more likely it is that an in-town prestige area can maintain a steady market for its rehabilitated dwellings.

Rehabilitators who enter the prestige market look first, then, for areas which combine historic associations with locational convenience. Although they must create a microcosmic environment by isolating their developments from the blighting influences which usually surround them, they can do so practically on a house-by-house basis. This is particularly true if the lot permits an enclosed garden and if access to the block is through a generally safe and attractive corridor.

Rehabilitation for the prestige market is exacting in its design requirements. Small units typical in this kind of rehabilitation require good open planning: glass doors opening on exterior patios, staircases that "float," and low room dividers that take the place of walls between living, dining, and cooking spaces. Air conditioning, in climates where the summer weather is hot or humid, fireplaces regardless of climate, and built-in bookcases enhance the marketability of rehabilitated structures, as do good quality kitchen and bathroom equipment and enough outdoor space for entertaining or gardening.

Georgetown in Washington, D.C., the Beacon Hill area in Boston, and the Rittenhouse and Fitler Square areas in Philadelphia are among the oldest and best-known examples of successful rehabilitation for the upper-income market. In each case, investment in rehabilitation enlarged the community's supply of housing, and produced excellent financial returns to the entrepreneurs who were involved. Differing markedly in size and appearance, these three areas shared the same advantages of a consistent and generally felicitous architectural style and a lingering air of gentility. There were a few other parts of Boston and Philadelphia whose high status attributes matched those of the Beacon Hill and the Rittenhouse and Fitler Square areas, but in Washington there was only one—Georgetown. This fact makes the successful rehabilitation of a large part of Foggy Bottom a remarkable example of entrepreneurial skill.

Even in its best period, Foggy Bottom was not a fashionable part of Washington. Some of its residences were not dissimilar in size and style to many in Georgetown, but they were more cheaply constructed and lacked fine details of design and many were little more than hovels crammed along both sides of an alley. But what is important is that the houses could be restored to look like Georgetown houses, and that they were close to the fast-growing nexus of State Department buildings and within walking distance of downtown Washington. Georgetown had long since been unable to accommodate all the upper-income people who wanted to live there; and if Foggy Bottom could be made to approximate the Georgetown look, rehabilitators believed they could tap the unfilled demand. In the years since World War II, they have been remarkably successful in doing so. Snow's Court and Hughes Court are successful examples of rehabilitation in Foggy Bottom.

The rehabilitation of Snow's Court started in 1953, of Hughes Court in 1954. The first was undertaken by amateurs, the second by professionals. This fact illustrates Nash's point that trained real estate operators usually get into prestige rehabilitation only after individual homeowners or inexperienced investors have led the way. The reasons are that the commercial operator is more cautious about risking his capital in an untried venture than the enthusiastic nonprofessional, and that mortgage money for rehabilitation is hard to come by until the tone and stability of an area are fairly well set.

The sixteen houses in Snow's Court were rehabilitated in two stages. The nine in the second group cost $27,000 to acquire and $80,050 to remodel; they sold for $135,000. The owner's $28,000 profit on the nine houses was 26.2 per cent of the sale price.

Financing was the biggest problem in the rehabilitation of Snow's Court. The owners needed $30,000 in cash to carry out the two-step project. They raised enough money for the initial purchase of seven houses and the contractor's first bill by assuming the existing mortgages on the properties, by borrowing from friends and relatives, and by putting up life insurance policies as collateral for a loan from a Georgetown savings and loan association. The contractor waited for his last payment until all the completed houses were sold, but the owners had to meet the second and third installments of his bill by selling two of the houses at cost before they were completed. After the project was finished, the owners were able to get small first mortgages for their buyers, provided they cosigned them. The mortgages ran to about $7,500 at 5 per cent for fifteen years. The second mortgages, amounting to the difference between an average equity of $3,500 and the amount of the first mortgage and carrying terms of eight years at 5½ per cent, the owners had to take back themselves. This meant that most of their profit lay in the future. More important, it also meant that their capital was so tied up they could not undertake any further rehabilitation unless they were willing to sell the second mortgages at discounts of 5 per cent or more.

The five houses in Hughes Court were only 12.5 feet wide. A real estate corporation bought them for $4,000 each, spent $9,000 per unit on remodeling, and sold them for $16,500. The $3,500 profit was 21 per cent of the sale price. The three members of the corporation used their own funds to finance the entire operation.

The most difficult obstacles apart from financing that both the "amateurs" and the "professionals" had to contend with were governmental ones: The District of Columbia provided no new public improvements for Foggy Bottom, not even street repairs. The residential character of the area was frequently in doubt when efforts were made by other interests to have the zoning changed. Finally, there was indecision among official agencies as to whether the Bottom should be declared an official urban renewal area.

Nonetheless, substantial sections of Foggy Bottom now stand, tastefully and profitably rehabilitated, against the backdrop of the Lincoln Memorial, the State Department buildings, and the Potomac River. The persons who bought and are still buying the houses reportedly are unconcerned by the fact that their property lies, to some extent, in the right-of-way of the District's proposed inner-belt expressway. The demand in Foggy Bottom for Georgetown style living is effective enough to override situations that would spell disaster to private investors in other areas.

With rare exceptions, it should be noted that prestige rehabilitation areas cannot be "created" by business initiative. The areas which will attract higher-income families are more likely to be "found." Their unique flavor first attracts artists, writers, and other nonconformists who are looking for cheap, but interesting, housing which they can improve by their own efforts. The more prosperous and socially conventional families come later. After the comeback of an area is under way, vigorous initiative by investors may speed its recovery. Broader-scale community efforts may yet achieve the same effect, though this remains to be proved.

Middle-Income Rehabilitation

Some of the best opportunities for the rehabilitation of housing for middle-income groups are to be found in the fringe development of a generation or more ago. Here the houses and apartments are larger than those closer to the downtown district and are rarely in as dilapidated a condition. Indeed, their loss of value is more often attributable to obsolescence and poor personal and municipal housekeeping than to serious structural defects or the intrusion into the neighborhood of deleterious commercial uses.

Many of the families that comprise the market for middle-income rehabilitation already own their homes in these areas, but as a rule the houses are deficient or obsolete on a number of counts. If owners can obtain the necessary financing, they frequently are eager to bring their properties up to a higher level of maintenance, to rearrange interior space, and to install modern equipment. As they do the job themselves or turn to contract remodelers to do it for them, their expenditures make up the largest dollar volume of all rehabilitation.

Another group in the market for middle-income rehabilitation is found among the families that live in apartments near the center of the city. After the birth of the first or second child the family needs more space and often will try to find it in an older, large house in a reasonably stable neighborhood provided that the house is well kept up, modern in its equipment, and available at a sales price or rent that is less than the going rate in the suburbs for comparable space. Many operative remodelers find this market a more sustained one for their investment than the prestige market.

Like the rehabilitator of properties for upper-income occupancy, the operative remodeler in the middle-income neighborhood has to be concerned with the level of amenities the neighborhood offers. Good community facilities and services are important. Unless they are available, rehabilitated units will not move in the market even if the vacancy ratio in the city is low. Financing terms for new single-family houses in the suburbs are too favorable for rehabilitated houses to be competitive unless potential customers can adjust their demands for space and modernity and a quick journey to work with their demands for a good environment for children. It is not surprising that operative remodelers in declining middle-income neighborhoods are usually strong proponents of civic improvement programs.

Operative remodelers in middle-income neighborhoods deal in three kinds of properties: obsolescent single-family houses which can be modernized to sell for single-family use; larger and often deteriorated single-family houses which can be converted into several units, one of which will be occupied by the new owner; and old-fashioned apartment houses which can be turned into modern apartments.

The first objective is to remove mechanical obsolescence. New wiring and an efficient heating system are installed along with modern equipment for the bathroom and kitchen. The design of the structure is not modified unless there is strong evidence that the potential market will stand the additional investment. What usually happens is that gimcrack trim is stripped off, a porch that darkens the adjoining interior space is removed, a non-load-bearing interior wall is taken out to increase the size of a room, built-in closets are added.

Remodeling of apartment houses proceeds along much the same pattern: essential repairs, new equipment, and plenty of paint. Often, however, elevators must be installed or replaced, and if the individual units are to be converted into smaller ones, major structural changes are required. The remodeler of apartment houses is more likely than the remodeler of single-family dwellings to rely heavily on the services of an architect or an experienced contractor.

The two immutable laws for profitable rehabilitation in the middle-income market are: never make a repair unless it adds value to the structure and never style the product above the normal consumption pattern of the prospective buyer or renter. The prestige rehabilitator, too, is usually careful not to make unessential repairs, but like the builder of new houses he can afford to lead his market with more imaginative design when the effective demand is high. But the investor who operates in the middle-income field must scale his product with infinite care. His customers are the average families for whom most advertisements, Sunday supplements, and television programs are produced. They are heavily in the market for new equipment, more clothing, and even a second automobile, but they are in the market for more housing only when it gives them a favorable balance between convenient location and adequate space, modern equipment and easy financing.

One of the most successful examples of rehabilitation of housing in the "gray" areas is in Boston, where since the mid-1920s a private entrepreneur has specialized in remodeling and selling houses for two- and three-family occupancy. Homes, Inc., operates on the belief that multi-family homeownership of this kind is the most sensible solution for lower-middle-income families, particularly in the age group between 26 years and 36 years. A two- or three-family house gives the owner his own dwelling and provides extra income to pay off the mortgage faster than would be the case with a single-family house.

Homes, Inc., sells its mortgages to Boston banks and savings and loan institutions, and gives the owner a low-interest second mortgage or a direct loan before letting him default on a single payment. Because the company redecorates only the owner's apartment, it makes a point of providing the services of one of its own staff to advise the buyer on finishing the job and sells him materials at cost or less. Moreover, the company sometimes provides the same service to adjoining homeowners in the belief that the more the neighborhood can be improved the higher will be the value of the remaining properties it holds in the area.

Unlike many rehabilitators, Homes, Inc., rarely expects to make more than about 3 per cent on its operation. This means that the volume of business must be large and the turnover rapid. Sometimes the company buys as many as seventy-five houses at a time. Like other successful rehabilitators, it keeps a full-time crew on the payroll, but subcontracts about half its work.

One of the company's typical projects is in the Dorchester section of Boston. Eight 3-family houses were bought for $75,000 from an estate and twelve adjacent houses from separate owners. The total purchase price was $201,000. Between $2,000 and $3,000 went into the repair of each of the twenty houses, which then were sold for less than $14,000.

Both contract remodelers and operative remodelers can make significant contributions to the improvement of middle-income housing. And, to the extent that their operations deter the loss of units from the market because of unchecked deterioration or obsolescence, they add to the supply of available housing. However, in declining areas their work must always be on a scale large enough to create an improved environment.

Low-Income Rehabilitation

Any kind of private rehabilitation requires new capital investment. Therefore, it almost invariably results in increases in the prices or rents of dwellings. Whether rehabilitation serves to increase the dollar price or the dollar rent or merely to prevent an otherwise unavoidable decrease in the price or rent of the dwelling is of little importance. In a profit economy, the investment presumably will not be made unless it increases the marginal return on the property and unless the return on the new investment is equal to that available from alternative investment opportunities.

Under these circumstances, private rehabilitation, even when it takes place under the spur of housing code enforcement, can serve only limited purposes in the housing market for low-income families. Its chief function is to improve the quality of low-rent dwellings which are already available to low-income families.

Almost all rehabilitation for low-income families is linked to official programs of housing code enforcement. Indeed, only the spur of court action and penalties induces many owners to make improvements. When the occupant is the owner, his only alternative to bringing the property up to legal standards is to let it be condemned and demolished or to sell it at a price low enough to compensate the new owner for the impending repair costs. When the owner is an individual investor or a company that deals in rental properties, additional choices are open. The structure may be remodeled for a higher-income market if one exists in the area or it may be held vacant until such a market develops or until the land can be shifted to a different use that will be more profitable.

Philadelphia provides a good example of what can happen in the private market when a housing code is widely enforced in a community. When values began to decline under the impact of enforcement, the small holders sold out to large investors. The new owners were not interested in remodeling the properties extensively because to do so would have required the use of equity money which could be more profitably invested elsewhere. But because they had bought at values deflated by code enforcement and had continued to draw rents at the higher original values, they were able to schedule enough improvements to comply with the requirements of the code. So long as the new owners improve their properties at a constant rate, the city allows them a generous period of time to do so. According to Nash, "Many dwelling units in downtown Philadelphia have received full facilities with complete redecoration at a reported cost of between $2,000 and $3,000 per unit. The rent increases have been limited by the market to about $10 per $1,000 added investment but the properties still yield a satisfactory though lessened return."

A different example of how the market responds to a code enforcement program is found in Charlotte, North Carolina, where between 1948 and 1956, 20 per cent of the city's housing supply was brought up to the standards of the housing code. The 11,000 units affected by the program were distinctly dilapidated wooden, single-family structures. Few of them had heating or plumbing facilities. All but a few of them were occupied by Negroes. Compared with the properties affected by Philadelphia's housing code, these dwellings would normally have been slated for demolition. A slum clearance program in Charlotte in 1948, however, would have created an impossible problem of relocation. The 1,661 units that were demolished posed problems enough. A balance had to be struck between the immediate alleviation of unsanitary conditions and future plans for clearance even if the code enforcement program might increase the eventual cost of redevelopment by its increase in property values.

Charlotte's code demands only minimum amenities and its administration provides a flexible time schedule for making improvements. So long as some improvements are made at a steady rate, owners are not brought into court. In the eight-year period between 1948 and 1956, only twelve owners forced the courts to act against them.

The first objective of Charlotte's code enforcement program was to get rid of outdoor privies. About $400 of the average improvement cost of $750 per dwelling unit went to the installation of an indoor toilet and running water. At this level of investment, rents increased about $6 a month. Some owners voluntarily made more extensive improvements: new kitchens, windows, doors, porches, and so on. In these cases, the cost of improvements ranged between $2,000 and $3,000 and the increase in rents was about $25 a month.

Before the program started rents in the area were only $2 to $5 per week, their prewar level, but the average weekly wage was between $60 and $75, almost double what it had been ten years before. It was clear that the occupants of the affected dwellings could pay higher rents without suffering economic hardship. In any city the enforcement of housing code provisions must bear some reasonable relationship to the consumer's ability to pay. Otherwise property owners probably will not undertake extensive repairs and, if they do, banks will be extremely reluctant to finance them, and public officials will face a major relocation problem when improvements finally take place and rent schedules go up. Charlotte avoided this situation by demanding only minimum improvements consistent with health and decency. Even if the real earning power of the tenants had not increased as markedly as it had, it is doubtful whether the $6 per month increase in rents would have been burdensome.

The important result of Charlotte's program, however, is not so much the elimination of 1,100 privies; it is the construction of new, reasonably priced rental and sales housing for Negroes both within the city and in the metropolitan area. As soon as it was evident that Negroes could and would pay a little more for improved housing in better neighborhoods, the private market responded quickly. Negro couples in the older age brackets did not want to leave accustomed neighborhoods and turned to new four-room units at weekly rents of $8.50 to $13.50 plus utilities. The young families bought new sales housing in areas outside the city.

St. Louis, another city with an active code enforcement program, has large residential areas that are not slums in the sense that Charlotte's were but which are seriously menaced by blighting conditions. Code enforcement officials decided, therefore, that they would require correction of only the most flagrant violations of decency and safety and concentrate on saving the somewhat better areas from further decline. Eventually clearance programs will eliminate the slums.

To test its theories, the city designated two pilot areas in 1955 for full-scale inspection and code enforcement. Both were lower-middle-income neighborhoods not unlike ones in Boston, Cleveland, Columbus, Chicago, and some other cities where operative remodelers were working without the spur of official improvement programs. No commercial rehabilitators had shown particular interest in the St. Louis test areas, however, and the question the code enforcement officers asked themselves was whether the residents could be induced to invest in the improvement of their own properties with only a minimum of legal pressure. According to Nash,

Inspections were the backbone of the program. St. Louis had consolidated its inspection so only one housing inspector looked for all code violations. However, if deficiencies were suspected in the electrical and plumbing systems, a special inspector was asked for his expert opinion before a violation notice was sent. The violation notice listed all violations regardless of which code had been broken. In addition, the notices carried a series of "recommendations" for improving the general appearance of the house which are not required by any code and are not legally enforceable.

The results were impressive. In the Cherokee area, for example, 6,791 of the 7,820 violations noted in 3,729 dwellings were corrected within three years. Moreover, 919 of the 1,301 recommendations for improvements over and above the legal requirements were voluntarily carried out by homeowners. The total private investment in improvements came to $800,000, apparently with little or no hardship to owner-occupants or renters, whose average annual income was about $3,600. A large part of the success of the program is due to the fact that the city spent about $200,000 to improve existing community facilities and to raise the level of its housekeeping services in the neighborhood.

Lessons for the Investor

Rehabilitation is economically feasible only when the investor believes that the returns from rehabilitated property are likely to exceed the returns from the property without rehabilitation, and if the cost of the repairs does not exceed the capitalized difference between the existing and potential rents or sales prices. Systematic programs to improve the setting for rehabilitation by providing more or better community facilities and by creating a stronger interest on the part of the consumer in maintenance and remodeling increase the opportunity for profitable rehabilitation and extend the useful life of the rehabilitated part of the housing supply. But outside the prestige field little new investor money is attracted to rehabilitation.

Common complaints of investors include difficulties in obtaining financing, and lack of cooperation from, or confusion of policy among, the governmental agencies with whom rehabilitators must deal. Many investors regard rehabilitation as an operation leading to doubtful returns. Lenders reinforce this attitude by taking it for granted that the remaining economic life of a rehabilitated dwelling is much shorter than that of a new dwelling. The FHA itself authorizes mortgages on rehabilitated dwellings for no more than three-quarters of their estimated remaining economic life. Since the period of amortization is shorter than that for new housing, the annual debt service charges are higher per dollar of debt. If the rehabilitated dwellings are rented ones, the rents have to carry the higher debt service charges. The liberal mortgage terms of Section 220, which Congress authorized in 1954, for financing rehabilitation in urban renewal areas have lured relatively few investors and lenders. The properties have to be brought up to FHA's minimum property requirements for rehabilitated dwellings which, though substantially less stringent than those for new construction, nevertheless are high.

Nor has FHA's other aid to rehabilitation—Section 221, which provides mortgage financing to persons displaced by public works and other government construction—attracted many potential investors despite its long terms and low interest rates. As with any mortgage financing it requires careful cost estimates for the job, title searches, and loans from a bank, savings and loan association, or other lender. By the end of 1959 only one-seventh of all applications for Section 221 mortgage assistance were to finance the purchase or rehabilitation of existing housing. Few owner-occupants even know about Section 221. But they do know about home improvement loans provided at high interest rates through finance companies and often by contractors. Much of the rehabilitation for homeowners is done with very high rate loans at often unnecessarily high costs to the customers.

The cost of rehabilitation financing and the difficulty in obtaining funds may be eased in the near future both because government is becoming more interested in encouraging rehabilitation and the building industry is becoming more interested in rehabilitation as a business. For example, the FHA's announced intention in 1961 is to devise easier and cheaper ways to finance home modernization. And many builders have discovered that in times when new construction slackens, such as the beginning of 1961, home modernization can keep their workers employed and their profits intact. Furthermore, the first national home modernization franchiser, with a training school and a variety of management services, began operations late in 1960. If rehabilitation is to succeed as a nationally organized business activity, consumers must have access to suitable loan sources.

If banks, savings and loan associations, and other financial institutions cannot be bolder in their approach to rehabilitation, they could at least be more imaginative. An unusual example of recognition of opportunity and community need is the decision of savings and loan associations in the District of Columbia to create a joint pool of funds from which loans can be made to owners who are required to bring their properties up to the standard of the District's housing code. This idea was pioneered in Baltimore in 1951 when bankers and real estate men provided the capital for the Fight Blight Fund in that city.

But favorable mortgage terms and low-cost money for rehabilitation are only part of the climate required to make rehabilitation work. The business of rehabilitation needs better and more sustained cooperation from local government and from the consumers themselves. Rehabilitation must have a neighborhood environment in which it is possible to function.

The individual homeowner often repairs and improves his house through special loans, such as FHA's Title I home repair program which costs borrowers 9.7 per cent interest and has a top limit of $3,500. Since he looks upon his house only partly as an investment, he may make these improvements without regard to the neighborhood and without regard to whether the cost of the improvements will result in an equivalent increase in sales price of the property. But even he is much more apt to rehabilitate when the neighborhood is improving.

The investor, however, *has* to emphasize in his calculations the impact of the neighborhood and the community. His possibilities for a good return depend on the proportion of dwellings in a neighborhood, which he (or he and other rehabilitators) can improve, on the elimination of the occasional slum structure, on new investment in schools, parks, and other public facilities, and on a high level of police protection and other municipal services.

Chapter 12

THE POTENTIAL CONTRIBUTION OF RENTAL HOUSING

Since the end of the apartment house boom of the mid-1920s the volume of rental housing construction has dropped tremendously and has been lower than the rental preferences of the market would suggest as desirable. As a consequence, most of the present supply of rental housing is more obsolete than sales housing and suffers by comparison with it. Among the causes of the decline in rental construction are low yields to investors, war and postwar rent controls, extraordinary tax and credit benefits for homeowners, and long capital return periods for investors. However, a modest revival of luxury apartment construction appeared in some areas in the late 1950s, and in 1960, 23 per cent of nonfarm housing unit starts were designed for rent.

A further strengthening of rental construction during the 1960s and 1970s may be anticipated as a result of the rapid growth of the number of younger married couples and of aged persons. The steady increase in managerial and white-collar occupations, and in the employment of women may support the rental market. The scarcity and increased cost of suburban land, and the extension of work journeys resulting from metropolitan growth may also favor a shift to rental types and locations.

These forces in the rental housing market must be supplemented with financial incentives if the potential is to be realized. More certain returns to equity capital must be achieved. Various tax discriminations might be eliminated by partnership treatment of rental housing corporations, accelerated depreciation for rehabilitation investments, and the equalization of income tax handling of renter- and owner-occupied housing expenses. Local discriminations in the assessment of rental properties for real property tax purposes should be removed. Finally, urban renewal programs may provide new opportunities for rental property investments.

The construction of new rental housing underwent a secular decline between 1930 and the late 1950s. In 1956 only 113,000 new units, 8 per cent of all new permanent nonfarm dwelling units that started that year, were in multi-family structures. By comparison, 44 per cent of the dwelling units built in 1927 were in multi-family structures. Going back further in time, more rental units were built in 1905 than in 1956 although the urban population of the country had tripled between those two dates. Since 1956, however, there has been a steady growth in the construction of rental housing. By 1960, as noted in the summary above, 23 per cent of housing starts, or 292,000 units, were slated as rental quarters.

Much of this decline in rental housing construction is doubtless attributable to a growing consumer preference for single-family owned homes. In turn, this preference may be partly attributable to the poor quality of a large part of the rental housing stock; much of it is made up of formerly owned homes, converted dwellings or apartments more than a quarter of a century old. A substantial proportion of rental housing is substandard in construction, lacks plumbing or heating and open space. Under these circumstances it is not surprising that rented dwellings are often in ill repute among those who have a choice, and that many think of owned homes as "better housing." But a study by the Federal Reserve Board in 1955 showed that although homeowners were generally more satisfied with their accommodations than renters were with theirs, a fifth of the owners would have preferred to rent if suitable quarters had been available. Millions of families thus appear to have been forced to buy houses, particularly in the early 1950s, because of deficiencies in the rental housing supply.

Why did investment capital shun the rental housing market for so long a period after the 1920s? Apparently because investors, after a generation of poor investment experience, were reluctant to enter a field where, traditionally, the risks are high and the yields low.

Investor Experience

The guiding principle of all investment is that prospective returns must be commensurate with risks. The developer of a new apartment house, particularly in an untried location, is aware of how vulnerable his investment is to the special risks of rental housing. The longest lease he can get from his tenants usually is for three years. Furthermore, current construction and operating costs for apartments require a higher monthly rental from the consumer than the equivalent for a single-family house.

Since his property has a presumed economic life of fifty or more years, the investor is faced with the possibility of major shifts in neighborhood characteristics. He has seen such shifts seriously depreciate the investment in rental housing of many of his predecessors. The Depression was disastrous for rental housing. High vacancy ratios and a decline in operating income forced many investors to default on debt service, particularly when they were heavily mortgaged. In addition, real property taxes stayed constant even though apartment vacancies went up and income went down. Most taxes of a manufacturing firm, on the other hand, usually decreased commensurately with declines in sales and profits.

In his study of elevator apartments in New York City (*Experience in Urban Real Estate Investment*), Leo Grebler, in 1955, showed that the free and clear return (net income before depreciation or debt service) on the original cost of properties acquired before the Depression was only 2.8 per cent in 1935 to 1939 and 2.2 per cent in 1940 to 1944. Of course, many of these properties were refinanced and the then current owners were receiving returns of 8 per cent or more. But those higher yields were possible only because of the great capital losses sustained by the previous investors. A sample of Chicago apartments, analyzed for this series of books, shows somewhat better experiences during the Depression. But even in Chicago, the free and clear return on original cost was only 3.5 per cent in 1936. The investor in rental housing has good reason, therefore, to fear a depression. But he also has reason to fear periods of prosperity: In such periods, the consumer turns to homeownership more readily than at any other time.

Another adverse situation for investors in rental housing is an emergency, such as a war, when they face rent control. Investors in other physical assets benefit from upward revaluations of their investment but the returns from rental housing are frozen. Rent control also widens the expected gap between the rents of old quarters and the rents of new units. As a result, consumers under rent control do not have the incentive to upgrade housing expenditures as their incomes rise. After World War II, consumers were horrified at what investors regarded as normal rents for new apartments. Their reluctance to accept higher rent-income ratios substantially reduced the market for new rental housing. A low-rent consumer psychology is bound to inhibit investment in rental housing. Inflation, and particularly the rise in costs of land and construction, makes it impossible for investors to build new apartments which can compete with existing apartments under rent control.

Poor earnings over the long run help explain the virtual disappearance of life insurance companies from the rental construction field. A major source of equity capital, in fact the only important source of 100 per cent private equity financing, became available when these giants embarked on apartment projects in the 1940s. By 1952 their investment reached $500 million. But, except for brief spurts, the rate of return was disappointingly low. By 1952 the net yield on book value of all rental projects of life insurance companies, after amortization, was below 2 per cent. Few projects were earning as much as 5 per cent on original investment. Since then a number of companies have sold their developments. If the incentives were there, however, life insurance companies could invest over $5 billion in rental housing under present laws. Their actual investment is less than 10 per cent of this legal limit and shows little sign of significant revival.

As a result of these experiences, investors rated rental housing very poorly until the last few years. In addition to the economic handicaps, they also had to reckon with social handicaps, like the traditional distaste of the tenant for the landlord. The longer these hesitancies persisted, the fewer became the number of investors who had had experience with rental housing.

Faced with what they regarded as excessive risks, investors responded to this situation just after World War II by demanding a higher return on their equity capital or by seeking some form of no-equity, no-risk government insurance. The largest volume of rental housing built just after the war was achieved under Section 608 of the National Housing Act. Frankly a device to stimulate rental housing in the tight postwar market, Section 608 cut risk and equity to nothing. "Windfall" profits resulted in a number of instances and the program was discredited to the point where it was canceled; but the fact remains that it served the purpose and, generally, the intent of the law. Experience under Section 608 indicates that builders can be induced to build rental housing when they are guaranteed the opportunity for a fast, high, speculative profit. Apart from "608" financing, investors in rental housing during the postwar years have required a prospective return of up to 20 per cent before they would proceed. They have been able to obtain such a high direct return as a rule only in choice market areas.

While the vacancy rate in rental units was only 2.6 per cent in 1950, from 1955 on it has not fallen below 5.3 per cent, and it reached a high of 7.6 per cent the last quarter of 1960. In 1960, however, 29 per cent of the vacancies lacked plumbing facilities, and almost 50 per cent rented for less than $50 rent per month. This suggests that a considerable proportion of the vacant rental units were undesirable to tenants, and not that the rental market had been satisfied. There were noticeable regional differences in vacancies, with a 10.2 per cent rate in the West, for example, and 4.6 per cent in the Northeast, in the third quarter of 1960. These vacancies do not appear to have deferred rental housing starts, which in the second quarter of 1961 promised a building rate unmatched since the 1920s.

FHA and Rental Housing

FHA's role in residential building probably has been more harmful than helpful to rental housing. The congressional act creating the FHA authorized a system of mortgage credit designed to encourage both rental and sales housing, but during most of its history the FHA has been administered to favor homeownership and especially homeownership in new suburban areas. By helping to make homeownership less costly than renting equivalent quarters, the FHA has undercut the rental housing market sharply. But, more serious, it has failed in the main to compensate for its support of sales housing with rental housing programs for the vestigial market for new rental quarters.

The FHA rental program has been the target of sharp criticism. But it must be recognized that there are inherent differences between the sales and rental markets which inevitably color FHA's administrative practices. The market for private houses has always been the larger and traditionally the recipient of more governmental aid, whereas the rental market has always been the smaller and the riskier. Aid to the renter is indirect and must be channeled through the investors. This means, as Louis Winnick points out in *Rental Housing*, that:

> Constant vigilance and strict regulation are required to insure that benefits will not be absorbed before they reach the intended beneficiary . . . when the FHA grants a long-term, low interest mortgage for rental housing, or when it reduces equity requirements to the vanishing point, some form of supervision is needed to make sure that the consumer benefits through lower rents or through more or better housing, and that government aid is not converted into excessive profits for sponsors or landlords.

By its very nature, an effective rental program must be risky and if the government wishes to stimulate rental housing it must bear the greatest risk. Stagnation in construction of rental housing, after the congressional investigation of the "608" program led to the termination of the program, showed that commitment terms and regulations had to be liberalized some way. The Housing Act of 1954 provided terms for urban renewal housing, under Section 220, that are almost as favorable as the "608" terms, although cost certification and other requirements make "220" less attractive to investors than "608" was.

The advantage FHA provides for the investor is mainly the opportunity of raising funds under terms that are more favorable than those of conventional mortgage loans. Aside from builders' profits, FHA mortgages enable private investors to speculate with small cash commitments on high-value real estate assets. A small rise in the price of the asset may lead to sizeable increases in the value of the equity. In addition, it is possible to get good operating returns on the small investment while the property is held in the hope of a capital gain. If the whole venture should be unsuccessful, the loss is relatively small.

When cash equity requirements and risks are effectively removed, as was the case under Section 608, and an attractive project can be developed from mortgage proceeds alone, the investor has little real concern with the marketability of the product. With a high enough mortgage, it becomes profitable to build rental housing anywhere. It can always be disposed of to the FHA. During the decade ending in 1955, probably more than half of all new rental units were built with FHA mortgages. By the end of 1960, FHA had insured almost 900,000 dwellings in multifamily developments.

Sources of Conflict between Investors and the FHA

On the whole, the FHA rental program has been characterized by improvisation; the trial and error nature of the program has undoubtedly had some adverse effect on the volume of production for the rental market. It has moved back and forth from very liberal provisions to excessively cautious ones. In return for the opportunity to make a profit and shift his risk, the investor must submit to a whole series of regulations, many of which he believes are unduly restrictive. Winnick has remarked that the FHA is not a partner in rental housing but actually acts more as a public service commission, regulating all the important management decisions of the projects it insures. "The turbulent history of FHA's relations with private investors and the successes and failures of its rental-housing programs illustrate," he says, "the problems arising from mixed or controlled capitalism where the government attempts to influence, by a system of carrots and sticks, the production and operation of property it neither owns nor manages. Delays and added costs do result, but they are part of a price paid by a free economy that willingly forgoes the possibly higher efficiency of social ownership in favor of social controls. Housing—especially rental housing—has been increasingly treated as a public utility but without full awareness of all the consequences, and—more important—without full development of the administrative apparatus and judicial processes that have evolved in transportation, communication, fuel, power, and other regulated industries."

A clash of objectives thus becomes practically unavoidable. The typical investor wants to put in as little cash as possible and maximize his earnings quickly and with a minimum tax liability. The FHA, on the other hand, seeks to limit the government's risk by obtaining as much initial equity as possible and insisting on high standards of construction and maintenance. In addition, it presumably has uppermost in its purpose the social goal of providing rental housing at rents lower than would obtain without government aid. Inevitably, the private and public goals are in conflict.

The fact that the program relies more on administrative discretion than on statutory provisions widens the area of disagreement. FHA's administrative regulations cover detailed supervision of site selection, site development costs, architectural design, accounting procedures, replacement reserves, and working capital requirements. After completion of the project FHA controls rent schedules, distribution of earnings, and changes in rents resulting from changing operating costs.

Rent schedules are a particular source of friction. The precise formula varies, but in general rents are set to provide a yield of 11 to 12 per cent on book equity, after operating and other costs have been paid. The formula provides a 7 per cent vacancy loss; if units are fully occupied the return on equity can rise to nearly 20 per cent. Rent increases for reasons other than increased operating costs or additional services are not permitted; and capital gains deriving from a superior location or a general rise in real estate values are not possible unless the investor refinances with a conventional mortgage.

FHA supervision over the distribution of cash in a completed project is another source of disagreement. FHA regulations require that 30 per cent of total book equity investment must be held as a permanent reserve. This regulation is intended to protect the investment and require more responsible operation. The typical investor, on the other hand, wants to withdraw his initial investment as fast as possible and at the least possible tax cost.

But for all the complaints of investors, the FHA has fashioned such liberal mortgage credit terms for rental housing that a small amount of equity capital can be multiplied into a tremendous investment. Also, with FHA assuming most of the investment risk, investors can try out market situations which might otherwise be financially hazardous. The fortune of the investor in rental housing is very much a function of FHA policies and administrative regulations.

The financial experience of the operators of two hundred FHA projects in the New York, Chicago, Washington, and Los Angeles areas has been studied by Louis Winnick for the period 1951–1956. His main findings were:

1. Earnings tended to go down through most of the period. The principal reason for the decline was an increase in costs and taxes that was insufficiently compensated for by rental income.

2. There was considerable variation in returns among the different areas. Chicago had the most favorable rate of return, New York the poorest.

3. High-quality efficiency and one-bedroom apartments did much better than walk-ups or elevator developments with family-sized units. In other words, those developments which competed most with homeownership did most poorly.

4. Real estate taxes were more burdensome in some areas than in others. In 1955 they accounted for 21 per cent of the rent dollar in the New York metropolitan area but only 10 per cent in the Washington, D.C., area.

5. The size of an FHA rental project does not seem to bear a consistent relation to the rate of return. In some areas the larger

projects have the highest return; in others, the smaller projects.

If the FHA rental housing program and investment psychology shift from quick windfalls to long-term operating returns, the value of such financial analysis as this will be particularly pertinent, for, as the next section indicates, new opportunities are developing which promise to alter investment climate for rental housing even more significantly.

The Future

Rental housing's future will be brighter than its past, and very likely brighter than its present. That part of the market which is most attracted to rental housing—single persons, newly married and childless couples, and older couples whose children have left home—will increase in the years ahead. In 1950 there were nearly 20 million potential household heads who did not own their own homes or apartments. Most of them were single persons—widowed, divorced, or separated. The Bureau of the Census estimates that by 1975 there will probably be 9 million primary individuals (i.e., single heads of households), or 55 per cent more than in 1955. That estimate compares with an expected increase of only 28 per cent in the number of primary families.

The gain in primary individuals will come mostly from older people, particularly widows and widowers. But young, unmarried persons, and divorced and separated ones, will also enter the housing market in greater numbers, especially if their incomes rise and they feel they can afford their own dwellings. In terms of age distribution, the 20-to-29-year age group—a principal group of renters—is expected to increase by 14.2 millions (from 22.5 to 36.7 millions). By contrast, because of the deficit in the birth rate brought on by the Depression, the 30-to-49-year age group has an expected net growth of only 2 million. But that is the group in the child-rearing, home-buying period.

These figures suggest a larger potential increase in demand for rental housing than for sales housing up to 1975. After 1975, the 20-to-29-year age group will move into the sales market of those 30 years old and over, and will eventually be replaced by the 38 million children who will still be between 10 and 19 years old in

1975. In fact, the number of persons between 20 and 29 will be even larger in 1985 than in 1975.

Persons over fifty years of age will increase by an expected 15 million in the next twenty years or so. A sizable part of this increase can be assumed to be potential renters. But if this assumption is correct, will these persons want small, rented single-family houses in the suburbs, apartments in the suburbs, or rented houses or apartments in the center of the city? The answer will depend in large part on the comparative advantages cities and suburbs offer as they change over time, and on the comparative costs—including tax costs—of living in one place or another.

Another trend that favors the rental market is the increase in the proportion of wives who work. Not only does prosperity provide more jobs for women but it stimulates their desire to help attain a still higher standard of living for the family. Many married women who work prefer not to have the responsibilities that go with ownership.

Still another trend favorable to the rental market is the shift to managerial and white-collar employment. Compared with an over-all expected increase in the labor force of 36 per cent in all jobs by 1975, professional jobs are expected to increase by 63 per cent, amusement and recreation jobs by 50 per cent, and business services by 49 per cent. Although these groups of workers show a high rate of homeownership, they also form an important sector of the market for apartments. Finally, continued migration to cities during the next decade will augment the market for rental housing.

But these anticipated changes in demographic and labor force characteristics do not ensure a greater demand for housing; nor do they mean that there will be a significant return to the city from the suburbs. They will be important to the rental market only if some of the current impediments to a more successful functioning of that market, particularly in connection with the renewal of our urban centers, can be overcome.

Possibilities for Overcoming Obstacles

For the reasons mentioned above, the rental market undoubtedly will show more improvement in the years ahead. But a much larger future market is both possible and desirable. The principal obstacle to it will still be uncertainty in the amount and cost of risk capital. If this deterrent is to be overcome, there will undoubtedly have to be a number of changes in FHA equity requirements and other regulations, and more effective methods than at present to widen the capital market and make investment more attractive to existing and potential sources of funds.

INTERESTING OF NEW INVESTORS

Equity capital is scarce and expensive in many parts of the country partly because of the poor organization of the real estate capital market. If the investment process were less cumbersome and if reliable facts were more readily available, a larger volume of investment funds might be forthcoming from the general public, who would probably be satisfied with lower returns than the professional investors demand. (The suggestions in Chapter 10 for facilitating mortgage securities are also applicable to equity capital.) Local and possibly national organizations are needed to serve as a source of "seed" capital and as a clearinghouse for investment facts. The Cleveland Development Foundation, sponsored by business and community leaders, has, with an investment up to January 1, 1959, of only $2,143,003, induced the public investment of $31,635,000 and the private investment of $100,922,000 in that city. Such a group can either float capital issues in its own name or lend backing to approved ventures.

IMPROVEMENT IN FLOW OF MORTGAGE CAPITAL

Periods of severe stringency in the capital market during part of the 1950s created problems for all sectors of the housing industry. While the supply of mortgage funds is responsive to higher interest rates, builders of medium-rent units are restricted by FHA's ceiling on interest rates as well as by tenant resistance to higher rents. One of the proposals which has been made to increase the supply of mortgage funds is to provide a rental-housing debenture carrying FHA insurance and a Treasury guarantee, thus making it equivalent to a Federal bond. Pension and trust funds and other potential investors might be attracted into the mortgage market if some such secure and easily obtainable instrument were available.

MORE FLEXIBLE FHA EQUITY REQUIREMENTS

FHA-insured financing will probably continue to account for the biggest part of the new middle-income rental units which are needed to meet consumer requirements and urban renewal programs. The terms under which such construction proceeds are therefore vital to future investment. Some conflict between FHA and investors over equity requirements and other regulations seems unavoidable. Experience has shown that some investor equity and risk is indispensable.

Under present legislation the amount of equity required for each project is determined by various appraisal standards, such as replacement costs and estimated value. The effective result of multiple appraisal standards is to permit FHA to vary requirements as a matter of policy. But these variations are not necessarily related to marketability. The alternative proposal is to adopt a uniform appraisal standard for all new apartment buildings which would establish the investment base, and then decide on the amount of cash equity by a scoring system which would take into account such market and risk factors as the quality of the community, the adequacy of the site and building design, and the reputation and past experience of the builder.

INCENTIVES AND REWARDS TO INVESTORS

Under present regulations, both builders and owners are faced with an array of restrictive regulations involving much red tape and delay. Some legislative and administrative controls are obviously necessary; others may be avoidable but are nuisances rather than positive obstacles to investment. A few present regulations seem unnecessarily restrictive and actually result in barriers to increased investment. The industry complains in particular about inflexible formulas which prevent rapid recovery of investment, rule out any chance of capital gains, and delay reasonable rent adjustments.

Greater flexibility, with some method for encouraging and rewarding successful projects, could certainly make apartment house construction more attractive to many investors without an undue increase in risks.

There are without doubt many persons who should rent, or prefer to rent, but become home-owners because the relative cost of owning as against renting appears highly favorable. Public tax policies which tend to favor ownership should be reconsidered; for example, the inequity of the Federal personal income tax law which permits homeowners (including holders of cooperative units) to deduct property taxes and interest on mortgage debt. Especially in the higher-income tax brackets, the savings may be large enough to affect choice of tenure. One possible solution would be to eliminate owners' deductions or to permit renters to deduct a given percentage of annual contract rent. Because ownership is so well entrenched, deductions for renters are the only really feasible means to employ in this situation.

Unequal property tax treatment for renter- and owner-occupied real estate is another important issue. Complete or partial tax exemption has been used in several states to lower rents appreciably. In effect, such exemptions are subsidies, to which there are numerous objections. If tax concessions are granted, they should be related to community goals, such as slum clearance and tenant relocation. An alternative is to remove some of the present discriminations in local tax assessments that favor ownership housing. In most municipalities rental housing is assessed higher than owned housing.

LOWERING OF FINANCING COSTS

The biggest problem in the rental market is how to provide enough new housing for middle- and low-income families. Efforts to encourage investment or to improve the quality of housing for this the largest sector of the rental market, are self-defeating if they result in higher costs and higher rents. Reductions in the present high cost of equity and mortgage capital will help to reduce rents. A reduction in interest costs would require direct public loans or a more favorable mortgage instrument. When the saving is achieved through the exemption of local bonds from

Federal taxation, the Federal tax loss is greater than the local savings.

Easier FHA repayment terms would be a more direct and less controversial method for reducing monthly rents. Shifting to a level-payment mortgage plan, such as is now used for Section 213 cooperatives, would mean lower rents on newly completed projects. Extending the repayment period would reduce rents even more. Under a sixty-year-level payment plan, annual debt service on each $10,000 is nearly $14 a month less than initial payments under the present forty-year increasing amortization mortgage. However, total costs over the full life of the development are much higher under a lengthened repayment period.

COMMUNITY NON-PROFIT HOUSING CORPORATIONS

If Congress is prepared, as it has been for ten of the postwar years, to approve FHA insurance on mortgages amounting almost to the full cost of rental housing projects, communities might establish nonprofit or limited-dividend corporations staffed with skilled businessmen to sponsor, build, and operate rental developments where needed. This would be a relatively small extension of the activity of present development foundations, referred to above, and might encourage the participation of philanthropic institutions. Minor changes in the chartering and supervisory regulations might permit lending institutions, like savings banks and savings and loan institutions, to serve as sponsors and owners or to participate in the equity. They would bring to such a function skills, a permanence of interest, and a reputation and stake in the community which the speculator often lacks.

EQUITY SHARES

An adaptation of the British builders' pool might prove useful in unlocking private investment for rental housing. Under the British plan, the builder leaves his profit in the properties to reduce the amount of the down payment required by the home purchaser. Adapted for American rental housing purposes, the same plan would enable the builder to obtain a mortgage on all out-of-pocket costs on rental housing construction, excluding profit which would take the form of equity shares. These shares would not be taxable to the builder as income, but after a period of years would be convertible to a long-term capital gain if the project proved to be economically sound and worth more than the amortized mortgage amount. This is a realistic economic approach since the equity on a project covered by a mortgage of approximately 100 per cent is in any real sense zero at the beginning of the project. The development of an equity would depend to a considerable degree upon the soundness of the location and design of the project. If judgments about them were valid, the equity which would develop should properly be taxable as a capital gain rather than a profit on construction.

COOPERATIVE HOUSING

Cooperative apartment developments are both a substitute for some sectors of the rental market and a means of providing a sector of the owner market with housing normally available only to renters. Regardless of whether such projects are built by nonprofit organizations or by speculators, it is the individual consumer who eventually holds the equity. The cooperative device has been used in some European countries as an important means to the ownership and management of housing. In some major metropolitan areas, particularly New York, the cooperative has long been used as a means for the ownership of central-city apartments. In recent years, however, many apartment buildings have been made cooperatives by a decision of the investor rather than by the desire of the occupants. In a tight housing market this has meant that tenants, who would have preferred to rent, have been forced to assume the risks and obligations of ownership. The cooperative had little momentum until the postwar period, when it began to be used in many parts of the country as a means of providing housing for upper and middle-income families.

The cooperative takes several forms. A cooperative corporation may be used to build new housing developments or it may be used as a device for perpetual ownership. The so-called development cooperative is a means whereby a group of people can get together in the joint development of a housing project in order to take advantage of the economies in land acquisition, design, and building which may be gained by group action. When the development phase of the project is completed, the cooperative is dissolved and the resulting units are sold to the individual members of the development cooperative.

The development cooperative may produce some cost savings to the participants since they assume the risk ordinarily assumed by the speculative developer. The members of the cooperative may avoid the builder's speculative profit although they will ordinarily pay the contractor a profit on the actual construction of the development. Under many circumstances, the contractor's profit will be substantially less than that of a speculator although few cooperative developments to date have been of sufficiently large scale to produce the economies in construction and the capable management obtained by the larger speculative builders. An advantage of a different, but none the less important, kind is the opportunity which cooperatives may provide for satisfaction of a distinctive architectural taste or locational preference.

In recent years the so-called builder-sponsored cooperative has been encouraged by the FHA with special mortgage insurance terms to builders who promote the development of cooperative housing projects before the ultimate owners have agreed to buy. The economic differences between this form of cooperative and the usual speculative development are slight. In November, 1959, the Commissioner of the FHA reported that over 55,000 families were living in cooperative housing financed with FHA's Section 213 mortgages for cooperatives.

An ownership cooperative is quite different, however, in that when the development is completed, the individual units are usually jointly owned by the cooperative corporation. Sometimes the cooperative retains full title to the property and the owners have a lifetime or indefinite tenure. Or, ownership may be on an individual basis with the property maintained jointly by the cooperative corporation. In either case, there are economies to be obtained in financing (usually one-fourth to one-half per cent on the mortgage interest rate), construction costs, and maintenance and operation charges. Under existing Federal income tax laws, the cooperative form of ownership has substantial advantages over renting because payments for local taxes and for interest on the mortgage may be deducted from the members' taxable incomes. This incentive alone should insure a growing future for the cooperative device and help expand the market for new housing for middle-income families.

The most successful cooperatives in the United States and other countries are those organized and supervised by a strong sponsoring agency—producer cooperatives, trade unions, religious or educational groups. Often they initiate a project with only a nucleus of the eventual ownership group. The famous Scandinavian cooperative housing developments are of this character. They are built by the central office of the cooperative movement which, although owned by consumers, operates like any large private corporation. In this country sponsors of cooperatives have the advantage of special provisions in national housing legislation which provide favorable mortgage insurance terms.

The nonprofit United Housing Foundation, established in New York in 1951, is a good example of current cooperative activity. It not only builds cooperative projects itself but through a subsidiary group—Community Services, Inc.—it provides contract services to other cooperative sponsors, such as negotiating loans, obtaining tax abatements, marketing of units, and so on. So far, however, it has not been able to extend its program beyond the New York City area.

As the population diversifies, it is quite possible that cooperatives like the United Housing Foundation will serve a variety of special markets in both the central cities and the suburban areas, particularly if they can offer community facilities such as swimming pools, tennis courts, and the like. Their great advantage is the opportunity they provide to build multiple housing in desired locations and to reach out to families who prefer ownership under any circumstances, but come into the market for the type of housing normally provided only in rental units.

URBAN RENEWAL

As in the past, a large part of the rental housing of the future will probably consist of single-family houses, the owner-oc-cupants of which have moved to other homes, renting their old ones rather than selling them. However, in the future not many two- and three-family rental units are likely to be built. Once they were a favorite investment of middle-income families and immigrants, and provided a significant portion of the rental-hous-ing supply. Nor is it likely that more than a relatively few rental housing units will be provided by converting large apartments and dwellings into smaller units. Few very large houses and flats are being built today.

The building of walk-up apartments and even of elevator apartments on outlying, vacant sites will undoubtedly continue. But a main opportunity for sites for rental housing will be the existing deteriorated areas in the middle of our central cities and older suburbs. It is these areas which provide most of the advantages of access to work, play, and shopping sought by the largest proportion of potential renters. Developers are beginning to take advantage of these locations and to provide in both town houses and apartments open space, play areas, and other features which many potential residents regard as crucial requirements in their decision to rent or own.

Blighted areas do not ordinarily become available as building sites through the normal processes of the market, but public urban renewal agencies can clear sites and make them available for private development at appropriate land prices. Recognizing that to the consumer dwellings are inseparable from neighbor-hood amenities and services, urban renewal officials are attempt-ing to revitalize whole residential areas with improved transpor-tation, schools, parks, and other facilities usually desired by the consumer and hence by the investor.

Urban renewal agencies and the business and civic leaders who serve as their commissioners should face the issue of just how im-portant rental housing is to the plans for the development of their communities. If it appears to be an essential component of the local housing supply, they must make decisions now about a number of critical problems. For example, should sites be cleared before there are developers to build on them? Which services and facilities will support the market for rental housing most effectively? Can rental and ownership housing be intermingled in the same area and reinforce each other economically? Which sites, if made available first, would best satisfy both the needs of the investor and the goals of the municipal government?

The upturn in rental housing construction apparently under way by 1960 suggests that public officials and investors will more and more consider specifically the ways whereby urban renewal and rental housing can reinforce each other.

THE FEDERAL GOVERNMENT

Chapter 13

FEDERAL CREDIT

Federal housing programs had their origin in the banking crisis and unemployment of the Depression of the 1930s. They have since been modified or expanded with subsequent national emergencies of war, reconversion, and recession. Providing shelter has often been secondary to stimulating or curbing the national economy. Federal aid has mainly taken the form of insuring deposits in savings institutions or insuring or guaranteeing mortgages. Chartering and supervisory activities of the Home Loan Bank System, direct lending under emergency programs or under the guise of the secondary market operations of FNMA have made important contributions. As a result, 35 to 50 per cent of postwar residential construction has been directly aided by FHA or VA, and a large proportion of the remainder has been indirectly aided by Federal deposit insurance.

These aids have broadly strengthened the position of private lenders and builders. In addition, subsidized public housing programs have provided a limited amount of housing for low-income families. In the 1930s, these programs demonstrated the feasibility of slum clearance and led to programs to foster urban redevelopment and renewal in the 1950s, with Federal and local subsidies.

While Federal aids have benefited the housing market, they reveal duplication of effort and lack of coordination. The use of housing policy as a countercyclical device for stabilizing the general economy has been at the cost of considerable instability within the building industry. And the effects of these swings in housing policy upon urban growth have largely gone unexamined.

A clear definition of national housing goals and policies and of means for achieving them is lacking. A wise government would develop and pretest new kinds of housing programs, appropriate to new problems rather than to the depression years in which existing programs had their origin.

In American politics, disagreements over the appropriate role of government in the economy are relative: how much action is needed; what is a proper level of taxes or public debt; which field of endeavor is more important than another; how shall aids be distributed and to whom. The evolution of Federal aids to housing illustrates all of these problems. It reveals a hit-or-miss search to delimit the areas where public action can best aid the economy, to balance such needs against their costs, and to define the general or public interest.

Precursors: 1900 to 1930

Although present Federal housing programs are of comparatively recent origin, the Federal interest in housing stems back to the latter part of the nineteenth century. In response to local interest in tenement and slum problems during the 1890s, congressional hearings were conducted on problems of slums and blighted areas in the major cities of the country. These hearings reflected a dawning national concern but they did not lead to any governmental program. It was not until World War I that the Federal government took direct action in housing and then it was for reasons of expediency. The Emergency Fleet Corporation was authorized to build housing for war workers near major shipyards. Later the United States Housing Corporation was chartered by the Department of Labor to build additional homes for munitions workers. The two programs produced a total of some 15,000 dwellings and 14,000 dormitory units, most of them completed after the end of the war. These units were later sold, thus ending the first Federal experiment in housing.

The acute shortage of housing after that war produced a flurry of congressional bills, none of them enacted, to provide a system of home loan banks and to make loans to veterans. At the state level, New York, Massachusetts, and a few other states authorized local tax exemption for veterans' housing. Then, during the 1920s, the Department of Labor continued earlier studies of the problems of housing for workers and the Department of Commerce established a Division of Building and Housing which conducted studies of home building and homeownership. The U.S. Bureau of Standards developed and promulgated uniform building codes, model zoning ordinances, and model state-enabling acts. These were so widely adopted by states and local governments during the late 1920s and the 1930s that they stand as the legal foundation for most of our present zoning, building code and city planning practices.

Home Loan Acts: 1932 to 1933

The major impetus for Federal action in housing came as a result of the banking crisis and unemployment of the Depression years. Residential building had begun to decline in 1925, following the mortgage bond debacle of the mid-1920s. The bankruptcy of a number of old and respected mortgage bond and mortgage guarantee corporations resulted in part from fraudulent practices in the financing of rental housing during the boom years. By 1931, it had become apparent that home building was on the road to a major disaster with a proportional decline in activity far exceeding that of other industries. In addition, local mortgage-lending institutions were in deep financial trouble and the beginnings of the banking crisis which was to follow were already apparent.

Because of these difficulties President Herbert Hoover convened the President's Conference on Home Building and Home Ownership, held in Washington in 1931 to consider the problems of the home-building industry. The eleven-volume report of the Conference is a monumental compendium on the state of the home-building industry and of mortgage lending at that time and is still a major reference source on the condition of the industry in the 1920s. However, the Conference produced no major conclusions on the mortgage-lending crisis. It divided sharply among those who demanded government action to rescue the collapsing savings and loan business, those who preferred other solutions to the financial crisis, and those who desired no Federal action at all.

In the fall of 1931, despite the inconclusiveness of the Conference's proceedings, President Hoover recommended that the Congress authorize the establishment of a Home Loan Bank System to provide a reserve credit facility for residential mortgages. Savings and loan associations had been the major source of residential financing and were in a state of constructive bankruptcy in most parts of the country. The national administration wavered between recommendations for a central mortgage discount bank serving all mortgage-lending institutions and more restrictive home loan bank proposals intended to serve only savings and loan associations. The issue acquired increasingly strong political overtones as the year 1932 progressed, but legislation was finally adopted for a home loan bank system in July, 1932. By that time the panic in mortgage lending had spread from savings and loan associations to other types of banking institutions, and mortgage foreclosures had become so widespread as to constitute an urgent national problem.

The Home Loan Bank Act of 1932 authorized the establishment of the Federal Home Loan Bank System, under the Home Loan Bank Board, and what became twelve regional Federal Home Loan Banks. These institutions were authorized to receive deposits from member savings and loan institutions and to extend loans to them in time of financial need.

The Home Loan Bank Board began its organizational activity in the face of the most acute financial crisis in the nation's history. In addition to the problems arising from the seriousness of that crisis, it encountered vigorous opposition from those parts of the industry which had hoped to obtain the establishment of a central mortgage discount bank instead of the more limited bank system which served only one class of lending institution. The Home Loan Bank System proved to have inadequate powers to meet the mortgage difficulties facing the nation.

The inauguration of the New Deal under President Franklin D. Roosevelt was quickly followed by the closing of the banks throughout the country and their reopening under Federal supervision. A system of deposit insurance was adopted, guaranteeing the security of deposits in commercial and savings banks. Tied to these measures was the second major step of Federal participation in housing finance. This was the passage of the Home Owners Loan Act of 1933 which led to the establishment of the Home Owners Loan Corporation, empowered to buy any mortgage threatened with foreclosure. The corporation eventually became the largest mortgage lender and the largest single property owner in the history of the United States.

The act had two purposes: first, to save the homes of families which were threatened with foreclosure, and second, and more important, to provide liquidity to banking institutions. At the time it was estimated that mortgages were being foreclosed at the rate of 1,000 per day. Hundreds of thousands if not millions of mortgages had already been foreclosed and the appeal of saving the homeowner was a powerful one. Many banking institutions were in solvent condition but had their assets tied up in mortgage loans which they were unable to liquidate to meet demands of depositors.

The Home Owners Loan Act was a dramatic step. It was predicted that the Federal government would lose most of the money which it was to loan. The Home Owners Loan Corporation received 1.8 million loan applications totaling $6 billion. It completed one million loans in an amount of over $3½ billion. Its eventual loan authorization was $4.75 billion. At the peak of its operations, it held 16 per cent of the mortgage debt of the country, and owned mortgages on 10 per cent of the owner-occupied properties. By the end of World War II, the Corporation had fully repaid its borrowings from the Federal Treasury and closed its operations a few years later showing a modest profit.

The Home Owners Loan Act also took a second step toward the long-range reform of the savings and loan business by authorizing the Home Loan Bank Board to issue Federal charters to savings and loan institutions and make loans to such institutions where needed. The Board's studies had shown that thousands of communities lacked adequate savings and loan institutions and that other areas of the country had too many institutions which were of too small size for efficient management. Federal chartering permitted the reorganization of these smaller associations into larger and more effective institutions and the organization of new institutions. Using HOLC funds, the Federal Home Loan Bank Board subscribed the initial share capital of newly chartered Federal associations. The Federal savings and loan system was, of course, part of a longer-range program of reform aimed at the strengthening of mortgage-lending institutions. While its activities grew slowly, by 1940 Federally chartered savings and loan associations accounted for half of the assets of all savings and loan institutions. By 1960, the 1,873 Federal savings and loan associations had assets of more than $38 billion, about 25 times the resources of the Federally chartered associations sixteen years earlier.

Since the 1930s, however, there has been no effort to review the adequacy of our system of savings and lending institutions and there has been no systematic analysis of the evolution of these institutions under conditions of a rapidly expanding economy.

The National Housing Act: 1934

The Home Loan Bank Act launched the government into a long-range program to reform and strengthen the savings and loan institutions. The Home Owners Loan Act provided emergency relief to homeowners and to mortgage-lending institutions. Neither of these measures had been effective, however, in providing an adequate stimulus to residential construction. Nor had they provided a means for encouraging the flow of loans into residential building from other classes of lending institutions. In 1934, the administration and Congress turned their attention to the problem of stimulating employment in residential construction. The National Housing Act of 1934 authorized the establishment of a system of mortgage insurance under the Federal Housing Administration.

To achieve its objective of stimulating employment, Title I of the act authorized Federal insurance of short-term loans for home repair and improvement. This insurance was offered free on any loan made by any qualified lending institution for any home repair or modernization purpose. It encouraged banks and other lending institutions throughout the country to extend credit to homeowners for the purchase of plumbing and heating equipment, home modernization, roofing, and other forms of repair.

To stimulate longer-range expansion in residential construction, Title II of the act authorized the establishment of an insurance fund for mortgages on homes built under Federal supervision or purchased after Federal appraisal. Under the act, as it still operates, the prospective homeowner applies to a local mortgage lender for a mortgage loan. The loan application includes evidence of the borrower's credit rating, the plans for the house, and an appraisal of it. The FHA field office reviews the plans, inspects the dwelling during construction, appraises the property, and rates the credit risk of the borrower. If it approves the mortgage loan, the FHA will then insure the loan when made by the applicant lending institution. The borrower pays a ½ per cent insurance premium. The insurance premiums are pooled in an insurance fund maintained by the FHA. If the mortgage subsequently goes into default, the mortgage lender forecloses the property, turning over title to the FHA. The FHA pays the mortgage lender the outstanding balance on the mortgage in debentures and sells the property or proceeds against the original borrower to recover its losses.

The purposes of the FHA mortgage insurance system were many. First, the FHA gave commercial and savings banks and life insurance companies a form of Federal aid comparable to that granted by the Home Loan Bank System to savings and loan institutions. Second, it improved mortgage-lending practices and construction standards. The depression years had revealed evidence of lax standards of appraisal, inspection, land planning, and mortgage lending which had intensified the foreclosure crisis of the early 1930s. It was believed that the FHA system with Federal appraisals and minimum property standards would provide a yardstick for conventional lending and would permit the government to establish criteria for construction, appraisal, land and site planning, and design which would be followed by mortgage lenders and builders generally.

The insured mortgage was admirably suited to the needs of national mortgage lenders, including life insurance companies, commercial banks, and savings banks. Because it could be purchased and sold it served the needs of institutions which required a higher degree of liquidity than that available in conventional mortgage loans. Because of its nationally standardized characteristics, it could provide an investment outlet for those Eastern and Northern institutions which had excess capital available for investment in other parts of the country. Because it was subject to a national interest rate, national standards, and a uniform guarantee, it could be an instrument serving a national mortgage market in contradistinction to the largely local mortgage markets which had existed before.

These three characteristics of the FHA-insured mortgage have had continuing advantages to both the consumer and the lender. The gain is in mortgage funds available in all parts of the country at a standard interest rate, longer amortization periods, and lower down payments. The consumer derives an indirect benefit in that the house he buys has been inspected or appraised by a Federal agent. While the owner receives no guarantee of construction quality he gets some assurance of minimum construction standards.

From the standpoint of the lender, the gain from FHA insurance is in the safety of loans at higher ratios of loan to value and over longer amortization periods than would be warranted or permitted on conventional and uninsured loans. A nation-wide system of appraisal, inspection, and risk rating makes it possible for local servicing agents to place loans and, under agreements to service them for a fee, to sell them in national markets. Not only has the FHA system thus opened up a national lending market, bringing credit to remote areas which otherwise would have had difficulty in obtaining residential mortgage loans, but it has equalized the competition among the several classes of lending institutions and gone far toward equalizing mortgage terms and the availability of mortgage credit in the various parts of the country. In 1959 almost $7 billion in residential loans (the bulk of which were for homes rather than projects) were underwritten by the FHA. In 1960 the total was more than $5.3 billion.

The National Housing Act of 1934 also authorized the chartering of national mortgage associations to issue debentures based on the security of FHA-insured mortgage loans. Despite the apparent attractiveness of the plan, and several efforts to assemble sponsors, no such private corporation was ever organized, largely because the low level of home building and high level of saving during the prewar and war years enabled existing institutions to meet the nation's mortgage credit requirements. However, the Federal National Mortgage Association (FNMA) was chartered under this legislation for the purpose of providing a secondary market for unusual types of FHA loans. The FNMA made mortgage loans and held them until the projects had demonstrated their earning power and risk characteristics. In most instances these loans were subsequently resold to private purchasers at a substantial profit. After World War II, the FNMA became a vehicle for Federal purchases of mortgages under a variety of circumstances wholly unrelated to its original purposes.

The United States Housing Act: 1937

The next major step in Federal aids to housing was the adoption, in 1937, of the United States Housing Act which authorized the nation's first long-range program of aid to public housing and slum clearance. The 1937 act had been preceded by an authorization under the National Industrial Recovery Act in 1933 for the Public Works Administration to make loans to nonprofit and limited dividend housing corporations for the construction of moderate rental apartments. Less than a score of acceptable loans had been made in the first year and a half, and so, in view of this unproductive experience, the Public Works Administration in 1934 started another program, this time for the direct construction of low-rent public housing projects in slum areas. Some sixty projects were built in more than fifty cities, each located in a former slum site and rented to families of moderate and low income.

But Federal ownership of the projects had created administrative difficulties, local opposition, and eventually legal obstacles. The result was the Housing Act of 1937. Under this act, earlier difficulties were resolved by authorization of Federal loans and annual subsidies to local public agencies for public housing where such agencies had been established pursuant to state enabling legislation and municipal action. Since passage of the 1937 act, almost every state in the union has adopted state enabling legislation and most of the major cities of the country have authorized the establishment of local housing authorities for the purposes of slum clearance and the provision of rental housing for low-income families.

The provisions of the United States Housing Act are administered by the Public Housing Administration (PHA), at an earlier time the United States Housing Authority. PHA is authorized to make loans to local housing authorities for the construction of public housing projects. Upon their completion, the local agency rents the dwellings to low-income families. Because these families can afford only a part of the full economic cost of the housing they occupy, the difference between the cost and rents established in accordance with family need is met by a subsidy. The Federal government contributes part of the subsidy in the form of an annual grant roughly equal to the debt service on the indebtedness on the project. The local government contributes the rest of the subsidy in the form of partial tax exemption which equals approximately half of the Federal contribution. Through the combination of Federal grants, local tax exemption, low interest rates on local authority bonds, and long amortization periods, rents are reduced to levels which permit even very low-income families and many charitable cases to occupy decent housing. At the end of 1960 there were 460,629 locally owned public housing dwelling units supervised by the Public Housing Administration.

The public housing program was our first national attempt to clear slums and provide new housing on former slum sites. It therefore provided the first model for a larger and broader program of urban redevelopment—our present urban renewal program. It also provided a workable means for rehousing low-income families in safe and sanitary housing, an essential part of any broad-scale program of urban renewal and slum clearance.

War and Veterans Housing

The housing programs developed during the depression years never succeeded in stimulating a full revival of home building.

They did, however, provide systems of aid which endured through the war and postwar years.

The outbreak of war in Europe in 1939 and the resulting armament programs led to a revival of the domestic economy. Home building boomed briefly until the United States entered the war and shortages of materials and labor necessitated curtailment. During the war years priorities and price controls limited construction to that essential for the war effort. FHA insurance was used to secure private construction where needed for war workers. Direct Federal construction of temporary housing was used in emergency situations. National programs encouraged the conversion of larger dwellings into apartments and the renting of rooms to war workers.

One of the important wartime achievements was the establishment of a single Federal housing agency which brought together some dozen agencies scattered in several Federal departments. The National Housing Agency regulated the wartime use of materials used in housing, and later developed postwar housing policies. Its administrator participated in Cabinet meetings and was the President's spokesman on housing policies. In 1947, the National Housing Agency became the Housing and Home Finance Agency (HHFA).

A second noteworthy wartime development was the coordination of housing and community facilities programs. Wartime experience demonstrated that the provision of schools, highways, health and recreation facilities, utilities, and stores has to go hand in hand with the provision of shelter. As a result, Federal aids to community facilities were established, some of which continue to be administered by the Housing and Home Fnance Agency.

The last, and most important, wartime development for housing was authorization by Congress in 1944 of a program of home mortgage guarantees for veterans to be administered by the Veterans Administration. With 12 million returning veterans, 3.5 million of whom had families and no separate housing accommodations, and with the acute housing shortage which then existed, it was evident that veterans' housing would be a major economic and political problem.

Under the veterans (G.I.) loan program ex-servicemen could

purchase houses with a mortgage of up to 100 per cent of the cost. The mortgages were guaranteed by the Veterans Administration without the payment of any insurance premium. The interest rate on such loans was fixed initially at 4 per cent and, because it was below the prevailing level, it thus conferred upon the returning veteran a substantial economic benefit. The VA system, although drawing upon the principles so successfully demonstrated in the FHA, lacked the FHA's existing organization for the approval of plans, inspection of construction, appraisal of values, and rating of consumers' credit risks. The annual volume of VA-guaranteed residential loans reached a peak of $7,154,000,-000 in 1955 and declined to $1,984,000,000 in 1960.

Postwar Housing Policies: The Housing Act of 1949

During the late war and early postwar years, the Federal government and numerous private groups began to develop proposals for a vast expansion of the housing market primarily in the belief that the postwar period would be characterized by a resumption of the conditions of depression and unemployment which had been typical of the prewar period. Many Federal policies were developed on this assumption, even though when they were finally enacted and placed in operation the country was enjoying conditions of unparalleled prosperity. Thus some of the major features of the Wagner-Ellender-Taft bill, later the Housing Act of 1949, including some elements adopted in 1946, 1947, and 1948, expressed a congressional desire to encourage expansion of the private housing market by providing the maximum possible opportunity to private builders and mortgage lenders to extend mortgage terms to prospective homeowners even at considerable risk. Indeed, by low down payments and the extension of amortization periods under the FHA Title II insurance program, the Federal government aided fourteen privately built homes for each publicly built home in both the prewar and postwar periods. Comparable improvements were made in the terms available for FHA mortgage insurance on rental housing of the limited dividend type.

The Housing Act of 1949 was enacted after four years of vigorous, and at times bitter, debate. The chief controversies were over public housing and urban redevelopment. The Title I urban redevelopment program authorized $500 million in Federal grants and $1 billion in Federal loans to enable local governments to acquire and clear slum areas.

Under the terms of the legislation a local redevelopment agency may obtain loans and a contract for capital grants to enable it to acquire and clear a blighted area. After acquisition and clearance of the slum, the community is required to install public improvements necessary for the new use and to sell the land for housing, commercial, industrial, or public developments. The cost of land acquisition and clearance in blighted areas usually exceeds the reuse value of the land. The resulting loss requires a subsidy of which the Federal government pays two-thirds and the local government one-third. The redevelopment program also includes authorizations for the acquisition and development of land which has remained vacant because of some topographic, title, or other defect. Originally the program authorized the clearance of residential, industrial, and commercial blighted areas only if a residential use was involved before or after acquisition: Residential slums could be cleared for nonresidential purposes; nonresidential blighted areas could be cleared for residential purposes. This provision was later changed to remove the residential qualification in part.

The Housing Act of 1949 also recognized that public housing is an essential part of a comprehensive local rebuilding plan in order to provide housing for families of low income and particularly for those dislocated as a result of slum clearance and other public works programs. The act, subsequently cut back, authorized a program of 810,000 units of public housing spread over a six-year period at the rate of 135,000 units per year. With minor modifications, the revised public housing program corresponded to that authorized by the Housing Act of 1937.

The 1949 act also authorized a broad housing research program. Put into operation the following year, it was first curtailed and then eliminated by appropriations actions in 1951 and 1952.

The Housing Act of 1954

Because all housing legislation thus far had been adopted under Democratic administrations there was some question after the 1949 act as to whether the legislation described above was in fact bipartisan in character and represented settled national policy.

After the inauguration of the Republican administration of President Eisenhower in 1953, that administration reviewed alternatives for housing policy through a broadly representative President's Advisory Committee on Government Housing Policies and Programs. The Committee's published report corresponds in many ways to the studies and findings of the earlier subcommittee on postwar housing under the leadership of Senator Taft and of the National Housing Agency. The policies outlined by the committee, and later recommended to Congress by the President and embodied in the Housing Act of 1954, confirmed and endorsed all the major features of earlier housing legislation and enlarged and extended many of the programs in important respects. The 1954 act clearly symbolized the permanent bipartisan character of Federal aids to housing, although controversy continues regarding emphasis and size of program.

The most important extension authorized by the Housing Act of 1954 was an enlargement of the concept of urban redevelopment to include rehabilitation, conservation, and other steps short of clearance as parts of a comprehensive program for the renewal of cities. The urban renewal program encourages local communities not merely to clear slum and blighted areas but also to develop programs for the rehabilitation and modernization of areas which are declining but are not ready for clearance, and the conservation of areas which are threatened with blight and may require spot clearance, rehabilitation, or code enforcement measures. These concepts, now included in the broader term of urban renewal, had been developed earlier in several cities, notably Baltimore, Chicago, and Philadelphia.

In order to develop broad local responsibility and support for urban renewal, the 1954 act required localities receiving Federal aid for their projects to develop comprehensive workable programs. The workable program includes the following elements:

1. Effective local codes and zoning ordinances
2. A master plan for the community's development
3. An analysis of neighborhoods, determining their need for renewal
4. Effective administrative organization for the execution of programs and for code enforcement
5. Adequate local financing resources
6. Available suitable housing to accommodate displaced families
7. Active citizen participation and support

The public housing features of the Housing Act of 1954, aside from minor perfecting amendments, served merely to maintain the public housing program at the low level of operation which had characterized it during the last years of the Democratic administration. Since this feature of national housing programs had always been highly controversial, its continuation under a Republican administration confirmed its bipartisan support.

The third major feature of the Housing Act of 1954 dealt with the problem of a government-supported secondary market for insured and guaranteed mortgages. These activities were centered in the Federal National Mortgage Association, then a wholly government-owned corporation which was originally chartered under the terms of the National Housing Act of 1934. Although first conceived as a private and fringe-purpose activity, FNMA had become a public and major-purpose activity by a process of evolution and improvisation. During the prewar and early war years, FNMA engaged in intermittent purchases of FHA-insured mortgages where private mortgage money was not readily forthcoming because of local credit shortages or the risky character of a project.

These fringe purposes attracted no particular attention until the early postwar years when "Fanny May" (as the FNMA is called) began to engage in heavy mortgage purchases to meet the needs for veterans housing loans in rural areas and for rental housing projects. In the years 1948 to 1950, when mortgage interest rates rose slightly, the 4 per cent maximum interest rate on VA-guaranteed loans became unattractive to mortgage lenders. Congress and the administration were unwilling to raise the allowable interest rate on G.I. loans and the mortgage lenders were unwilling to lend freely at the authorized 4 per cent rate. In order to prevent a sharp curtailment in the G.I. loan program, "Fanny May" was authorized to purchase loans. In three years it issued commitments to buy $2.7 billion in mortgage loans, largely those guaranteed under the G.I. program. These commitments were nearly ten times the total commitments issued by "Fanny May" during the preceding decade and they made "Fanny May" a major element in the residential mortgage market. In the years 1951 to 1954, "Fanny May" issued commitments averaging $600 million per year. As a consequence of these actions and intermittent sales, the "Fanny May" portfolio rose from $200 million in 1948 to $2.4 billion in 1954 and to over $6.3 billion in 1960, an all-time high.

The debate over the appropriate role of the Federal government in the so-called secondary mortgage market raged bitterly during these years, as Charles Haar shows in his study in this series, *Federal Credit and Private Housing*. In general, veteran and builder groups contended that the veteran had the "right" to a 4 per cent mortgage loan and the government had an obligation to sustain this rate, if necessary by making direct mortgage loans or what was economically the same thing—commitments to purchase mortgage loans from private lending agencies.

Home builders generally adopted the position that the Federal government was under no obligation to make direct mortgage loans but that it was under an obligation to provide a steady and ample flow of mortgage funds. Bankers, on the other hand, argued that the Federally fixed interest rates inevitably produced difficulties over yields in the mortgage market which would alternately attract private mortgage lenders and then drive them out of government-guaranteed and -insured mortgage lending.

President Eisenhower's Advisory Committee on Government Housing Policies and Programs and, later, the administration adopted a compromise solution on the problem of the government secondary market. The Housing Act of 1954 changed the Federal National Mortgage Association to a quasi-public corporation. Borrowers were required to buy shares in "Fanny May's" stock currently equivalent to 1 per cent of borrowings. The Treasury supplied the rest of the capital stock. The corporation was authorized to borrow directly from private lenders on the security of its mortgage portfolio. Since a decade or more would elapse before the share investments of private stockholders reached significant levels, this change of the organization of the corporation was largely a semantic one involving no real difference in economic policy.

The Housing Act of 1954 failed to take any decisive position on the appropriate long-range role of the Federal government in the secondary mortgage market. Despite this fact, it is clear that an impressive body of experience and custom has developed during the decade of the 1950s which would make it exceedingly difficult for the Federal government to extricate itself from what amounts to direct mortgage lending on a very large scale in times of mortgage credit shortage.

During the postwar period, another group of lesser activities also became fairly permanent parts of the Federal government's program of aid to housing. The College Housing Program authorizes loans at favorable interest rates to colleges and universities for the construction of dormitories for college students and faculty. There is a similar program of loans for community facilities, continuing several programs which had been carried on under various authorizations since 1932; a program for the advanced planning of public works; and a program of grants to local communities or states on a matching basis for metropolitan or city planning, and for demonstrations of urban renewal techniques. The Voluntary Home Mortgage Credit Program helps obtain private mortgage credit for FHA-insured and VA-guaranteed loans in areas of capital shortage.

During the years following 1953, the Housing and Home Finance Agency was reorganized to include five major organizational units. These are the Federal Housing Administration, the Public Housing Administration, the Urban Renewal Administration, the Federal National Mortgage Association, and the Communities Facilities Administration. The Office of the Administrator of HHFA coordinates and supervises the operation of these constituents. The Home Loan Bank Board and its affiliated agencies were removed from the Housing and Home Finance Agency by congressional action in 1955 at the insistence of savings and loan organizations.

The Impact of Other Government Policies

This brief history of the Federal government's direct intervention in housing describes only some of its policies which influence housing. More general policies of government may have an equal or greater impact upon the housing industry. Of these the most important are tax policy, fiscal and monetary policy, and selected aspects of defense, natural resources, and transportation policy. Some of the most important of these are identified briefly here.

Tax policies of the Federal government have a profound influence on the housing industry. Perhaps the most direct are Federal income tax allowances for local property taxes, interest payments, and the deferment of capital gains taxes on owner-occupied houses. In combination these features of the personal income tax make the Federal government contribute, through tax deductions, a fifth or more of the costs of homeownership, depending upon the income tax bracket of the individual. For example, a person with a $12,000 income in the marginal 30 per cent rate group, owning a home bought at $23,000 with a $20,-000 mortgage and a $400 local property tax bill, would find the government contributing roughly $40 a month to his housing expense. No comparable deductions are available for the person who rents his dwelling. If the homeowning family has owned the house for a decade, and enjoyed an inflationary gain in the value of the property, it faces a substantial capital gain tax unless it continues to own. Tax policies like these have contributed substantially to the growth of homeownership in recent years.

On the other hand, Federal corporate income tax policies probably do not go far enough in distinguishing the peculiar position of home builders. Building differs from other manufacturing enterprise in its lack of heavy, fixed, long-term capital investment, and the resulting absence of opportunity for advantageous depreciation accounting. Perhaps tax policy should be used to encourage greater investment in building corporations. There have been efforts to convert building profits into capital gains, but they do not match the incentives built into the tax laws in other fields, notably by depletion allowances.

Furthermore, the distribution of tax resources among Federal, state, and local governments in this country seriously affects the economic position of housing. For historical, political, and technical reasons the Federal government draws its major revenues from personal and corporate income taxes. This leaves local government largely dependent upon the real property tax, a tax which falls heavily on housing. Federal and state budgets, though drawn primarily from urban areas, are spent largely in rural and farm areas. Thus the net effect of state and Federal grants does not appreciably diminish local government's dependence on the property tax.

National fiscal and monetary policies have dramatic effects on the housing economy. The short-run monetary policies of the Treasury and the Federal Reserve Board alternately reduce or increase the cost and availability of mortgage credit, and the volume of building. Long-range policies of inflation or deflation materially alter the equity position of homeowners and the security or value of mortgage loans.

Other national policies may have less sweeping effects, but the location of defense plants, for example, may mean rapid growth for some areas and decline for others. River and power developments can have similar consequences. And the national highway program may double or triple the geographic spread of the suburbs of cities within two decades, just as failure to provide corresponding aids for rail transportation may eventually mean the decline of central areas of some cities.

The Growing Role of Government Aids

Unquestionably the most significant factor in housing finance in the last twenty-five years has been the emergence of the Federal government as a major force in the housing industry. Starting from relatively small beginnings in the depression years, Federal aids to housing now affect 35 to 50 per cent of all new residential building. The proportion of new residential construction which is directly aided by FHA mortgage insurance and VA mortgage guarantees is shown in Chart 18. The proportion varies widely from year to year but has ranged from a third to a half of all new residential construction during the postwar years. In addition to these more directly measurable aids, a very large proportion of the remaining new residential construction is financed through savings institutions whose deposits are insured by the Federal government. Thus, the direct and indirect impact of Federal aids on housing accounts for a majority of all new houses built and may affect three-quarters of the total in some years.

Federal aid for the refinancing of the existing supply of hous-

Chart 18. Proportion of permanent nonfarm dwelling unit starts aided by Federal government, 1935–1959

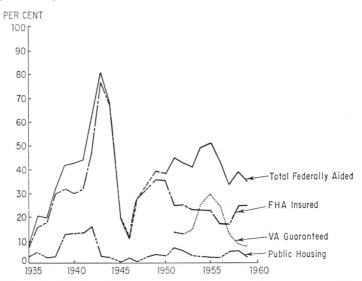

Note: Statistics for VA-guaranteed dwelling unit starts are not available for the years 1945–1950. Thus the total of dwelling units aided by the Federal government is understated.

Source: Housing and Home Finance Agency, *Thirteenth Annual Report*, 1959, tables A-1 and A-7, pp. 286–287; 293.

ing has always been proportionally less significant than that for new housing. Nevertheless, insured and guaranteed mortgages probably account for more than a quarter of outstanding mortgage indebtedness on older houses; the total outstanding insured and guaranteed portfolio in 1960 accounted for a third of total mortgage indebtedness.

Despite recurrent concern with the role of housing in the national economy, it is notable that national housing policy has usually failed to be a significant factor for promoting stability in the national economy. The volume of Federal participation in residential building varies closely with the volume of economic activity generally, tending to rise as business conditions improve or to decline or stay at low levels as business conditions deteriorate, although housing starts did move countercyclically in the earlier postwar recessions and expansions.

The housing programs of the 1930s pioneered in methods intended to stimulate a large volume of employment but were unsuccessful in reaching this objective. There is considerable evidence today that the housing aids used to help solve the postwar shortages of housing contributed as much to inflation as they did to the solution of the housing problems of returning veterans. In 1950 and in other years, when housing was looked to as a device to curb inflationary pressures, Federal policies failed to curb housing booms until the inflationary pressure was well past its peak.

But the evolution of Federal housing aids from 1932 on is characterized by a growing recognition of the complex phenomena with which the aids deal. If there is still little recognition of the close relationship between the supply of existing housing and the supply of new housing or between housing in central cities and housing in suburban areas, such a device as the workable program, required as a part of urban renewal, is helping to clarify the separate but complementary roles of the Federal and local governments and private enterprise.

One of the most notable features of Federal aids to housing finance is their almost total reliance on private sources of funds. More than 90 per cent of Federal financial aids to housing to date have been drawn from private sources through private institutional savings channels. Indeed, our system of mortgage-lending aids is largely a system of aids to various classes of mortgage-lending institutions. Much of the evolution of all Federal aids to housing can be attributed to competition among these lending institutions for Federal benefits which would improve their position vis-à-vis other classes of lenders.

Federal aids have had three major effects on the sources of funds for mortgage loans. They have strengthened local lending institutions, they have provided a type of mortgage instrument which enables national savings institutions to lend fairly readily on a nation-wide basis, and they have developed a type of mortgage instrument which enables major credit sources, such as commercial banks, to enter the mortgage market with greater ease than in the past.

While these institutional developments have brought huge additional sources of capital into the mortgage market, and have thus enlarged the sources of capital potentially available to the housing industry, they have also contributed to the instability of the flow of funds into housing. It has been argued that if the yield on government-insured and -guaranteed mortgages were free to follow the market rate, instability would be considerably reduced. On the other hand, it is contended that Federal aids should not be made available to mortgages with uncontrolled interest rates. During the early postwar years when mortgage funds were abundant and insured and guaranteed mortgages were selling at substantial premiums, there was evidence that institutional factors make mortgage interest rates quite sticky and very slow to respond to changes in the money market. This history encourages the belief that a number of institutional factors, including consumers' expectations, the needs of lenders to service other industries as well as housing, and the desire for a diversification of portfolio, may be influences resisting flexibility in mortgage interest rates and tending to produce ample funds for housing investment at some periods and shortages at other periods.

On the other hand, as pointed out above, fixed interest rates on government-insured and -guaranteed mortgages have made mortgage credit available in the South and West for the first time on terms approximating the terms available in the North and East. During the postwar years the opportunities opened to larger capital pools to lend on a national basis through insured and guaranteed mortgages have also served to equalize the flow of funds to different parts of the country and to eliminate some of the most acute shortages of mortgage funds which formerly existed in the so-called debtor areas of the country. Although the competitive effects of insured and guaranteed mortgages have not eliminated interest differentials between different parts of the country on conventional loans, they have reduced the differentials which formerly existed.

The three decades of Federal housing activity are characterized by dramatic changes, remarkable successes, and dismal failures. Federal efforts to make fundamental changes in the structure of housing finance established institutions of unprecedented strength requiring little continuing aid. But once entrenched, these institutions have resisted changes in credit practices.

Chapter 14

THE FUTURE OF FEDERAL POLICY

Federal credit policies in housing have been used to counter economic trends at the expense of the stabilization of the housing industry. Since these countercyclical policies appear to have failed or to be unattainable, an alternative policy of stabilizing residential construction volume at a level commensurate with population growth and obsolescence rates should be tried. Such a policy would require a reconsideration of existing programs, eliminating some and adding others.

Stabilizing residential building at a high volume would require an expansion of the private housing market so that more of the population could share widely in new sales or rental housing. Such a policy would require reductions in costs of construction, operation, land, and financing, diversification of product, expansion of rental construction, and, probably, new forms of government insurance or loans. Present mortgage insurance and guarantee programs were conceived to be actuarially sound, but they have been increasingly directed toward social objectives for which they are ill adapted. They might better be curtailed or redirected toward attainable objectives while new programs designed to serve more essential purposes are adopted. An expansion of market, financial, and technological research would assist in clarifying the aims and methods of Federal credit aids, and in distinguishing areas requiring aid from those which the market can now serve.

There is wide agreement in the United States that housing is not just another economic good, but a social necessity requiring public regulation and affirmative assistance. Just as most organized groups from labor to bankers accept the need for municipal controls over housing and urban development, using the police power to protect health, safety, and welfare, they have come also to accept Federal credit aids as essential to maintain and enlarge the production of new houses and to aid the rehabilitation of old, in order to provide an adequate supply of housing.

Under these circumstances there is little prospect that government intervention in housing will be reduced or terminated. But there is still much debate on a wide range of choices as to the specific purposes and methods of housing credit aids, and as to how they shall be administered and who will benefit directly or indirectly from them.

Is the primary objective the replacement of slums or the provision of housing for low-income families? Is it the stabilization of the building cycle, or the lessening of unemployment in times of recession? Should housing objectives be achieved through a larger volume of construction for higher-income families who require only a little help, or for lower-income families with more urgent needs, but requiring substantial subsidies? How much housing must be provided by public agencies, and how much can be provided by private business? Each of these questions illustrates choices in policy which are open for discussion. Each choice offers different benefits at different costs. Some objectives, and some methods, may be in conflict, as when we want to maintain a large stock of housing for low-income families, and at the same time to clear slums in order to rebuild cities.

Federal policies, adopted over a thirty-year period, reflect the political responses of different times. Each has tended to become a "permanent" program, supported by its particular beneficiaries. It is essential, therefore, that all policies be reviewed periodically in order to make sure that each is essential, is the most efficient means for achieving a desired end, and is consistent with the others. In such a review, competing claims must be reconciled and adjusted.

TABLE 9.   GROSS PUBLIC CREDIT USED UNDER FEDERAL NONFARM HOUSING
PROGRAMS: 1933–June 30, 1957 (in millions of dollars)

	Authority to make loans, grants, purchase mortgages, insure loans and expend from public debt receipts	
	Total current authority	Cumulative gross total authority used
Urban Renewal		
Loans.................................	$ 1,000	$ 132
Capital grants........................	1,350	105
Federal National Mortgage Association....	5,523	4,246
Public Housing		
Loan authorizations...................	1,500	4,584
Grants and appropriations..............	336	400
College Housing........................	925	214
Public Works and Planning*.............	32	87
Federal Housing Administration		
Home improvement insurance...........	1,750	10,147
Mortgage insurance...................	28,084	34,829
Defense, War, and Other Emergency housing and public works*...........		2,587
Home Loan Bank Board		
Federal Home Loan Banks.............	1,000	
Federal Savings and Loan Insurance Corporation.......................	750	
Home Owners Loan Corporation........		3,499
Veterans Administration		
Guaranteed loans.....................	*	22,477
Direct loans.........................	881	672
Total.............................	$43,131	$83,979

a Does not include miscellaneous appropriations or administrative expenses.

b Appropriations included.

c Limited only by number of veterans using aid.

Source: Adapted from *Congressional Record,* July 11, 1958, p. 12,319.

During the postwar years the FHA assisted nearly one-third of new mortgage lending. FHA and VA together aided about 40 per cent of all mortgages issued in the period of 1948–1958. The total Federal loan, grant, and insurance authorizations from 1933 to mid-1957 exceeded $83 billions, as is shown in the accompanying table. Less than $3 billion represent appropriations of tax dollars, the rest being for loan or insurance authorizations, largely supported by income or offset by assets such as mortgages. Ninety per cent of the total derives from postwar activity.

Under these circumstances it may be questioned whether still further Federal aid to housing will be politically or economically desirable. But if there is no prospect for a major reduction of Federal intervention in mortgage lending, there are very clear-cut demands, discussed below, for fringe additions to Federal programs which might bring increases or changes in Federal activity in the fields of chartering, secondary market operations, and aids to middle-income housing. Together these changes would not radically increase the proportion of housing subject to direct and indirect Federal aids. They might change the character of the aid offered and they might affect an additional 10 or 15 per cent of new-home building activity.

The issues that must be evaluated are ones that affect the housing industry and its capacity to enlarge and improve the housing supply, and ones that affect American cities and their capacity to undertake renewal and development programs. They are, in broad categories: (1) the building cycle and monetary policy; (2) the levels of building and maintenance required to raise housing standards; (3) the market for middle-income housing; (4) rental housing production; (5) the risks and responsibilities of government and private industry; (6) urban development policy; (7) research, technology, and training; (8) public housing; (9) Federal administration.

Housing in National Economic Policy

National concern with housing policy emerged because of the credit crisis and unemployment of the early depression years. Throughout the 1930s, government aid to housing was used to stimulate investment and employment. During the war years, this policy was reversed; rigid controls were imposed on residential construction to husband building materials and labor. Prices and rents were controlled to prevent inflationary increases.

The intimate connection between housing and economic stability was clearly recognized by the Housing Act of 1949. One of the major objectives of that act was the maintenance of economic stability, full employment and consumption. During the years since the passage of that act, the Federal government has recognized the importance of housing in the national economy by attempts in 1950–1951 and 1956–1957 to cut back or hold down residential construction because of the threat of general inflation.

But the use of government aid to housing to promote economic stability has never been systematic. To the extent that we have developed general stabilization policies, we have neglected to consider their repercussions upon the housing industry. Although national legislation from 1932 to 1958 is replete with admonitions concerning housing and economic stability, national policy has been improvised, usually ineffective, and often clearly erroneous. Two issues in particular illustrate this: first, the role of housing construction in maintaining full employment and, second, the role of mortgage credit in national fiscal policy.

The economic philosophy which prevailed from 1933 on involved a number of major assumptions which proved to be wrong. First, it was assumed that the major problems of the economy were those resulting from underemployment and deflationary pressures and that Federal housing programs should therefore be concerned principally with stimulating residential employment. This attitude prevailed even after nine years of war and postwar prosperity when the pressures in the economy were inflationary rather than deflationary.

A second major assumption was that residential construction somehow could be reduced in periods of boom and stimulated in periods of depression by manipulating Federal credit. This was disproved during the 1930s when, despite credit aids, residential construction remained at levels only 50 per cent of those attained in the boom period of the 1920s. Studies of the rate of expenditure of public works funds, including housing, during the 1930s show that building activity responded very slowly to legislative authorizations or changes in credit policy. Indeed, the known time lag in the building industry is often of the order of two to four years from the decision to invest, through site selection, land purchase, design, engineering, finance, permits, bidding, and contract letting, to actual employment. This fact alone should long since have given pause to those who insist that housing can be turned on to meet the needs of economic stabilization.

It is equally clear that housing cannot easily be turned off or cut back. Rigorous priority controls limited residential construction during World War II, but short-run credit regulations at the time of the Korean War did not prevent a boom in residential construction. These experiences suggest that it is exceedingly difficult, if not impossible, to restrain residential construction when building materials and labor are so scarce as to create strong inflationary pressures.

On the other hand, credit conditions have produced some longer range countercyclical effects in the postwar years. When credit has been tight, in boom years, the interest-rate ceilings on Federally insured and guaranteed mortgages have been below market rates, and activity under these programs has been curtailed with a resulting decline in housing starts. After credit conditions had eased and business activity declined, insured and guaranteed mortgages became attractive, and housing starts rose. Conventionally financed residential building has been relatively stable in its growth pattern, apparently, in part, because of greater interest-rate flexibility. As a result of its dependence upon credit, housing appears to have been held back, in boom periods, more than most other industries. There is no question about the need for stabilization measures. The incidence of these measures, as between small and large business, and upper- and middle-income families, and housing and other industries needs much more investigation.

For social reasons we have increased mortgage amortization periods to the limit of economic feasibility and reduced down payments to zero in periods of inflationary pressure. But this leaves us without economically sound credit terms to sustain residential construction in periods of declining economic activity. Because we have rather low incentives to use economic restraints in periods of boom, we tend to deprive ourselves of economic incentives for use in periods of depression. Therefore, other measures, including direct loans, deferred amortization, deferred interest, and housing inventory policy must be considered for use in periods of depression.

The Federal government has engaged in direct lending of some magnitude in the guise of the secondary market provided by the Federal National Mortgage Association ("Fanny May"). Twice in the postwar years, 1948 to 1950 and 1957 to 1958, it provided direct credit to sustain mortgage lending. However, in 1957, an increase in "Fanny May" purchases combined with lower down payments did not prevent an additional decline in the volume of FHA and VA housing starts. The situation improved in 1958 in large part because competing demands for credit eased. Although this action constitutes a considerable precedent, no permanent Federal policy resulted and residential construction continues to vary from year to year, in part because of fluctuations in the availability of credit. On the other hand, the direct loan programs of the Veterans Administration and the special assistance loans of the Federal National Mortgage Association would seem to indicate that it is settled government policy to assure a steady flow of mortgage funds in some areas and for some purposes, like cooperatives, defense housing, and urban renewal, which Congress apparently considers affected with a greater degree of public interest.

At the same time, it will be noted that where the government has made mortgage loans, whether under the guise of direct mortgage lending or under the guise of secondary market purchases, it has tended to adopt terms which correspond fairly closely to those of the private mortgage market. This policy has been justified on the grounds that such loans would be held only temporarily by the government and would be of such a character as to be susceptible of sale on a private market at some future time. In 1948 and 1949, "Fanny May" committed over $2 billion to purchase VA-guaranteed mortgages at 4 per cent. The market rate was then about 4½ per cent, a rate at which FHA loans were being made in unprecedented volume. Congress clearly intended to maintain a 4 per cent G.I. rate even at the expense of having the government purchase through "Fanny May" almost a fifth of all loans made.

How many other veterans could not buy a house because the rate was not raised to 4½ per cent? How many might have been disadvantaged by a ½ per cent increase in the cost of mortgage money? The increase was authorized later. Such questions have been rarely asked and never answered, but the fact remains that the great bulk of Federal National Mortgage Association mortgage purchases since 1948 have been at times when an increase in the insured or guaranteed rate would have accomplished the same purpose, and this without any examination whatsoever of the number of beneficiaries of the fixed rate who would be priced out of the market by the increase.

In other areas of activity, like low-rent public housing, college housing, and urban renewal activities, Congress has concluded that these functions can be achieved only if funds are made available at interest rates which are substantially below those offered by private mortgage lenders. The government extended loans directly from the Treasury, or guaranteed local public bonds, so that favorable terms could be available. "Fanny May's" special assistance loans to cooperative, defense, disaster, and urban renewal housing also appear to be instances in which a special problem has justified a special aid. It must nevertheless be stressed that these are the rare cases, and account for only a fraction of lending activity.

In the light of such examples as these, it is fair to ask, as Charles Haar does in his study of Federal credit in this series, just what is the purpose of Federal housing policy? To get more houses built? To raise the level of homeownership? To give aid to veterans regardless of their ability to pay? To help renew cities? To keep the economy stable? Should "the lens of judgment," Haar wonders, "be that of the profitmaker or of the welfare houser?" If Congress distributes its favors too liberally, he says, it cannot be effective in meeting particular problems. And if it does meet those problems effectively, the general market will have to fend for itself much more than it does now.

But when the housing market fends for itself in any marked degree, it becomes more vulnerable to sudden shifts in the economy than do other industries. Arthur Burns, a former chairman of the President's Council of Economic Advisers, suggests that this is so in stating that when general credit restraints were used to hold back inflationary pressures in 1956 and 1957 housing suffered disproportionately. In actual fact, the Federal Reserve Board's strictures on credit had little effect on industries that then engaged in a capital building boom. They continued to finance their capital requirements, in large part, out of earnings or proved able to pay higher rates in the bond market. Borrowing for consumer purchases continued to mount—except for housing: residential construction dropped by more than 30 per cent. General credit manipulations clearly had a differential impact. The implication was clear, however, that the Federal Reserve Board took the position that in determinations of national economic policy one industry cannot be exempted from controls imposed on all even if varying effects result. From the hindsight of 1958, it could be argued with some cogency that the credit restraints of 1957 failed to cut back industrial expansion at a time when curtailment of industrial expansion would have been advantageous to the economy, and cut back residential construction at a time when the expansion of residential construction would have been advantageous socially and perhaps even economically.

These experiences suggest that we are still far from reconciling the social objectives of housing programs with national economic needs for stability and growth. Some characteristics of the housing industry make it ill suited for countercyclical uses, except perhaps in periods of prolonged depression. If countercyclical use of housing policy is unattainable and inconsistent with social objectives, is stabilization of residential construction at a high level attainable and consistent? We shall return to this theme.

If the interest rate continues to be used as a major device for limiting economic activity, can discriminatory consequences be avoided? Presumably freeing the government-aided rates would reduce the wide fluctuations of recent years, but at a substantial price to consumers in later years. Could these consequences be offset by direct loan programs for "social purpose" housing, or by temporary secondary market operations of a central mortgage bank? Here selective programs may be more effective and less costly in achieving both economic and social objectives.

Little attention has been directed to the public issue of whether or not to sustain residential construction during temporary or prolonged declines in the market demand for residential housing. The boom years immediately preceding the recession of 1958 seem to demonstrate that residential construction may be operating at levels far below those required to provide adequate housing for the American people. In these years the economy was advancing steadily. In constant dollars it grew by over 30 per cent from 1950 to 1957. But residential building averaged one-fifth lower than the 1950 peak. Housing demand among families in the market was being met at current price levels by a volume of construction which was not adequate to eliminate the use of substandard units. It is equally clear that a large volume of public housing for low-income families is not likely to be a popular device for meeting large employment or housing needs. This suggests that other programs should be explored with the view to sustaining residential construction during periods of declining markets, in order to effect the replacement of obsolete and substandard houses, upgrade the stock, and build that reserve "cushion" of space needed to provide flexibility in the supply. The means for attaining such objectives have scarcely been examined or suggested, much less given serious attention by economists and housing officials.

Ever since the 1920s various groups have proposed a central mortgage bank as a means for solving some problems of credit flow for housing. Current studies by private research groups are directed toward clarification of the issues involved. Such an institution cannot, as some hope, suspend the normal competition for funds in our economy. On the other hand it might well even flows, particularly in short-term fluctuations, provide for desirable flexibility in the mortgage market, and perhaps further reduce geographic differentials in the availability of mortgage money. Further, such an institution could help to tap new sources of savings, and could help to distinguish market-guided and fully economic programs from those which require more clear-cut Federal help.

Stabilizing Residential Building

A high and stable volume of residential building, coupled with an expansion of maintenance and remodeling activities, is indeed required if there is to be any real progress toward the elimination of blight and the raising of housing standards. The homes not built in periods of residential recession can never be occupied by families now living in shacks and slums. In short, low production in home building guarantees that old, substandard houses will continue to be the only ones available for many American families, that relocation will be difficult, and that the prices of old houses will be too high for profitable rehabilitation or for occupancy by low-income families. The volume of residential building and remodeling required to achieve a better housing stock is, therefore, a crucial question for housing and renewal policy and one that is closely related also to the problem of economic stability.

Charles Haar sees the problem in somewhat different terms. According to him, "the goal can no longer be to maximize the number of houses per se. Rather, it is to concentrate limited government aid to meet the needs of those specialized groups of which the free market takes little account." The extension of Haar's argument to its logical conclusion would mean, at the least, sharp curtailment of the basic FHA and VA programs. If the general housing market were thus to be abandoned as a matter of Federal housing policy, Haar believes the present system of mortgage insurance could be restructured in any one of a number of ways to induce the flow of private money into special areas like rental housing, housing for the aged, housing for minorities, and so on.

But by specific declaration in the Housing Act of 1949, and by actions in the years since 1932, it is clear that the Federal government is committed to provide credit and other aids in such form as is necessary to maintain a substantial volume of new residential construction. The Home Loan Bank Act, the National Housing Act, the United States Housing Act, and the Housing Act of 1949, clearly express this as national policy. In addition, the authorization, almost without debate, of $2 billion in "Fanny May" loans in 1958 suggests that Congress is unwilling to permit residential construction to fall below a level of approximately a million units a year. On the other hand, Congress has never stated what level of residential production it conceives to be desirable.

To pursue such an approach, let us assume that the elimination of slums and blight and the provision of decent homes for American families require new residential construction of 1,500,000 homes a year and the substantial rehabilitation of 500,-000 more each year for the next five years, with a higher rate thereafter, probably exceeding 2 million new units annually in the seventies. Could Federal aids be used to achieve such a level of construction, with fluctuations of not more than 10 or 15 per cent? What kinds of measures might be indicated? Could these be adopted without prohibitive expense, utilizing largely private instrumentalities, and without serious competition with or reduction of present volumes of purely private and Federally aided private construction and mortgage lending?

Presumably any such program would require, first, that steps be taken to assure maximum private effort. Some of these have been discussed in preceding chapters.

Freed from arbitrary interest rates, present aids to private building and mortgage lending might compete more effectively for capital under changing money market conditions. If such a policy had been pursued in recent years, it would have relieved the government of the need to purchase approximately $5 billion in mortgages. These funds might have been used for loans to stimulate the building of homes which otherwise could not be produced or for market groups which otherwise could not be served. The feasibility of such a program has not been examined by government in recent years. The Housing and Home Finance Agency is the only major Federal agency which until 1961 lacked a staff of economists to make such an analysis. The following sections review some of these important problem areas.

Housing for Middle-Income Families

Despite the large expansion of Federal aids in the last twenty-five years and despite the continued extension and improvement of the terms on which homes are made available with Federal credit aid, it is apparently true that the private housebuilding industry serves only a fraction of the American public. This is not always true, nor is it true in all communities. There is evidence that, in some parts of the South and West, residential construction costs and the costs of operating a home are proportionally lower in relation to family incomes than they are in other parts of the country. In these areas, the upper half—or even more—of the income distribution may be in the effective market for new housing. It is also true that the price increases of the postwar decade gave many families a substantial equity in a home which later enabled them to upgrade their housing without assuming debt obligations beyond their means. With these reservations, most data indicate that half or more of all families have incomes which do not permit them to rent or purchase new homes.

The problems of providing housing for families in the middle-income third of our population, of providing housing for low-income families, of increasing the volume of replacement of obsolete housing, and of maintaining stability in residential construction are wrapped up in the fundamental issue of the breadth of the housing market. To the extent that the housing market can be greatly broadened, it may be possible to sustain a high level of residential construction. This would mean that middle-income families would have access to better quality housing at lower prices, and a larger supply of older housing would be available at low prices for occupancy by low-income families. With lower prices of old homes, their rehabilitation or conversion would be possible on a more widespread and economically sound basis. The resolution of this complex of problems requires the adoption of a national policy with respect to the new housing market and a national policy with respect to filtration.

The expansion of the housing market to serve middle-income families must be approached through a product that is more attractive to the consumer and through reductions in the cost of constructing and operating the home, reductions in taxes, and reductions in the cost of land. It must also be approached through reductions in the cost of financing. No single device is likely to yield all the answers. The ultimate solution will probably be found in a combination of financing incentives which will encourage cost reductions on the part of house and apartment builders. Although the discussion here is directed solely toward financing devices, other cost-reducing methods described elsewhere in this book must be linked to them to secure an adequate broadening of the housing market.

Several approaches to the financing problem may be identified here. One approach would provide for a privately financed first mortgage loan of a relatively long amortization period and covering half the cost of the home. Such a loan would be backed by a low-interest-rate government second mortgage which would not be amortized until the first mortgage had been paid off. In effect, the government would provide half of the funds at the cost of money to the government for the first half of the ultimate amortization period. This method has been used in some of the Scandinavian countries.

A second approach is a return to the unamortized loan. The unamortized loan came into disfavor as a result of excesses during the 1920s and the liquidity crisis among lending institutions in 1930–1932 which forced the foreclosure of many otherwise sound loans. Under certain economic assumptions, including that of a slow, steady depreciation in the value of money, the unamortized loan has much to commend it. The rapidly changing characteristics of American cities suggest, however, that a wholly unamortized home mortgage loan may be very risky for reasons associated with urban growth and change.

A third alternative to financing housing for middle-income families is a loan whose interest rate is subsidized. Presumably such loans might be made through normal private channels at the current conventional rate, with a subsidy from the government on the interest rate for some part of the ultimate term. The direct subsidy device would have the advantage of recognizing the actual cost involved which other devices tend to conceal.

A fourth alternative would be a direct government loan for a long amortization period at the cost of money to the government. Such a loan would achieve a lower cost to the consumer than any of the other alternatives enumerated here. It would involve the use of government credit for fully repayable loans. The loans could be serviced through conventional private lending channels at the usual service fee and could be converted under certain circumstances to the servicing agent's portfolio. A number of European and South American countries use this kind of government loan in various forms for similar purposes.

The main features of such a program already exist or their administative forms have already been established in the direct loans of VA and the secondary market activities of "Fanny May." For illustrative purposes, if the Federal government were to make available mortgage loans for amortization periods of forty years at an interest rate of 3 per cent, such terms might bring into the market for new homes an additional half million families a year. Such a program could presumably be administered through private mortgage-lending institutions as "Fanny May" commitments are administered today. The mortgages could be held by private banks as agents for the Federal National Mortgage Association. Price and income eligibility limits would be necessary to protect normal markets and prevent dissipation of benefits in credit-induced price increases.

Other approaches to the middle-income housing problem include subsidies to families on the model of those used in the Scandinavian countries, direct government loans for private rental housing, and local tax exemption. Some of these schemes have been employed by New York, Connecticut, and Illinois. An early example of a middle-income housing program was the program of direct loans to veterans authorized by the state o Connecticut after the war. This program authorized loans at ar effective interest rate of little more than 1 per cent to veterans who otherwise could not afford to purchase homes under the G.I. program. Because the state did not impose a sliding scale for the loans based on the cost of money, for example from 1 per cent to $3\frac{1}{2}$ per cent, it was liable to fairly serious fiscal risks. On the whole, however, the program made homes available to veterans who would otherwise have been unable to afford such homes.

So far the discussion of housing for middle-income people has stressed homeownership. The second major area for possible expansion is in the field of rental housing, including cooperative housing. Rental housing is of particular importance because it constitutes the major form of tenure in central-city areas which are scheduled to be renewed. Rental housing has been the most significant failure of housing finance for a quarter century. Since Chapter 12 is devoted entirely to rental housing, it is not discussed in this chapter. Similarly, since public housing programs for low-income families are covered in Chapters 5 and 16, they are not included here.

Government Risks and Responsibilities

Federal housing legislation indicates that the government looks to private business to meet most of the housing needs of this country but that government will seek to reinforce and aid private business to fulfill a larger proportion of the total responsibilities of our society in housing. To the extent that private enterprise cannot meet recognized housing needs, legislative policy indicates that the Federal government is committed to additional aids to private enterprise and to local and state governments to meet such remaining housing requirements. Under these guiding principles, the scope of governmental responsibility is heavily influenced by the effectiveness of private business activity.

Yet the history of Federal housing legislation strongly suggests that it will be exceedingly difficult for government to maintain such a policy of restraint in the face of growing demands for government aid to housing. In recent years the industry has steadily urged smaller down payments, longer amortization periods, billions of dollars in governmental purchases of mortgages, and new types of mortgage insurance. All of these require the government to assume risks which private business is unwilling to assume. The effect is to provide substantially riskless loans to mortgage-lending institutions and to enable the home-building industry to engage in large building operations with a minimum of working capital and virtually no permanent investment. Congress has been content to go along with this expansion of governmental activity. There has been no systematic examination of the possibility of making structural changes in the organization of the industry which might enable it to assume functions now assumed by government.

Thus, savings and loan organizations have demanded a new form of mortgage insurance to meet their particular needs and to relieve them of the necessity for assuming certain risks. This despite the fact that as early as 1948, John Lintner in an examination of mutual savings banks (*Mutual Savings Banks in the Savings and Mortgage Markets*) demonstrated that a similar class of lending institution could have adequately safeguarded its mortgage portfolios by self-insurance at modest cost. Unfortunately, both the administration and the legislative branch of Congress have been far too willing to take on additional responsibilities of this type rather than face the difficult task of devising methods for encouraging or, indeed, requiring private institutions to assume the same responsibilities. With government investments and contingent liabilities in housing exceeding $80 billion a systematic review of the whole subject is clearly indicated and desirable.

Government may also have been too prone to use devices of mortgage guarantee or insurance or mortgage purchase in instances in which the use of the more traditional regulatory powers might have served the same purposes. In each of the government programs these problems arise. The Home Loan Bank Board can assume the risks of somewhat less rigorous supervision through its deposit insurance funds. The FHA may reduce the probability of loss by compelling the builder to adhere to more rigorous standards of design, construction, and location or it may assume a larger share of those risks through its insurance funds. The normal tendency of the administrative agencies is to minimize the amount of supervision or regulation on critical issues at the expense of greater risks to insurance funds. Thus, there is a whole class of administrative actions under which the government may assume responsibilities or can take risks without assuming the corresponding responsibilities for exercising appropriate supervisory control.

Some of these problems have been largely concealed by the postwar inflation and prosperity. The most important of them is the question of responsibility for appraisals and risk rating. It was originally presumed that both the FHA and VA programs were coinsurance programs under which the risk of the mortgage loan was divided between the Federal government and the mortgage lender. As the programs have evolved, however, the risks are very largely assumed by the Federal government. The mortgage lender runs no real risk of loss. So long as there was a risk of private loss, it was presumed that the lending institution would scrutinize appraisals and evaluate credit risks with the care customary in conventional loans. With the coinsurance feature virtually eliminated from the program, however, this is no longer true. Many classes of private lending institutions rely entirely upon the Federal guarantee. Some institutions do not even bother to appraise property or review the standing of the borrower. Under these circumstances, grave questions arise as to the responsibility for the risks assumed.

Although the FHA has done what is generally regarded as a most creditable job of professionalizing and systematizing the inevitably hazardous business of appraisal and risk rating, there have been some scandals and some problems of recruiting skilled personnel, particularly during periods of prosperity. The early Veterans Administration program involved some outrageous practices which had a very clear inflationary effect and provided Federal aid for some of the worst-built housing in the history of the country. Although the VA program has improved greatly in recent years, it still relies heavily upon fee appraisers who may often be confronted with situations involving conflict of interest. To the extent that private lenders abdicate their responsibility for appraisals and credit and risk rating, the mortgage insurance and guarantee programs become programs which are largely administered by Federal agencies rather than private lenders. They become programs which are "private enterprise" in name only and in which the major decisions, the major responsibilities, and the major risks are all undertaken by the Federal government with private lenders serving merely as executors of the program. If the major purposes of programs are merely to relieve private business of risk, their continuation may reasonably be called into question.

Another important problem in Federal aids to housing finance arises because of the very marked tendency to shift from actuarially sound risks in the direction of programs involving increased social responsibility. The original FHA program was intended to be an actuarially sound program of mortgage insurance. Despite the lack of experience which would justify the establishment of an insurance rate which was in fact actuarially sound, subsequent experience has demonstrated that the insurance premium charged has largely met these criteria. Indeed, the study of FHA insurance reserves by Ernest M. Fisher and Chester Rapkin (*The Mutual Mortgage Insurance Fund*, 1956) suggests that the rates may have been a little higher than were necessary to serve the purposes of actuarial soundness. Unfortunately, the FHA system was so successful that in the postwar period the VA system of mortgage guarantees was adopted by Congress without any insurance premium. At this point, the insurance system became a guarantee system and the concept of actuarial soundness went out the window. Congress was voting to assume a risk of unknown magnitude as a form of benefit to veterans and to defer responsibility for facing up to the cost until some later date.

Successive postwar modifications in the FHA program have had quite similar effects. They have required the FHA to insure ever larger mortgage ratios—now up to 100 per cent—and ever longer mortgage terms—now up to 40 years—to accomplish certain public purposes despite the fact that these were dubious economic risks. The FHA is now required to insure homes in blighted areas under renewal programs, to insure housing projects on Army bases for Army personnel, and to insure mortgages on homes for the aged, despite the fact that there is no actuarial experience on which to base such insurance programs. Further, these mortgages involve greater risks of loss to the government but the terms are more favorable to the builder or lender.

In all these cases, it is probable that the social purpose is a worthy one. There is a real question, however, whether the social purpose is soundly served by the mortgage insurance or mortgage guarantee instrumentality. There is also a question whether such socially necessary purposes are best served by a device conceived as an actuarial risk, when the risks involved are larger than those which could normally be tolerated by any workable insurance premium. In addition, the insurance device is incapable of serving some of our most urgent needs. It rarely works effectively for any but the higher-income families. In effect, public policy has become a matter of using the wrong instruments for the right purposes in order to defer the recognition of the potential costs. The risks in such a policy have been concealed to date by twenty years of inflation. It is quite possible that as a result of the passage of time and the conditions of inflation, the costs may never have to be borne directly by the public.

As national housing programs broaden there should be a constant re-examination by Congress and by all others concerned with the goals of housing policy of the use of the mortgage insurance device for social purposes involving substantial risks. It is clear that the insurance and guarantee system is one of the finest economic inventions ever devised, but it appears that other devices might better serve some of the more important social purposes of contemporary national housing policy.

The Federal government has a vitally important role to play in the development and renewal of cities. It plays this role in partnership with many forms of private business and many types of local government. As new programs are developed to serve newly recognized needs, policy makers must be alert to eliminate older programs which have done their job, and to make sure that public action is necessary in fact to serve public purposes.

Other Federal Housing Activities

Federal programs of aid to housing and urban renewal provide a wide range of aids, but they leave other important areas untouched. The Housing Act of 1954 took important steps toward comprehensive renewal and filled gaps in the 1949 Act with its provisions for a "workable program," demonstration grants, authorization for experimental nonresidential renewal, and grants for city and metropolitan planning. Some of the more important remaining gaps are identified below.

Although the workable program requirements of the urban renewal program make the development of a general city plan a requisite for Federal aids to urban renewal, similar requirements do not attach to other Federal aid programs, including G.I. mortgage guarantees, FHA mortgage insurance, and, of perhaps the greatest importance, the Federal highway program. If all these programs were made subject to the requirement that a city have an effective general plan in operation as a condition to Federal aid, dramatic progress in city planning and development would probably result.

A closely related problem is the quantity and quality of personnel for city planning and urban renewal. These professional activities are comparatively new. Although the number of schools giving graduate training in city planning has increased threefold during the postwar years, the demand for trained city planners still far exceeds the supply. The Federal government has given recognition to comparable problems in the fields of the sciences by offering graduate scholarships. A modest program of scholarship aid to graduate study in housing, urban renewal, and city planning is clearly needed.

There is also growing evidence of Federal recognition of the important role of community facilities in urban development. This recognition began with public works programs in the 1930s and the wartime need to provide community facilities for isolated centers of war industry. In the postwar period Federal aid took the form of loans for the advanced planning of public works and loans for the construction of community facilities in Federally affected and rapidly growing areas. Doubtless, the most important development in the near future in this field will be the adoption of a Federal program of loans and grants for school construction. Such loans in the past have been administered through the Community Facilities Administration of the Housing and Home Finance Agency. If this administrative tradition is maintained in some enlarged program in the future, it will serve to reinforce a broad Federal concern for urban development expressed administratively in the Housing and Home Finance Agency.

Federal grants for community facilities such as water, local health, fire, police, park, recreation, library, and other services do not appear to be urgently needed if local governments can be relieved in greater degree of the major costs of highways and schools. Federal and state aids in these two strategic areas would free local tax resources for the support of the other, smaller but more numerous, functions required to service residential areas. On the other hand, suburban communities, which must accommodate a growth of 60 to 100 million people in the next two decades, may face impossible fiscal problems in borrowing funds to build facilities for future population growth, facilities which such growth can later support. There is ample precedent for an open-end program of Federal guarantees of local bonds to meet these requirements.

Among the metropolitan growth problems is the reservation of land for future industrial, residential, and other private uses, and for permanent public uses. While the housing acts of 1949 and 1961 contain some provisions for these purposes, they are yet to be implemented.

The Federal government has clearly recognized its concern with the economic health of cities and its willingness to provide large Federal grants to aid local government in coping with the deterioration of cities and their rebuilding. The willingness of Congress to continue the program of Federal grants for urban renewal shows that this principle is now firmly accepted in national policy. Although the original terms of the Housing Act of 1949 limited the urban development program to residential areas, the subsequent acts recognized that cities must be treated as whole economic units and that urban redevelopment techniques pioneered in housing may advantageously be applied to commercial and industrial areas of the city. Some expansion of the proportion of urban renewal funds which may be utilized for nonresidential renewal projects will help cities to develop the tax and employment base required to support local government services.

Federal credit aids may be essential to the market but should be coupled with state and local actions which take account of complex and interrelated problems of city planning, zoning, interim land uses, local tax revenues, and local government powers. Here, private interests and Federal and local government require joint agreement on actions yet to be devised.

Research

No major industry in the United States is as deficient in systematic research as the housing industry. Building materials manufacturers, almost alone in the industry, do development work on specific new products, but builders, land developers, mortgage lenders, and real estate brokers conduct virtually no research. As a result, a $20 billion industry which, to be comparable with other industries, should be spending from a half billion to one billion dollars annually on research is almost at a technological and scientific standstill. The low progress rate of the industry is doubtless directly related to its inability to use the resources and skills of modern scientific institutions. As Chapters 7 and 9 point out this unhappy situation in housing stems in large degree from the small scale of the business units which comprise the industry. In agriculture, where a comparable situation has always existed, the Federal government's research program has produced scientific miracles which have revolutionized agriculture during the last seventy-five years. The U.S. Department of Agriculture currently spends $240 million annually on research; the Housing and Home Finance Agency so little that it does not even account research expenditures separately. When Federal commitments, grants, guarantees, and loans on housing exceed $5 billion annually this situation is hard to understand.

A large-scale research program in housing and urban development could include technical research on the assembly of structures, on land and facilities development costs, on the processes affecting the growth or decline of cities and of neighborhoods, on housing markets, and housing finance. It could use the services of hundreds of research groups throughout the country, some of which are now engaged in small efforts in this field.

It is sometimes charged that government aids support marginal producers and thus slow the rate of growth of the more efficient. This whole problem should be the subject of careful study. In addition, it is frequently contended that the FHA insurance program impedes the adoption of new materials, methods, and designs. FHA's conservatism, like that of lenders, stems from an understandable caution about the durability or acceptability of new features which often must last for twenty years or more. But such hazards can be specifically insured against, and when FHA has an insured portfolio amounting to $33 billion (1960) it should be under a positive mandate to insure the property owner against loss on some new developments of an experimental character. Such insurance, without additional cost to the owner, might apply to a few thousand homes a year for the specific purpose of giving every possible encouragement to builders and materials manufacturers to develop and try innovations as promptly as possible.

Probably the most spectacular deficiency of the housing industry is its lack of adequate market data. The census of the farm population and farm housing involves the expenditure of $1.90 per capita on the farm population. The corresponding census of urban housing and population involves an expenditure of only $.45 per capita on the urban population. We have precise data on the agricultural land use of every county in the United States but we lack the most elementary data about urban land use. We have better data regarding the number of pig and chicken incubators in the United States than we have on the number of urban factory buildings or urban stores. Our major industries conduct systematic and detailed surveys of the buying habits, incomes, residential locations, and social characteristics of their purchasers. They use all the elaborate methods of modern market research to diagnose consumer preferences and tastes. No such information is available in any city in the United States for the markets and customers of the housing industry. If the housing industry had market information corresponding to that available for other industries of corresponding economic importance, it would reveal large unserved markets and many business opportunities for the industry. Unless the Federal government takes the lead, it is unlikely that such market research will be done.

Problems of Federal Administration

Another important unresolved issue in Federal housing policy is the problem of coordinating Federal housing and other programs. Although the Housing and Home Finance Agency administers, through its constituent agencies, programs of aid to private and public housing, urban renewal, home rehabilitation and improvement, public housing, urban redevelopment, community facilities, secondary credit, and direct loans, there has been little effective coordination among them. In addition, the Federal government has failed to coordinate urban housing policies with its programs of aid to water supply, sewerage, and stream pollution, and its Federal highway program and other programs aimed toward industrial or economic development.

This lack of coordination is most evident in urban renewal programs. Administered by the Urban Renewal Administration (part of the HHFA), they are dependent in large degree upon the mortgage credit aids administered by the Federal Housing Administration, a constituent of the Housing and Home Finance Agency. Approval of an urban renewal project by the Office of the Administrator of HHFA and by the Urban Renewal Administration provides no assurance that the Federal Housing Administration or any other agency will provide the essential mortgage insurance or credit. Other parts of the Federal housing credit system, including the Home Loan Bank System and its member institutions, have even less direct concern with urban renewal programs. This lack of coordination is a reflection, of course, of the weakness of legislative enactments and of the lack of effective policy control over its operating agencies by the Office of the Administrator of the Housing and Home Finance

Agency. That Office is an instrumentality of the President and Congress, created for coordinative purposes; but its constituents are in large degree responsive to the special interests which support them and provide the political pressure necessary for their continuation and expansion. Many groups have suggested that the Administrator of the HHFA be given Cabinet status and thus the influence required to coordinate housing activities and the broader programs of aid to urban areas conducted by other departments.

Perhaps the most conspicuous example of duplication in government programs is offered by the existence of the FHA and the VA mortgage programs. Both of these agencies insure mortgages, both have nation-wide systems of field offices to inspect and appraise homes. Their separate regulations and procedures require builders and lenders to maintain dual sets of accounts so that the duplication extends not merely to government but also to private agencies. The Hoover Commission (the Commission on Organization of the Executive Branch of the Government) recommended that the administration of these programs be combined in the FHA at great savings to the government, a recommendation bitterly resisted by veteran groups and some lenders.

Finally, the administration of Federal aids involves the granting and occasionally the denial of substantial economic benefits. Although these types of grants have not been traditionally subject to review by the courts, they are susceptible of being administered inequitably or in a discriminatory manner. Administrative appeals and review machinery ought to be developed to give business firms and others opportunities to have proposals reconsidered.

This, and the preceding chapter, have traced the evolution of Federal aids to housing through the last quarter century. These aids have become a permanent feature of government, influencing most new home building and supporting the program of urban renewal. Powerful lobbies have developed to maintain and expand them and to influence their administration. National political leaders, trade associations, and citizens have an obligation to scrutinize them carefully to be sure that they still continue to serve public purposes. Some programs appear to be serving chiefly private businesses. If this is true, perhaps they can be turned over to private business in actuality. Other programs appear to support inefficiencies rather than promote the development of business patterns which will not require continuing help. In the light of the expansion of the economy a review is in order.

Chapter 15

POLITICS AND PRESSURE GROUPS

National housing policies have evolved largely from the competing demands of special-interest groups. Arguments about the public welfare often reflect the demand of some groups for competitive advantage over others. The major housing controversies have not been over public housing but over how different segments of the industry were to share the housing market. The cumulative effect of special pleading has led to a steady expansion of programs, since each interest is willing to sacrifice the other interests' programs but not its own.

Despite this tendency, pressure groups have often supported ideological positions; that is, they have opposed their own welfare to sustain some real or imagined general principle. Skilled industry leaders have sometimes overcome ideological obstacles to find ground for mutual agreement on housing programs, but have often found their organizations too rigidly committed to positions to adapt to changing conditions. Pressure groups support and are supported by Federal agencies, and sometimes secure their objectives through administrative means. A thorough airing of the objectives sought by different groups, and information and knowledge concerning housing conditions, the industry, and its markets are required for constructive debate.

For nearly a century housing has been a matter of public and community concern in the United States. During these years groups representing all kinds of interests—recreation, public health, business, municipal efficiency, and the like—have slowly come to join at least a part of their effort in programs designed to improve conditions of urban life, to prevent or eliminate slums, and to provide better housing. In earlier days these groups sought to achieve their objectives through education and private philanthropy, later through the use of the powers of local government. It was not until the Depression and the years following World War II that housing policy came to be recognized as an integral part of national economic policy.

Political Issues in the Housing Economy

The politics of housing and urban renewal form a fascinating chapter in national development because of the thin line that separates public from private objectives in housing policy. During the last twenty-five years new forms of partnership between government and business have emerged in housing which illustrate both the possibilities and the problems in a mixed economy. The continuing debates over the course of national housing programs illuminate the roles private groups and government play as they settle important policy issues, and they bring to sharp focus the means a democratic society employs to resolve important political issues regarding the nature of social organization and the means to be used in achieving public and private purposes.

Beginning in 1930 those who were concerned with improving national housing conditions progressively succeeded in obtaining the intervention and assistance of the national government on behalf of their objectives. But even a measure of national agreement upon the desirability of Federal intervention brought arguments as to how Federal powers and policies should be brought to bear on housing and urban renewal. There are some who hold that Federal aid should first be allocated to those people who most need aid and can least afford to take care of their own housing. Others contend that the cost of providing good housing for all the indigent families is beyond our national fiscal capacity and that our economy will benefit most by providing government aid to the more prosperous families who need it least. Relatively minor governmental expenditures, it is argued, will provide incentives for these families to seek even better housing and in doing so to enlarge the total housing supply. By this means more good housing will eventually filter down to families who cannot now afford it.

The most bitter arguments arise, however, over the distribution of the benefits of government programs as between different business interests. Savings and loan groups seek to advance their welfare and their share of the total mortgage market through the Home Loan Bank System. Other classes of lending institutions which benefit more from the Federal Housing Administration want to see its activities maintained, and consequently oppose, or at least do not support, other programs. There is controversy between those sections of the building industry primarily interested in sales housing and those sectors of the industry primarily interested in the construction of rental housing. The ancient arguments between borrowers and lenders which have persisted throughout our national history find their counterpart in the politics of housing, with those representing borrowers arguing for longer amortization periods and lower interest rates and those representing savers and lenders arguing for higher interest rates and more restrictive credit policies.

A more fundamental, more obscure, but basic controversy in national housing politics is the struggle between those who try to enlarge the housing sector of the economy and those who compete for the consumer's dollar in other fields. The historic decline of consumer expenditures for housing reflects the rapid expansion and overwhelming competitive strength of services and other consumer durable goods. The shift of consumer expenditures from housing to automobiles has resulted, at least in part, from huge governmental expenditures for the facilities automobiles require—roads and highways. Those concerned with the housing economy argue that housing is a far more essential commodity in our society and that massive governmental expenditures to facilitate the use of automobiles and to increase consumer expenditures for them do not deserve the priority they receive. But the automobile industry, organized into vast industrial giants, effectively uses the power of advertising to create public demand for its products. As ever more roads are necessary to enable consumers to use their automobiles, the industry gives powerful support to campaigns for prodigious amounts of Federal aid to highways. The housing industry, fragmented and divided, has had no similar resources to create a climate of consumer demand either for its products or for the aids which government might provide to make them more effectively available.

Another fundamental political issue is the conflict of interest between those concerned with suburban and rural areas and those concerned with urban and central-city areas. Our basic systems of housing aid give enormous advantages to people who like to live in suburban and rural nonfarm areas and offer few comparable economic advantages or incentives to people who like to live in central cities. Policy makers, concerned about central-city development, slowly have come to recognize these differentials in aid and now seek to redress the balance by obtaining more nearly comparable aids for urban and central-city districts.

Broad political issues such as those outlined above are rarely debated on their merits. In the four-year controversy that preceded the Housing Act of 1949 they were, it is true, well aired in two congressional elections and one presidential election, but more commonly they are argued from the standpoint of special programs. A debate over the terms under which FHA may insure existing residential properties masks, for example, a struggle between different classes of lending institutions to secure a larger proportion of the home mortgage market. An argument over "Fanny May's" discount rates is one between borrowers and lenders and between different classes of lending institutions. The controversy as to whether the FHA shall insure mortgages on rental properties at 90 per cent of value or 90 per cent of necessary current costs is at base a struggle between developers and lenders.

The Pressure Groups and Their Organizations

The political processes involved in reaching agreement on housing issues may best be illustrated by a description of the organizations that were involved in the debate from 1944 through 1949 over the Wagner-Ellender-Taft bill which, when the legislative dust had settled, became the Housing Act of 1949. The debate arrayed two great coalitions against each other: a score of business groups and well over fifty so-called public-interest groups. The debate really revolved around relatively minor issues, for there was a wide measure of agreement on some fundamental matters by both sides; but it brought into play trade and reform organizations which used many propaganda and pressure techniques on behalf of the positions they favored. The public record of their activities provides a remarkable acount of political action in housing.

According to the published hearings of a committee of the House of Representatives, twenty-three business organizations took a position in opposition to the Wagner-Ellender-Taft bill. Their opposition was directed not at the proposed aids to private enterprise, but at the bill's public housing provisions—and to a lesser degree to its urban redevelopment and research proposals.

Four organizations formed the core of the opposition: the National Association of Real Estate Boards, the United States Savings and Loan League, the National Association of Home Builders, and the United States Chamber of Commerce. Closely allied with this group and following it on major issues of policy were five other organizations: the American Bankers Association, the Mortgage Bankers Association of America, the Building Products Institute, the National Retail Lumber Dealers Association, and the Associated General Contractors. Still other allies were thirteen organizations representing apartment house owners, building materials manufacturers, specialized subcontractors, prefabricators, and the like.

The supporters of the Wagner-Ellender-Taft bill were an even larger and more diverse group. The core of this group was the National Housing Conference, the National Association of Housing Officials (now the National Association of Housing and Redevelopment Officials), the American Federation of Labor, and the Congress of Industrial Organizations. Closely related to them were five veterans' organizations: the Veterans of Foreign Wars, the American Legion, the American Veterans

Committee, the Jewish War Veterans, and the Catholic War Veterans; organizations representing the three major religious denominations; the United States Conference of Mayors; the League of Women Voters and the American Association of University Women; the Urban League and the National Association for the Advancement of Colored People. Allied to these organizations were fifty-four others representing public health and welfare, settlement houses, churches, cooperatives, and so on.

The composition of the two coalitions changed from time to time as organizations defected or shifted position. The following descriptions are of the core organizations on each side and some of their influential supporters.

The National Association of Real Estate Boards, an organization with a reported 44,000 members in 1,100 communities, supported a Federally chartered mortgage discount bank in the 1920s and early 1930s. In 1934 it came out in favor of the FHA mortgage and later it encouraged the introduction of the first proposals for Federal aid to urban redevelopment.

The National Association of Home Builders was established during the war years as an affiliate of the National Association of Real Estate Boards, but a few years later broke away from its parent and became an independent organization. By 1950 it had 16,000 members organized into 130 local home builder associations. Its propaganda strenuously opposed the public housing program as "socialistic" or "communistic" and as being in direct competition with private home-building activity, and just as vigorously supported the expansion of the FHA mortgage insurance program, the VA mortgage guarantee program, and the liberalization of mortgage terms available under both FHA and VA. Its primary interest was in the development of single-family, detached suburban houses.

The United States Savings and Loan League, organized in 1892, represents most of the savings and loan associations in the United States; it had 3,600 members in 1950. Savings and loan associations promoted and supported the Home Loan Bank Act of 1932 and expansions of it in 1933 and 1934. They opposed the establishment and later the extension of the FHA mortgage insurance system. Although the savings and loan institutions of the country had been the primary beneficiaries of Federal aid during the 1930s and had benefited directly from the activities of the Home Owners Loan Corporation, by the late war years the League proposed the early liquidation of the Home Owners Loan Corporation's remaining portfolio at some expense to the government and at a substantial prospective profit to the member institutions. This action incurred the strenuous opposition of the Home Loan Bank commissioner of that day and promoted dissension among the members of the League. As a result a rival organization was set up. The National Savings and Loan League urged the re-establishment of the Home Loan Bank Board as a quasi-independent agency and, when this proposal was incorporated in the Wagner-Ellender-Taft bill, lent its support to the bill.

The United States Chamber of Commerce with its 2,600 local chambers was actively opposed to the Wagner-Ellender-Taft bill, and there is some evidence that the Chamber's Construction Division served as a coordinating agent for the opposition at certain crucial periods. The Chamber's opposition to the bill was based largely on its opposition to any further expansion of governmental expenditures or financial commitments. The Chamber did support, however, the expansion of the FHA system of mortgage insurance, as it has perennially supported other aids to business.

The Mortgage Bankers Association of America with 1,200 member mortgage bankers and brokers supported a continuation and expansion of the FHA mortgage insurance system but opposed the public housing and slum clearance features of the bill. Its members are mortgage brokers who engage very heavily in the writing and servicing of FHA-insured mortgages, particularly for life insurance companies and commercial banks. The American Bankers Association, representing 15,000 commercial banks in the United States, took a similar position. On the other hand, the National Association of Mutual Savings Banks, representing the mutual savings banks in the Northeastern part of the United States, supported the major features of the bill, including the public housing and urban redevelopment titles. In this respect the mutual savings banks reflect the fact that business opposition to the legislation was far from unanimous.

The National Housing Conference played the role of coordinator for the interests that supported the legislation. This organization, consisting of 3,000 individual members, had been established in the early 1930s to promote public housing legislation; later it broadened its interests to include urban redevelopment and renewal. The NHC had support from a few business leaders and labor, veterans, and religious, welfare, and other civic groups.

The National Association of Housing Officials was a closely related organization. Its 4,000 members were chiefly members and employees of local public housing agencies. Organized in the early 1930s, its primary purpose was the development and expansion of the public housing program and the advancement of the professional status and interest of those engaged in that program. It later extended its interests to urban redevelopment and renewal.

The two major labor organizations of the United States, the American Federation of Labor with 7½ million members and the Congress of Industrial Organizations with 6 million members were strong advocates of the Wagner-Ellender-Taft bill. The American Federation of Labor's position rested in some degree on the special interest of its building trades department in employment opportunities in construction, but it gave vigorous approval to urban redevelopment proposals and Federal mortgage insurance, particularly for cooperative housing projects. The Congress of Industrial Organizations had no such special membership interest in the bill's employment aspects and spoke chiefly on behalf of its members as consumers of housing.

Allied with these core organizations supporting the Wagner-Ellender-Taft bill were municipal, civic, religious, and veterans' organizations of considerable importance. The American Municipal Association representing the officials of 9,500 cities through state leagues of municipalities consistently supported the bill although it did not engage in aggressive lobbying. The United States Conference of Mayors, representing the larger cities of the nation, fought hard for the bill.

Protestant, Catholic and Jewish groups supported the bill

through the Federal Council of Churches of Christ in America, the National Catholic Welfare Conference, and B'nai B'rith. Because of their wide representation, they were regarded as being highly influential even though they did not engage in the intensive propaganda activity typical of more single-purposed organizations. The same was true of the American Association of University Women and of the League of Women Voters.

The veterans' groups were among the important supporters of postwar housing legislation, apparently recognizing that comprehensive housing legislation was the means of obtaining housing assistance for lower-income veterans. The American Legion supported the Wagner-Ellender-Taft bill even when some state chapters opposed it vociferously. Indeed, the struggle within the American Legion between proponents and opponents of the legislation was among the most dramatic of the struggles over the adoption of the legislation.

Finally, there was a pressure group among the Federal agencies involved. The Federal bureaucracy tends to reflect the divisions of opinion which exist in the political world outside Federal agencies. Relative influence, the state of readiness for political action, and willingness to exercise pressure varies from agency to agency and from time to time. During the late war years, the staffs of the National Housing Agency, the Federal Public Housing Authority, and, in lesser degree, the Federal Housing Administration, conducted a number of studies which provided much of the factual background for the Wagner-Ellender-Taft bill and presented their findings at hearings conducted by Senator Robert A. Taft.

In addition, because it is fairly usual for counsel for the several housing agencies to serve as advisers to the Senate and House Banking and Currency committees, both their knowledge of the legal problems involved and their judgments as to desirable courses of action doubtless exercised strong influence on the course of the legislation. There were also unquestionably times when the field offices of the several Federal agencies served a staff or intelligence function for the pressure groups who were contending for legislative change.

Critical support or opposition came at different times from the Department of Commerce, the Department of Labor, the Federal Reserve Bank, and other agencies of government not directly involved in housing legislation but having strong peripheral interests in it. In the closing hours of debate on the 1949 Housing Act which the President was supporting, the Federal Works Agency appeared with the opponents of the redevelopment title to urge that the program be modified and vested in that agency rather than in the National Housing Agency. Thus does the executive establishment speak with several voices reflecting different interests.

The Balance of Power

The effective political power which was mustered by the two opposing coalitions proved to be surprisingly evenly balanced. The opponent coalition was able to provide a considerably larger full-time staff in Washington during the four years of debate than could the proponents, and their propaganda material was of a far higher professional quality. The hearings of the House Committee on Lobbying indicate that their financial resources were considerably greater, too. The Realtors' Washington committee, which was merely one organizational wing of the core group of the opponents, had a national budget in 1949 of more than twice the annual budget of the National Housing Conference, the central organization for the supporters. On the other hand, the numerical strength of the opponents was considerably smaller than that of the proponents.

However, some of the opponent groups had the advantage of effective grass-roots community organization. Thus, the thousand-odd local real estate boards and the chapters of the National Association of Home Builders and the United States Savings and Loan League constituted powerful instruments for political pressure in the home communities where it counted most. For many years it had been the practice of local savings and loan institutions to elect members of Congress to their boards of directors. This fact doubtless contributed to congressional understanding of the problems of the savings and loan industry and to congressional interest and responsiveness to the organized representatives of savings and loan interests.

The supporting organizations, on the other hand, claimed to represent a majority of the people of the United States but by no means spoke for a majority of those that knew or cared about the bill. The 60 million American citizens in towns and cities represented in Washington by the United States Conference of Mayors had almost no direct personal interest in the activities of the Conference. Similarly, most of the 13 million members of the two major labor organizations or the 50 million or more Americans represented by the three major religions whose national organizations supported the legislation had very little direct interest in the campaign which their leaders were supporting.

There were dissenting opinions in both camps. The narrower the purposes of a voluntary special-interest organization, the more likely it is to reflect the members' views accurately. Hence very broad purpose organizations—like those for labor, veterans, and religious interests—may not be so representative of members' views on specific problems. If this is true, it raises a fundamental problem in the politics of housing, for the special interests of certain businesses are always actively served by the national organizations that represent them. The citizenry as a whole is rarely represented and seldom aware of the problems involved. Almost all producers are organized, but few consumers are. Those who seek a public dollar are apt to be on hand where legislative decisions are made; the citizenry, whose dollar is sought, is likely to be home mowing the lawn.

Local interests and issues in housing differ from those on the national scene, but on the whole they typify the same organizations, controversies, debates, and solutions. The principal difference is that local organizations are much less concerned, as might be expected, with the ideologies involved—much as they may use ideological slogans—than they are with strictly local issues growing out of neighborhood composition and small-business activity.

This is nowhere better exemplified than in Chicago where

immediately after passage of the Wagner-Ellender-Taft bill a controversy over the selection of public housing sites broke out and raged for two years with extraordinary bitterness. Instead of Congress, the target for action was the city council which had to give its approval to sites proposed by the local housing authority. In much the same manner as occurred in the national arena, council members were highly responsive to the local pressure groups which they favored. However, none of the four core groups opposing national legislation played a major role in the local battle in Chicago. Even the United States Savings and Loan League, whose chief executive in Chicago was a leading member of a national antipublic housing lobby, saw no great advantage in direct intervention in the local situation. Nor, apparently, did the national labor unions or veterans organizations which had supported the national legislation. Indeed, there was often a switch from national to local attitude on the part of members of both groups. Some powerful members of the local banking fraternity and real estate group took a stand on public housing's side or stayed aloof from it entirely, and there were members of unions and veterans groups who, from within their neighborhood associations, strongly opposed public housing. The field office of the national Public Housing Administration was at times opposed to PHA's stand in the situation and vice versa. In the end, when compromise was finally reached, practically every organized group had shifted its ground at least once and sometimes more frequently.

Ideology and Interest in National Housing Legislation

In democratic societies it is fashionable to draw a contrast between special interests and the public interest. But what is the public interest? And how may the public interest be ascertained save through the kind of political controversy, argument, and public debate described above? Organizations to carry on such activities are essential to the functioning of a democratic society. They constitute the means through which public policy issues are brought to the attention of the nation and its communities, examined, debated, and eventually decided.

The so-called special-interest groups do sometimes engage in self-seeking activity. But very often they are motivated by broader ideological conceptions of the role of government in society. This fact is illustrated by several switches of position which occurred during the postwar debates on national housing policy. Consider, as an example, the Urban Land Institute which was organized to promote the redevelopment of central cities. During its formative years, it was instrumental in conducting a number of surveys on the need for urban redevelopment in central cities and in the development and introduction into Congress of one of the first bills seeking a national program of Federal aid for urban redevelopment. Despite this fact, it joined with its sister organization, the National Association of Real Estate Boards, and others in opposing Federal legislation to this end, apparently as a result of ideological concerns over the extension of Federal government activity into a new field and the increased public expenditures which would result.

Similarly, there is no question but that building materials manufacturers would profit from any enlargement of housing construction, public or private. The Producers Council, representing major manufacturers of building materials, pointed toward such a position in its preliminary discussion of postwar housing policy. But in the end it joined with the opposition in attempting to curtail Federal aids for public housing and urban redevelopment.

Similar changes of position occurred among the supporting groups. Outstanding among them was the action in 1946 of the American Legion in disavowing further support of priorities for veterans' housing. This led to the elimination of such priorities despite the fact that they were clearly designed to make available to veterans homes which might otherwise have gone to nonveterans. This action might be described by some as the assumption of temporary control of the Legion's housing policies by those who were more interested in profits from home building than in the welfare of the veterans. The American Legion later supported the bill.

Ideology and interest may be variously defined. For example, who is to say that home builders or mortgage lenders or labor or any other group will be best served in the long run by a particular kind of Federal activity or a particular level of Federal expenditures? Will the manufacturers of building materials benefit more from a different distribution of our economic resources, or will they benefit more from an expansion of Federal housing activities? Clearly, there must be at least a minimum level of semantic honesty if debates over policy are to expose the issues at stake. Generalized debates on whether urban renewal is socialistic or communistic mask the real issues and produce more heat than light. In the development of national housing policy, the issues revolve around questions of how much debt the Federal government can afford to carry, how much local communities can and should contribute to efforts to improve housing standards, what classes of people will benefit from resulting housing, and what classes of business will provide it. If it is true that the efforts of some of housing's interest groups to liquidate controls on housing in 1946 helped advance the interests of other sectors of the economy, it can justifiably be argued that the national welfare would have been advanced by a little more self-interest on the part of the home-building industry and the manufacturers, mortgage lenders, and other groups who participate in it.

The claim of some groups that they oppose the enlargement of Federal activities and programs is difficult to support. At no time in the last twenty-five years has any of the groups opposing the expansion of Federal aids to housing generally opposed the expansion of Federal aids specifically to its sector of the housing economy. Thus, "opposition to government expansion" really means opposition to government expansion of aids which would be of primary benefit to other groups and support for aids which would be of particular benefit to the group immediately at hand.

One of the conclusions that might be drawn from these observations is that there is little probability that the aggregate of Federal activity will ever be reduced, since the aggregate impact of all pressure groups is for continued expansion of all programs. Only if some groups were willing to sacrifice their own special interests by advocating the elimination of programs which are of special benefit to them would there be any real prospect that

Federal activities could or would be reduced appreciably. Viewed in this light, the central concern must be for an honest appraisal of the benefits and costs of each program. Most people have little concern whether savings and loan institutions or mutual savings banks or mortgage bankers or commercial banks or life insurance companies have government mortgage guarantees, or whether any one or several of these groups should have their competitive interests advanced vis-à-vis the others by a governmental program. But it is their concern that there should be prompt, economical, and efficient mortgage service in all parts of the country through whatever institutions can most efficiently provide it.

The quality of leadership involved in pressure groups may exercise a decisive influence upon their success or failure and upon their contributions to national policies and programs. In the history of national housing legislation some leaders stand out as men with a clear sense of strategy, prodigious tactical skills, and a readiness to exercise their influence to shape national housing programs effectively. As they gained experience they repeatedly sought to develop accommodations with their opponents in an effort to advance viable national housing policies. At the height of the controversy over the Wagner-Ellender-Taft bill, for example, one National Association of Real Estate Boards leader tried hard to develop a common program with the CIO for cooperative housing. Too often, however, an organization finds itself so heavily committed to ideological positions that it is unable to adapt itself to the strategic changes or tactical shifts signaled by a farsighted leader.

The positions of almost all of the pressure groups in housing have shifted with changing circumstances and changing concepts. In the depression years representatives of the building industry expressed little opposition to the expansion of governmental programs. Any aid was helpful when all were unemployed. But there was intense competition as to who would get aid. The widely held assumption that the Depression would resume after the war produced considerable agreement on the need for a full complement of Federal aids to private housing, urban redevelopment, and public housing. The Wagner-

Ellender-Taft bill might have been adopted almost without controversy in the fall of 1945 or in early 1946. But then it became clear that the postwar period was to be one of prosperity. The building industry promptly disavowed government aids for slum clearance and demanded only government mortgage insurance and guarantees and an opportunity to compete in a boom market. Booms do not last forever, however, or they produce excessive demands for money which reduce the mortgage funds available to home building. When these circumstances arose, industry opinion divided again: Builders wanted credit even if government lending ("secondary market support") was needed. Lenders wanted higher interest rates and resisted the extension of credit aids. Then in 1953 and 1954, when housing production was down by 20 per cent, some of the most vigorous and sincere opponents of public housing and slum clearance discovered rehabilitation and ended by agreeing on an urban renewal program that, on a much narrower basis, they had opposed earlier.

In no small degree many modifications of positions or reversals of positions come from a clearer perception of the effects of various proposals and a clearer understanding of the problems involved. Often the staff work of advisers to leaders in pressure groups is an important element in developing better programs. But even so, the leaders of all groups are from time to time misinformed or lack information essential to an intelligent analysis of the problems at hand and the solutions proposed to those problems. At times the Federal government has been extraordinarily helpful in shedding light on housing problems by providing a comprehensive set of facts and an appraisal of alternative possible programs. At other times it has failed almost wholly to provide adequate data for intelligent judgments. In recent years the amount of factual knowledge available for public decision-making on housing and community development has diminished rather than increased.

Pressure Groups and Administrative Action

It is widely recognized that Federal administrative agencies tend to become subservient to the interests of the particular groups they serve. Thus, the Federal Housing Administration enjoys the most vigorous and sustained support of home builders and certain classes of mortgage lenders. The Home Loan Bank System enjoys the support of savings and loan associations. The Veterans Administration's loan-guarantee program draws support from veterans' groups, and so on. These administrative agencies understandably tend to respond to the administrative and policy suggestions of their support groups. As a consequence, the pressure groups can often achieve changes in policy through administrative action or through administrative support of legislative proposals.

Where the administering agency is subject to dual or conflicting pressures, it may be forced to consider alternative policies and to weigh the public costs and benefits involved in those policies. But where the administering agency is not subject to conflicting pressures it unquestionably tends to sacrifice broader public purposes in favor of the narrower interests of its supporting groups. As a consequence of the sustained interest of business groups in the FHA program and the almost total absence of any countervailing pressure from consumer groups, the Federal Housing Administration has since its inception tended to improve benefits available to mortgage lenders and to the builders of sales housing. By contrast, it has developed few effective means to further the rental housing program—the pressure is simply lacking; or to improve the quality of its protection of consumers—again, pressure is lacking. Similar administrative practices can be cited with respect to other Federal agencies.

Because of this tendency of administrative agencies to represent and reflect the special interests of their clientele, it is easy for them to lose sight of their broader general purposes. One of the most serious problems of Federal administration is how to interpose some higher supervisory authority as a watchdog of public concerns. The only effective limitation upon demands for ever larger budgets comes, in the case of the several Federal housing agencies, from the Administrator of the Housing and Home Finance Agency, and the Bureau of the Budget, and the White House. Their supervisory and policy control attempts to assure that the broader public purposes intended by Congress in its original authorization are not slowly subverted and undermined in favor of the narrower purposes of support groups. The need for such supervision can be modified to the extent that there are built into each agency's program countervailing pressures which force the agency to balance and reconcile pressures on it.

The Role of Political Leadership in Housing

Two axioms of contemporary political theory are demonstrated with considerable force by the history of Federal intervention in housing. These are the concept that executive power considerably exceeds legislative power in the modern state, and that the multiplicity of interests embraced by the two major political parties precludes basic changes in our laws unless both parties agree.

Executive political leadership, specifically that of the President, was largely responsible for our basic housing programs. The Home Loan Bank Act, drafted in President Hoover's Department of Commerce; the Home Owners Loan, National Housing, and United States Housing acts, drafted in the executive offices of President Roosevelt; the Housing Act of 1949, also drafted in the executive offices of President Roosevelt and supported and adopted under President Truman's administration; and the Housing Act of 1954, drafted by a committee appointed by President Eisenhower, bear witness to this leadership. Although the legislative branch has been able to block, ratify, or modify legislation, it has rarely initiated major changes. Not only is it the responsibility of the executive branch to respond to public needs by proposing necessary action to meet them, it is only the executive branch, with its institutionalized access to data and opinion, its permanent experts, its systematic methods of examination, and its operating experience, that can effectively analyze the complex forces at work within the economic and administrative system and judge the desirability and workability of new proposals.

Housing legislation has been bipartisan legislation through most of its history. From 1945 on, major bills have almost invariably had bipartisan sponsorship, always bipartisan support. In Democratic and Republican Congresses minority votes have been indispensable to passage. Democratic support has usually been proportionally greater than Republican. Northern Democratic senators and congressmen and some nationally known Southern Democrats have usually combined with the Northeast urban Republican senators and congressmen from urban areas to support housing legislation. Opponents of housing legislation are drawn from Southern Democrats and Midwest and rural Republicans.

The platforms of both parties traditionally reflect this bipartisanship. While Democratic platforms have often been more specific in their housing pledges, Republican platforms have made generalized statements construed as support for all types of existing housing legislation. The bipartisan character of housing support might have come under question, because so much of it was adopted initially under Democratic administrations, if major programs had not been continued or extended under the Eisenhower administration. The very balance of exterior pressures gives political leadership in both parties freedom for maneuver. If either business or consumer groups carried a preponderance of power this opportunity might not exist.

It has been said that the most effective means of adult education is public controversy. Whether or not this is true, it is clear that the active participation in public decisions by organizations representing different interests and groups helps to clarify policy by informing the public—or publics—on the issues. Only through politics and political pressure can a democratic society define goals and select the appropriate means to carry out a policy, whether for urban renewal or any other public purpose.

In these efforts, however, it is indispensable that the facts be available so that the debates on public policy are based upon an accurate understanding of the problems, the resources available for their solution, the alternative means of solving problems, and their costs and benefits. This means that there must be fact-gathering and fact-analyzing organizations able to carry on the continuing investigation which is essential for reasonable discussion and decisions on housing and urban development.

Where vigorous political pressures are absent, there is usually inaction. If public leadership is timorous, weak, or inept, it is usually because private leadership is lacking.

THE COMMUNITY

Chapter 16

MUNICIPAL PROGRAMS
FOR URBAN DEVELOPMENT

In fifty years the annual expenditures of local governments in the United States rose from $1 billion to over $30 billion. This increase resulted both from urban growth and from the pressures on government to maintain an efficient, livable environment. Cities require transportation systems, trained workers, recreation spaces, welfare systems, space and facilities for commercial and industrial growth, and safe housing. As citizens and businesses seek new services and higher service standards, cities face higher maintenance expenditures and more rapid replacement of facilities.

Municipal governments have steadily broadened their powers and programs to meet the demands of an expanding economy. Early regulatory actions and public utility programs have been supplemented by new measures of planning, public housing, redevelopment, code enforcement, and capital programming. "Urban renewal" has come to mean not only specific Federally aided activities but also the coordination of all municipal efforts for urban improvement and development. Coordinating numerous complex programs and obtaining financing for them out of local, state, and Federal funds are main tasks for municipal politics and administration.

During the nineteenth century the leaders of American communities became aware of the importance of some kind of community action to improve housing conditions, particularly those of poor families. The first efforts were educational and were conducted by religious and welfare groups in an attempt to bring the conditions in slums to the attention of a wider public.

The immigrants and the migrants have always had the poorest housing. In 1835, Gerret Forbes, city inspector of New York, called attention to bad housing conditions in that city, particularly among recent immigrants. The first systematic analysis of the slum appeared in Lemuel Shattuck's census of Boston in 1850. In one of the documents which served to awaken America's conscience to the problem of housing blight and to launch the public health programs and social reforms which developed in the last half of the nineteenth century, Shattuck described the slum conditions under which Boston's immigrants lived.

During these same years there was intensive agitation for housing reform in Europe, particularly in Great Britain. Utopians stimulated the public imagination with descriptions of ideal communities in which all would be housed well, and (in some cases) in which wealth would be shared by all members of the group. Utopian settlements in the United States constitute an interesting chapter in our national development.

All these expressions of concern led in the second half of the nineteenth century to the formation of associations for the improvement of conditions of the poor. The specific purposes of the associations were numerous. Some groups agitated for the establishment or improvement of county poorhouses where paupers might be housed, clothed, and fed. Others sought to enlighten industrialists and persuade them to construct company housing. Still other groups examined and publicized housing and environmental conditions in the slums and blighted areas of cities, and worked through churches and other institutions to educate the poor and the foreign-born and to combat drink and other vices commonly associated with slum living.

One of the fruits of this movement was the establishment of settlement houses in Boston, New York, and Chicago where education, recreation, and general information were constantly available to the neighborhood. As settlement houses expanded their resources and their activities, they became community centers through which the slum dwellers had access to means to improve their situation.

During the same years, philanthropists, particularly in Boston and New York, began to build housing for the poor. Groups of prominent persons established limited-dividend corporations which built, owned, and operated tenements. Well-meaning as these efforts were, they produced no significant volume of new housing. But limited-dividend corporations were pioneers in the development of apartments or tenements which provided light and air to interior rooms. This advance was in sharp contrast to the tenements being built by speculators. Often these were six rooms deep and had windows only in the outer rooms.

The most lasting effects of these reform movements were the adoption of building codes to ensure the structural safety of dwellings and later, at about the turn of the twentieth century, laws to guarantee light, air, and sanitation in newly built tenements. In New York, in particular, thousands of tenements were built under so-called "old law" regulations of this kind. They met the law requiring that each room have a window leading out on the air shaft, but the air shaft was usually four stories high and only two feet across between adjoining and abutting buildings. The standards were raised at a later time to require that air shafts must open to the front or the rear of buildings. This change provided interior rooms with more effective light and air. The basic tenement house law also insisted for the first time that all buildings have some sanitary facilities. Each apartment did not have to have them, however; legally, they might be in the basement or rear yard.

Although regulatory measures such as these markedly improved newly built tenement houses, they left a large number of existing tenements untouched. It was a half century later, after World War II, that many American cities began to adopt ordinances requiring old buildings to be brought up to such minimum standards of health and sanitation as had been governing new construction for many years.

Tenement laws, building codes, and plumbing and electrical codes had one effect which was not anticipated: they increased the cost of new construction substantially. When the higher costs occasioned by conformity with the codes were added to the higher building costs that followed World War I, the effect was to make it practically impossible to build new housing at rent levels or prices within the reach of the lowest income groups. Although some new tenements were built in the early years of the twentieth century, the fact that they were allowed to become overcrowded from the start intensified efforts to control excessive occupancy by law. The building of tenements for initial occupancy by poor families was brought to an end in the early 1930s by the combined effects of construction standards and occupancy standards.

Actions which evolved steadily in the first half of the twentieth century included the beginnings of city planning, laws to regulate the uses of land, and the provision of community facilities. Governmental housing programs as such (except for those temporary ones generated by requirements of World War I) were not inaugurated until the depression years. Programs for the large-scale regeneration of communities through consolidated actions in housing and building regulation, slum clearance, rehabilitation, the provision of community facilities, and other efforts, did not start until after World War II.

Regulatory Devices

All the regulatory controls devised by local government—tenement laws, building codes, housing ordinances, zoning and subdivision regulations—have as their principal purpose the prevention of abuses: people must not be allowed to live in unhealthful and unsafe buildings, land values must be protected, the community must not be made to pay unwarranted costs for speculative land development.

The police powers were invoked to protect public safety, often in emergency cases. For this reason the legal tradition recognized that the property of an individual might justifiably be sacrificed, sometimes, to protect the public without compensating the individual for his losses. Today police powers have been broadened to cover many problems from the control of poisoned food to requirements for bathrooms in houses, and the zoning of land for agricultural use. In some cases the controls impose real financial burdens or otherwise deprive individuals of actual or potential property rights. Because society does not compensate the individual for these real or imagined losses, the police powers are surrounded by elaborate legal, administrative, and other safeguards. In addition, the degree of control is usually minimal. Thus housing codes may require the installation of a toilet, but not a full bathroom, or the installation of screens, but probably not exterior paint. For similar reasons the enforcement of codes is also often minimal. They are applied in extreme cases and violation is tolerated widely in the less noticeable cases.

As urban renewal programs expand, municipal government faces two problems, first that of enforcing codes which have long been on the books and developing more effective administrative apparatus for widespread enforcement, and, second, that of regularly revising the standards of what is to be enforced. In most cities enforcing staffs are so small that scores of years would be required to inspect every dwelling even once. Much larger enforcement staffs will be required to do a complete and continuing enforcement job. But even as present codes are being enforced, rising standards of living, broader public understanding, and greater resources make higher code standards possible and publicly acceptable. If we were willing to pay the economic and political costs of compliance, we could enforce these higher standards today. Since we are not, apparently we content ourselves with minimum standards, and seek to use other inducements to encourage individuals to adhere to the higher standards. Here the police power blends in practice with urban renewal programs in wholly new types of public action.

City Planning

Many of America's earliest communities—Savannah, Philadelphia, Washington, D.C.—were planned cities in that they were laid out from their start according to a physical scheme for streets and land subdivision. Rapid urbanization and the prospects of fast profits in land speculation brought to an end the idea of the community planned from its founding, and city planning in the United States largely disappeared during most of the nineteenth century. It was not until after the 1893 World's Columbian Exposition in Chicago that there was a national revival of interest in city planning.

The City Beautiful movement, partly the outcome of the Fair, was initially concerned with the development of civic centers, parkways, and parks. Its supporters promoted the establishment of independent city planning commissions to coordinate and plan these developments for municipal governments. But even the earliest of these city planning efforts usually included in their goals the elimination of slums and blight even though the commissions were powerless to do anything about it. The city planning movement developed parallel to the rise of regulatory devices. It has taken fifty years to bring the two together, as they are now in urban renewal programs.

Until the 1930s both civic and housing improvement remained fringe programs in city government. Not until the necessity to revive the national economy focused attention on them as having a high economic potential did city planning begin to provide the bridge between urban change for economic development and urban change for aesthetic and humanitarian objectives.

As a contribution to city government, the community planning agency gathers and analyzes data on employment, population, income, land use, transportation, trends in residential development, trends in commercial and industrial activities, and changes in consumer behavior. It often carries on continuing market analyses for housing, education, recreation, cultural services, and commercial facilities, and in other ways performs an intelligence function for the community, alerting it to changes and potential changes. It invites and stimulates public expression of possible community goals and then points out the logical consistency or inconsistency of each. In its ideal form, it can explore alternative means of achieving community goals and point out the costs and benefits of each.

In its general plan, the planning agency proposes a strategy for economic development and a distribution of land uses and population densities to meet the community's social and governmental requirements. A typical city plan usually allocates funds and land to highways, parking facilities, port, harbor, dock and railroad facilities, schools, parks, playgrounds, health and welfare centers, water, sewerage, gas and light facilities, and other community services like libraries, museums, auditoriums. The plan is a guide not only to public actions but also to private development.

An essential feature of most city plans is the delineation of residential neighborhoods, industrial districts, a central business district, and subregional and neighborhood shopping centers. The plan answers directly or by implication questions such as these: Is the city to be rebuilt at high densities with a hope of holding great numbers of people close to the center, or is it to be rebuilt at lower densities, thus displacing population ultimately into other areas? If high densities are chosen for some areas of the city, will they be competitive with other areas, and hold their planned population? Are they to consist predominantly of residential areas occupied by low-income families, or are they to contain enough pleasant features to attract or hold middle- and high-income families? If additional space is needed by business and industry, should such uses take precedence over residential uses and where? What combination of land uses and distribution of business and residences will best serve the objectives of the major groups in the community? Since urban renewal is the basic tool for preserving or changing the land use and density pattern of the city, it is essential that these basic questions be resolved through comprehensive planning or other public deliberations so as to guide specific renewal projects.

Public Housing

It is not surprising that the administration of local housing programs should have been vested in a special commission or authority. Commissions were widely used in American municipal government for new functions. The special authority seemed to have particular advantages, however, for the purposes of administering the public housing program. Since the authority was to receive most of its funds from the Federal government, a large amount of Federal supervision of local action seemed appropriate, presumably without raising conflicts between different levels of government.

Despite their antecedents of social reform, the first public housing programs in the United States were strictly employment measures intended to provide jobs for the unemployed and markets for idle building materials manufacturers. Because of depression conditions, hundreds of thousands of families had doubled up in the 1930s and hundreds of thousands of other families had returned to rural farm areas where they might at least scratch a living out of the soil. There were widespread vacancies in housing at all price levels, but vacancies were particularly high in slum areas where many old dilapidated buildings had been abandoned and boarded up. The population of major cities was static or declining. All of these conditions made the clearance of slum areas and their rebuilding with low-cost rental housing an attractive way of providing employment and stimulating recovery of the national economy.

When Congress adopted a permanent public housing program in 1937, the Act required that one substandard residential unit be demolished for each new one built and that the resulting dwellings be made available to low-income families who had previously occupied substandard dwellings. Thus, while the program was directly oriented toward clearing slum sites and rehousing slum dwellers, it was careful not to interfere with the private market for new housing. The fact that the public housing program did not add to the supply of housing, combined with the fact of its low-rent limitations, was assurance that housing would not be provided through public enterprise to families who might afford privately supplied dwellings.

By the end of World War II, conditions in the housing market were almost totally different from those which had accompanied the establishment of the public housing program. The nation faced its greatest housing shortage. All habitable dwelling units in any price class were fully occupied and three to five million families were doubled up. The greatest building boom in the history of the nation was under way to meet this unprecedented need for housing. To complicate matters further, a fast-rising level of personal income helped produce the greatest wave of births in the nation's history and a huge migration of families from farm and rural nonfarm areas into cities.

Under these circumstances, the construction and operation of public housing projects was very different indeed from the program local housing authorities had operated in the depression years. The clearance of slums became an acutely difficult and painful task involving the relocation of one or more families for every dwelling demolished, with the resulting further intensification of the housing shortage for all families. The relocation of families from slum sites became one of the most critical limiting factors in the public housing program. Where vacant sites were available local public housing authorities often found themselves in competition with private builders who were willing, sometimes eager, to build accommodations for high-income families on sites proposed for low-income families. To the extent that local authorities sought to avoid intensifying the housing shortage by building their first postwar projects on vacant land they often came into conflict with neighborhood groups who strongly resisted the introduction into their neighborhood of public housing projects with the accompanying "undesirable" low-income families.

Another problem arose when urban renewal programs began to make their demand felt for redevelopment sites. Some cities found that public housing built in the 1930s occupied land that in the 1950s logically required other uses. At the end of 1959, Buffalo, New York, successfully petitioned for the right to convert a state-subsidized low-rent public housing project to a middle-income cooperative. The reason advanced was that without this action the adjoining water-front area could not undergo the major upgrading proposed in renewal plans. This, in spite of local statements to the effect that there was no surplus of low-income housing units and that 20,000 substandard units still remained.

But boom conditions had other unforeseen consequences upon the public housing program. Under conditions of full employment most normal urban families made too much money to be admitted to public housing, which by law is restricted to the lowest-income families. However, hundreds of thousands of families from rural and farm areas, most of them unskilled in city occupations and many of them Negroes, were flooding into the larger cities. Since no new housing was being built for them and since they were usually discriminated against on account of their race or obvious lack of urban skills and education, they overcrowded the older areas of cities and in doing so contributed to their rapid deterioration. Slums began to expand as families doubled up in marginal areas and spilled over into double and triple occupancy of slightly better areas.

These facts meant that many of the applicants for public housing were those who had broken homes with no full-time wage earner, those who had health problems which deprived them of an average income, aged couples living on very small retirement benefits, and those who were usually both unskilled and discriminated against—Negroes, Puerto Ricans, Mexicans, and Orientals. Whereas in the 1930s the occupants of public housing were families showing distinct social improvement when compared with those still living in slums, as measured by declines in delinquency, crime, and disease rates, in the 1950s they were problem families revealing many of the same behavior characteristics as slum dwellers. Public housing could provide decent safe and sanitary housing but it could not overcome the social pathologies of such groups.

The problems of local public housing authorities have been further complicated by their obligations to urban renewal programs. By law and common consent, families relocated from any urban renewal, highway, or other public works project have a first priority for admission to public housing projects. In the 1930s local housing authorities could select the most deserving, the most ambitious, or the most eager for self-improvement among those who needed assistance; since then local housing authorities have had to take whoever was displaced by some other government agency's action—usually those who would not and could not be housed by anyone else. Inevitably these conditions put local public housing authorities in the middle of political controversies of the most intense sort. Far from being detached from local politics, housing authorities became involved in activities, such as relocating low-income Negroes, which are among the most controversial of municipal government.

The changed conditions which altered the circumstances under which local public housing authorities operate forced its strongest advocates and those responsible for its administration to review the character, scope, and administrative arrangements for the public housing program and point up both some past deficiencies and some new opportunities.

In many cities it is now widely believed that large public housing projects should be abandoned and that most future ones should be of small enough size to fit easily into the existing structure of neighborhoods in order to reduce the differentiation which exists between public housing projects and contiguous private residential development. Smaller-scale projects should also help the families which occupy them to become accepted by the surrounding community more quickly.

In the early years of public housing, preference in tenant selection was almost always given to families with children on the principle that future citizens should be favored. Recently, however, these preferences have shifted to the aged, partly because current legislation in response to the growing number and proportion of old people provides for them. In addition, this shift is partly due to the reluctance of public housing officials to fill their units with unwed mothers and other problem families who dominate the lists of potential tenants. Local political opposition to public housing diminishes when it is earmarked for the aged and so an increasingly high proportion of the projects which pass political screening now are for them.

In some cities it is also held by housing and welfare officials that the limitation of public housing to low-income families serves to deprive public housing projects of the kind of leaders and pace setters who helped lift the social standards of tenants in the thirties. Unless a neighborhood contains some families who are more ambitious than the general level, have higher standards of personal behavior, perhaps earn a little more money, and can provide leadership for community organizations, it will tend to deteriorate to the level of those with low aspirations. In recognition of these facts, Chicago officials award a year's free rent to the family that contributes most to an improvement of living standards in public housing and shows qualities of neighborhood leadership.

If existing public housing projects are to be a leavening influence they must have some leaven. If so, the arbitrary income limits which now force the upward mobile families to leave public housing projects must be relaxed so that those who wish to may remain. For these purposes, some cities believe that it would be desirable to permit public housing projects to charge full economic rents for higher-income families or for some proportion of them. It may also be desirable to permit the sale of public housing projects or parts of them to occupants whose incomes rise. Such a program of limited sale of public housing projects would also have the advantage of holding down or reducing the total proportion of the housing stock that is in public ownership even though this proportion is small.

Most American families in most cities obviously prefer single-family dwellings. There appears to be no good reason why public housing should not be built on scattered sites, as separate dwellings or small apartment houses, or should not consist of older dwellings bought and rehabilitated by local housing authorities. Nearly one hundred cities have embarked on scattered site projects, and in 1959 Philadelphia bought 200 row houses for rehabilitation. The first two-story brick house with basement to be rehabilitated in the pilot program was badly deteriorated. The cost of the house and its rehabilitation came to $9,500, considerably less than the cost of new construction.

Public housing programs are being reorganized. In some communities public housing agencies have already been combined with redevelopment or renewal agencies. In other communities they have come under the supervision of a mayor's coordinator of all housing and urban renewal and development activities. Whether through reorganization or through coordination, the broader community purposes to be served by public housing cannot be achieved by independent local housing authorities unless they are closely integrated with other municipal programs.

Urban Redevelopment

The urban redevelopment program authorized by the Housing Act of 1949 was conceived during the war years. It was designed to clear slum areas, reduce the cost of cleared land through public subsidy, and sell the land for appropriate private uses, principally housing. The program was based in considerable degree on public housing's experience with slum clearance in the depression years. The real estate and housing groups that backed the 1949 act reasoned that if public powers could be used to clear slums for public housing they could also be used to clear slums for other purposes. They recognized that in most instances the appropriate use for a slum site was private rather than public and sometimes nonresidential rather than residential. They urged that slum clearance and public housing be separated. Looking back to the social and economic imperatives of the depression years rather than ahead to those emerging for the postwar period, state and Federal urban redevelopment legislation foresaw little more than isolated blocks which, cleared of slums, would be sold for appropriate public or private uses.

As a consequence the organization of redevelopment agencies followed the earlier pattern of public housing. A special commission or authority was established pursuant to state law and appointed by the mayor with the approval of the city council, presumably to provide assurance of appropriate independence from political interference. The redevelopment authority could borrow funds from the Federal government or borrow funds directly with Federal guarantees and would have corporate flexibility in buying and selling properties. It also would attract as its commissioners a high quality of unpaid citizen leaders from business and civic circles. And because redevelopment authorities would deal in many instances with private investors, the authority form of responsibility would seem to create an atmosphere in which negotiations with private interests might be conducted most fruitfully. For all these reasons, most state enabling laws for urban redevelopment authorized redevelopment commissions which were to be constituted as special authorities by each municipality. (Sometimes public housing authorities were reconstituted in title and function to include redevelopment.)

The character of the first urban redevelopment programs seemed to confirm these expectations and to encourage the idea that the independent redevelopment authority was an appropriate municipal agency for carrying out the program. But it soon became clear that the conditions under which the first urban redevelopment projects were undertaken were far different from those of the depression years. The acute shortage of housing made relocation a major issue from the start. Competition among different claimants for land involved municipal governments in controversy and required the intervention of mayors and city councils. If slum sites were to be used for higher-income housing or for nonresidential uses, the housing shortage would be more acute. If displaced families were to be crowded into not yet wholly blighted areas, slum conditions would probably result. In addition the prevailing shortage of housing and the high occupancy of substandard housing were pushing the cost of slum clearance far higher than prewar experience had suggested would be the case.

The problem of marketing cleared redevelopment sites proved to be a complex one. In some communities where caution prevailed, sites were rarely cleared until a buyer was under contract. This usually meant that redevelopment was restricted to small sites where some peculiar feature created an opportunity for private investment and suggested that the availability of an interested investor rather than any over-all plan or strategy for the community should dictate priorities in urban development. In some communities where a policy was adopted which involved the acquisition and clearance of slum sites before any redeveloper was available, sites stood idle for several years until an investor appeared who was willing and able to acquire and develop them. Such situations understandably provoked community concern and intensified the hostility of persons who had been displaced from the area.

As communities began to develop a more systematic approach to urban renewal, along with programs for the eventual clearance of the whole blighted core of the city, the limitations of the urban redevelopment program and of its administrative machinery became increasingly apparent. It followed that some one municipal agency should be responsible not only for analyzing the existing supply of housing, but for planning its rehabilitation and conservation in order to serve the needs of the whole market; and not only for removing obstacles to private residential construction, but for actively helping to open new opportunities for all kinds of private investment. Urban renewal appeared to be the required formula for this complex meld.

Urban Renewal

In the Depression and early postwar years a few communities had begun to experiment with the enforcement of housing and sanitary codes on an area basis to abate the deficiencies of housing in blighted areas. They tried rehabilitating structures in relatively small areas and encouraged the spontaneous rehabilitation and upgrading of slightly better residential areas. In communities like Baltimore, where major efforts were undertaken to utilize all of the code enforcement powers of the community to improve neighborhoods, these experiments were undertaken in conjunction with parallel programs of urban redevelopment and public housing.

But these programs revealed serious problems for municipal administration. Code enforcement powers were scattered among health departments, building departments, fire departments, and departments of licenses and inspection, none of which was willing to surrender its code enforcement function to another. It was the rare municipality, indeed, that could muster the resources necessary for a systematic, unified code enforcement campaign in which all enforcement powers were brought to bear on an entire neighborhood through a single set of actions.

Even the best community programs in this field demonstrated that code enforcement was only one aspect of a comprehensive program for urban renewal. Enforcement might compel some property owners to bring their properties to minimum standards, but it could not induce others to improve their properties above the level of a minimum code. The inducement needed to evoke higher standards of improvement might necessitate rechanneling traffic around a neighborhood, or the installation of new community facilities such as schools and playgrounds, or the use of public powers of condemnation to clear out spots of hopeless blight in otherwise salvageable areas.

Moreover, codes with standards limiting the maximum occupancy of dwellings meant the provision of housing outside of blighted areas to accommodate the families who were living there at densities clearly in excess of the code's minimum. Enforcement raised problems of relocation just as did clearance.

Experiences like these led directly to the concept of urban renewal as it was expressed in the report of President Eisenhower's Advisory Committee on Government Housing Policies and Programs, and later embodied in the Housing Act of 1954. The requirements of that act for a "workable program" (later changed in title to a "program for community improvement") clearly recognized that all the available powers of municipal government must be brought into play to achieve a systematic attack on slums and blight. These included building and housing codes and their enforcement, and zoning and subdivision controls and their administration. The powers of condemnation available under urban redevelopment legislation were needed not merely for the clearance of large blighted areas but also for spot clearance and for the acquisition of properties which could be rehabilitated. Systematic programs were required for relocation housing. Public costs must be incurred for the provision of community facilities to prevent decline of basically sound areas as well as to encourage rehabilitation in deteriorating neighborhoods. And to augment, support, or demand the use of these public powers, well-informed citizen groups were essential. Appropriately enough, Plymouth, Massachusetts, was, in September, 1959, the one thousandth city to have a workable program approved by the Administrator of the Housing and Home Finance Agency. That approval brought 54 per cent of the urban population under local workable programs. By the end of 1960, Federal grants of about $1.9 billion had been reserved by the Urban Renewal Administration to assist 870 slum clearance and urban renewal projects.

The broad concept of a workable program for urban renewal reinforced the earlier view that all of these efforts desirably should be conducted in accordance with a comprehensive city plan for land uses, community facilities, traffic and transportation, other capital improvements, and housing. Further, as the new concept embraced not only slum clearance and rebuilding but the conservation of good areas, the arresting of blighting influences in areas just starting to decline, and the rehabilitation of areas which were already on the downgrade but still salvageable, the earlier concept that slum areas were somehow fixed in size gave way to the recognition that blight was a pervasive and growing influence and that continuous municipal and private action was required to control it.

Some communities recognized early that the level of new residential building in suburban areas is an important element in the rate at which and the extent to which blight spreads in a central city. Only through a high level of new construction can the supply near the top be increased enough to permit less good existing housing to filter down the income ladder. When the demand for older houses slackens, their prices go down. More housing then comes into the price range of that large proportion of low-income families who are not served by public housing, and some of it at least serves as a source of supply for families who must be relocated because of renewal and public works programs. Finally, rehabilitation of deteriorating structures becomes economically feasible. Thus new urban and suburban home building decisively influences a city's urban renewal program.

Municipal programs for large-scale urban renewal may require bulwarking with aids that are available only through state government. Greater discretionary power in effecting metropolitan organization would be helpful in some places as would be more flexible state limits on local taxes and debts. In lieu of fiscal self-determination, some states are diverting state-collected revenue directly to the purpose of local housing and renewal programs. In New York, for example, the state passed the Mitchell-Lama Limited-Profits Housing Companies Act in 1955 to provide $50 million of state monies for direct loans to builders of middle-income or cooperative rental housing projects. Under this act loans may be for 90 per cent of the cost of a project and tax exemption is allowed for 30 years up to one-half of a project's total value. Builders' profits are limited to 6 per cent of equity. The state authorized an additional $100 million of state money to limited-profit companies in 1958 and a year later amended the act to provide for a limited-profit housing mortgage corporation. The corporation is a vehicle to obtain $200 million of investment funds from insurance companies and banks to mix with state funds on a one-to-two ratio. Lending institutions participating in the corporation's program receive 30-year self-amortizing certificates bearing interest at 5½ per cent per year. By combining state and private funds the amount of middle-income housing built with state aid is expected to triple in New York communities.

The adoption of comprehensive urban renewal programs has brought into question most of the earlier forms of municipal organization for urban renewal. When public housing, redevelopment, code enforcement, rehabilitation, city planning, community facilities, capital programming, and state aids are all involved in a renewal program, the administration of them by separate, independent, and semiautonomous municipal departments, agencies, and authorities creates such obstacles and problems of coordination as to jeopardize the success of the entire venture. As a result, many municipalities are re-examining their municipal organization. Some municipalities have merely provided a mechanism for coordinating the programs of a number of independent agencies. Others have undertaken wholesale reorganization.

Philadelphia led the way for coordination and Baltimore for reorganization. The urban development coordinator in Philadelphia is an appointee of the mayor. He and his small staff are responsible for coordinating all programs of renewal, development, and redevelopment, for supervising area-wide code enforcement programs and other similar neighborhood demonstrations, and for advising on capital budgeting for the provision of community facilities.

In Baltimore a new agency was set up to develop programs of municipal aid to private development, both residential and nonresidential. To the new agency was transferred responsibility for urban renewal, public housing, area code enforcement, and relocation. Baltimore thus places in one central agency the responsibility for the core functions of urban renewal. Other functions like the provision of schools, parks and playgrounds, streets and street lighting, which can help create a climate to stimulate private investment and rehabilitation in residential areas, remain in their own departments but are integrated with the renewal program by a special assistant to the mayor.

No single scheme will be effective in all types of government. What works under a strong mayor plan of government may prove unsuccessful under a city manager plan. The commission form of government has its own peculiar problems. Major cities like Philadelphia, New York, and Chicago have very different problems from those of smaller communities like Decatur, Illinois, or Richmond, California, or Gadsden, Alabama. Three conclusions, however, are clear. First, urban renewal is being less and less considered on a project basis. It is no longer concerned with this or that isolated spot of slum or blight. Second, urban renewal has come to be recognized as the application of all the powers of municipal government to the treatment of the problems of the urban environment. It involves private investment, private maintenance, public investment, and public maintenance and operation. It necessarily involves almost all the departments of municipal government. Those functions which are central to urban renewal, including the use of the condemnation power, the provision of public housing, code enforcement and relocation, can no longer—according to an increasing number of public officials—be treated as isolated parts of renewal programs. Third, since this is the case, urban renewal requires the supervision of its various programs by the central authority in municipal government which makes major political decisions. In some cities this authority is the mayor or head of the dominant political party, in others the city manager and city council, and in still others, a commission. Urban renewal cannot be isolated from local politics. Indeed, it is central to local politics and will probably become an increasingly important issue in political campaigns.

Relocation and Assimilation

American cities have become a twentieth century melting pot for hundreds of thousands of families from rural and farm areas whose problems of assimilation are similar to those of European immigrants half a century ago. A generation hence many of them will have learned the skills and ways of urban society, but today this is true of only a few. Their problems are only intensified by the fact that many of them are Negroes. Otherwise they share many of the characteristics of earlier immigrants: low incomes, relatively low skills, and a transitional culture from a rural, familial, and static society to an urban, nonfamilial, and dynamic society. Many of them are eager to prosper, but they live under conditions which severely hamper their efforts.

On the other hand, wherever they go, low-income people bring with them problems of education and community organization and increased requirements for police, health, and welfare services. The fact that they are actively unwanted in most parts of a city is the central problem in urban renewal and other programs that involve displacement and relocation.

Some of these problems can be met by new forms of education and training for urban living, an urban version of the agricultural extension service. In other situations the use of social institutions and services, settlement houses and welfare centers, can help new or problem families to adapt themselves to new ways of life. But all of them are closely related to housing and the neighborhood. Thus if housing and renewal agencies are to achieve their purposes of eliminating the social slum as well as the physical slum, they must become either coordinators of or partners in a broad range of social services. These new purposes, too, require a broader view of housing and renewal, and their involvement in the central policy decisions of local government.

When urban renewal is conceived in this comprehensive way it becomes the major means by which cities carry out a city plan. The city plan, while it is usually couched in terms of the distribution of land uses, is also the community's plan for the distribution of population, determining as it does the density at which people live, the types and quality of residential areas they will occupy, and ultimately what they will pay for housing and community services. Thus, urban renewal programs must face the problem of how urban populations are to be distributed. This is not likely to be a temporary or short-range relocation problem. Rather, it is at the core of many of our most important urban functions.

Historically, relocation has been treated as an incident to other programs, as has the broader question of the distribution of the population throughout the metropolitan area. Since the war relocation has been accomplished largely by squeezing displaced families into the existing supply of housing. In Chicago, during the decade 1948–1958, 86 per cent of relocated families were accommodated in private housing.

In 1961, the commissioner of the Urban Renewal Administration announced that from the beginning of the program of Federally aided slum clearance and urban renewal in 1949, through June 30, 1960, over 85,000 families of the nearly 94,000 formerly living in project areas were rehoused; the others were in the process of moving. Less than 8 per cent moved to substandard dwellings but the whereabouts of some were unknown and might increase this proportion. Though the quality of housing for the relocated families seems to have improved, their expenditures for housing were undoubtedly forced upward.

Public aid to families specifically requiring relocation merely serves to give them preference in obtaining the limited number of vacant units available, thus depriving others equally in need of housing but not being relocated with government assistance. These relocation policies may result in accelerating the deterioration of the areas forced to accommodate the displaced populations. It is only rarely that communities can build new housing on vacant land just to house families displaced by renewal programs. The seriousness of the situation is augmented by other improvement and construction activities. The Federal highway program, for instance, is creating a relocation problem at least equal to the one arising from urban renewal. And as communities build new schools, parks, and playgrounds the relocation requirements stemming from these types of public works will grow, too.

There is still another aspect of relocation that requires clarification of public policy. Almost all renewal and capital improvement programs either physically displace business concerns or, particularly if they are marginal enterprises, remove their markets. Just as the community requires policies for the distribution of urban population, the community also requires policies for the distribution of economic activity. Originally, the relocation of business was not recognized as a governmental responsibility in connection with urban redevelopment and renewal programs. Now at least relocation payments to business establishments have been authorized under Federal legislation. Since business provides the economic lifeblood for any urban area, it is essential that urban renewal planning provide opportunities for desirable business expansion and economically fair means for relocating businesses that have to be moved as a result of public works.

Beginning with their use of regulatory devices and going on to comprehensive urban renewal activities, it is evident that municipal leaders must develop clear-cut policies for housing and community development problems if they expect to solve these problems in any short time. By the end of 1960, eleven years after passage of the Housing Act of 1949, only 41 of the 870 projects approved for Federal urban renewal aid in 475 communities had been completed. On the whole, most city officials still try to deal with problems of slums and blight by treating the sore spots—a little code enforcement here, a little clearance there. This usually transfers the problems from one area to another as low-income families are shifted about. Instead, organized local interests and business must join more energetically with government in finding ways to make the housing market work more dynamically.

Only if additions are made to the housing supply for all income levels will we be able to sustain the total volume of new construction needed to permit filtration. And it is through the filtration of the normal supply that most of the housing requirements of our communities will be served. But filtration will work only if the housing market provides enough houses to go around and enough extra ones to create vacancies so that families can have freedom of choice and price in moving from one neighborhood to another.

Thus public agencies concerned with housing and urban renewal must consider housing market areas as a whole. Few communities have adequate data to do this. In the 1930s under the auspices of the Works Progress Administration many cities undertook real property inventories which were invaluable planning and policy aids as long as they were kept up to date. If every community with an urban renewal program made an annual housing market analysis part of its workable program, the returns in reliable data on which to base project determinations and resulting needed relocation housing would alone be worth the cost. In Newark, New Jersey, the City Planning Department has entered on IBM cards all data from a reassessment of property values. If, in addition, such cards could record relevant information on the housing market, it would be possible to measure by a quick statistical process housing improvement in terms of the relative effectiveness of different types of treatment in different areas. A constant inventory would be so valuable to real estate interests and investors that they might be ready to contribute to its cost.

As the units of government closest to popular pressures, municipalities have been compelled to create new programs, invent new agencies, and devise measures for their administration. The varied experiences of municipalities suggest that new forms of organization are required if public response to emerging development problems is to be effective.

Chapter 17

METROPOLITAN
ORGANIZATION AND
RESIDENTIAL EXPANSION

*Population growth has flooded across municipal boundary
lines into suburbs and unincorporated parts of urban areas, dramatically changing the distribution of population and the form
of cities. Problems of housing, highways, water supply, police
and fire protection, parks, transit, taxes, land use, schools, and
commercial and industrial growth do not end at municipal boundary lines. They run across them linking city to suburb, and
suburb to surrounding country.*

*Local zoning and building code decisions affect metropolitan
housing and industrial expansion, impose diseconomies upon
builders, and produce widely varying standards of local service
and local taxes for consumers. Many observers believe that some
form of metropolitan government may be essential to eliminate
these inequities and provide for metropolitan-wide services and
development opportunities. Others argue that local differences
provide greater freedom of choice or are so deeply cherished as to
be ineradicable.*

*Between the two extremes lie other possibilities: intergovern-
mental cooperation, joint programming of public improvements,
special districts, and service contracts. No one solution is likely to
prevail. Each has its costs and its benefits. Too rigid adherence to
existing local government forms may lead to further state and
Federal intervention where metropolitan-wide service or cooperation is essential to a metropolitan economy. Federal, state and local
agencies concerned with urban development in metropolitan areas*

314

are beginning to seek a better definition of the limits of their actions and responsibilities.

By 1960, 113 of the 180 million American people were living in the nation's 212 metropolitan areas, each such area consisting of one or two central cities and numerous surrounding suburbs.

Urban areas began to spread out long ago as people moved along railroad lines to small suburban communities. The movement was limited in the main to the well-to-do who concentrated in compact and exclusive residential suburbs. The growing use of the automobile, which was accompanied by new road systems, made a further spread possible after World War I. The rate of population growth during the depression years was slow, however; not many people could afford new housing anywhere. During those years urban growth drew upon land already supplied with streets, water, and sewerage systems, and it made use of community facilities built for an earlier generation either in the central city or in its immediately adjoining suburbs.

After World War II the pent-up force of housing demand, coupled with almost universal automobile ownership and an expanded network of highways, made it possible for builders to put up millions of new homes on the cheapest land available in the outer suburbs. The developed land was used up in the first few years following the war and existing community facilities were strained beyond their normal capacity. Fast-rising incomes combined with generous financing terms under FHA and VA made it possible for millions of families to buy the new houses. Most of these new homeowners had moderate incomes compared with those of the earlier suburbanites, but they were accustomed to urban services and expected them in the new tract developments that had recently been open countryside.

The shift to an urbanized metropolitan existence has caught us unprepared. Nowhere is our unpreparedness more apparent than in the failure of governmental policy to deal vigorously with the present results and the probable future consequences of this massive extension of the urban population and its housing. Involved are such questions as land use, fiscal capacity, community facilities, relocation, economic development. Confronting, but not solving, these problems are 16,210 independent governmental bodies: 256 counties, 2,328 townships, 3,164 municipalities, 2,598 special districts, and 7,864 school districts. The largest concentrations of governments are in the New York and Chicago metropolitan areas which have 1,074 and 954 governments respectively. As the accompanying table shows, Philadelphia comes next with 705 and even the least in the list, Detroit, has 250.

TABLE 10. NUMBER OF LOCAL GOVERNMENTS IN SELECTED
STANDARD METROPOLITAN AREAS, 1957

Standard metropolitan area	Local governments
New York–N. E. New Jersey	1,074
Chicago	954
Philadelphia	705
Pittsburgh	612
San Francisco–Oakland	414
St. Louis	400
Portland (Oregon)	337
Los Angeles–Long Beach	319
Detroit	250

Source: U.S. Bureau of the Census, *Census of Governments*, 1957, vol. I, no. 2.

Metropolitan Consolidation and Housing

In their study in this series, *Government and Housing in Metropolitan Areas*, Edward C. Banfield and Morton Grodzins singled out the effects that changes in the structure of government might have on the quality, quantity, and price of housing in metropolitan areas, and came to the conclusion that while changes might alleviate some of the problems of urban expansion, including those of housing and urban renewal, they could not solve them. In the view of Banfield and Grodzins, changes in government policy are far more important than changes in the structure of government.

The main points where governmental structure in metropolitan areas is often said to have adverse effects on housing and urban renewal are: (1) the lack of metropolitan planning, (2) multiple zoning, subdivision, and building regulations, (3) the limited legal powers of local governments, (4) tax deficiencies and inadequacies, and (5) the poverty of civic leadership.

LIMITATIONS OF METROPOLITAN PLANNING

Advocates of metropolitan planning claim that economies in public costs for facilities and services such as sewers, water systems, transportation, and schools will result from planned development of the metropolitan complex at predictable rates of growth; that metropolitan planning will ensure an adequate supply of development land served by suitably located highways and utility systems; that it will aid the relocation problem by viewing the housing situation throughout the area; and that it is an essential communication device between public and private interests which must rely on its fact-gathering and analysis as a basis for decision.

Only about half the states authorize metropolitan-wide planning. Most of such planning comes under one of these categories: a comprehensive plan of land use to guide the area's future development in respect to water and sewerage systems, recreation, highways, and the like; *ad hoc* plans for special projects like flood-plain control and river development, airports, and interurban rapid transit; technical assistance on matters of zoning, subdivision control, and building regulation to jurisdictions in the area which do not have their own technical staffs.

Banfield and Grodzins acknowledge that "progress in community development (and the housing that goes with it) will be facilitated by marshalling facts, pooling expertise, and ensuring collaboration among those concerned." They say, however, that the power of decision in metropolitan areas is too widely scattered to allow a high degree of coordination, and without metropolitan government there is no mechanism to enforce metropolitan plans. And they add, "people who argue for metropolitan planning are frequently arguing in effect not so much for planning as for a government having the powers to do what they want done."

MULTIPLE HOUSING CONTROLS

There is almost no uniformity among the zoning, subdivision, and building controls that are operative throughout a metropolitan area. As a result there is frequently a mixture of land uses that is unsightly and costly; there are severe diseconomies to the builder, who cannot easily assemble land in quantity or build to consistent specifications; and finally, there is an inequitable allocation of housing and community facilities. There is no doubt that suburban zoning, subdivision and building regulations help maintain the density of the central cities by making access to new residential areas more difficult. However, this problem would not necessarily be quickly solved if there existed a metropolitan government. Housing measures—such as relocation or a change in density—which are politically infeasible on an intercity basis do not become feasible merely by enlarging the area. Furthermore, the imposition of minimum standards throughout a metropolitan area may easily go beyond their necessary purpose of safeguarding the health and safety of the community to infringe on the essential freedom of the individual by requiring him to buy more housing and related facilities than he wants.

NARROW LEGAL POWERS OF LOCALITIES

Municipalities are under-represented in state legislatures; their ability to act efficiently and economically is frequently much curtailed. Moreover, state limitations on municipal debt deprive municipalities of necessary fiscal independence. Banfield and Grodzins believe that statutory and constitutional debt limits should be abolished. But they point out that complete municipal fiscal independence is unwise; instead there must be much closer coordination in taxing and spending policies between states and municipalities and between the Federal government and municipalities.

TAX DEFICIENCIES AND INADEQUACIES

In all metropolitan areas there are great inequities in property-tax assessments. These result from the decentralized organization of the tax system, and many experts believe that there should be a single tax jurisdiction to deal with revenue sources of the metropolitan area as a whole. Banfield and Grodzins agree that segmented tax jurisdictions and the resulting inequities of income and service are genuine impediments, "yet the consequences are not so overwhelming that they lead necessarily to a drastic structural reorganization of metropolitan government."

THE POVERTY OF CIVIC LEADERSHIP

The poverty of leadership is acute in many central cities. Many officials in these cities complain that business and professional people who might become civic leaders do not do so because they live in the suburbs. However, the roster of members of almost any important civic group in almost any large city shows that many men and women who live in the suburbs do concern themselves actively with development and improvement programs in the city. It is on official municipal boards and commissions that such people are most often missed; local laws frequently prohibit persons not living in the city from membership on city planning commissions, urban renewal authorities, and the like.

There is no doubt that these five conditions frequently impede effective metropolitan development. Some of them probably contribute to inequalities in service and to unjustified variations in the cost or quality of housing. None, however, would cease to exist if a metropolitan government were enacted. The fundamental causes of unsatisfactory housing, as other chapters in this book have shown, are poverty, discrimination, imperfections in the capital market that discourage the ready flow of investment into housing, the high cost of land, and the failure of consumers to demand, and builders to provide, a better product.

Government can improve matters by judicious policies: but it is thoroughly unlikely that any structural changes—not even consolidating 250 or a thousand political jurisdictions in a single metropolitan-area government—will do much to change the attitudes of people or the workings of the economy. Too many observers of the housing situation oversimplify it by seeking formal administrative changes rather than by rethinking basic policies.

Simplicity, uniformity, and symmetry in governmental structure are not necessarily admirable goals. Furthermore, we often take it too much for granted, Banfield and Grodzins point out,

that the presence of a large number of independent local governments in a single area means waste and duplication. That there may be even administrative advantages in decentralization is often overlooked entirely. Beyond problems of efficiency and economy, issues of community independence, sociability, and status are involved. Technical considerations concerning optimum areas for given services must compete for priority with political issues concerning the best organization for the public control of public officials. Issues of philosophy intrude: when does self-government in one locality impede self-government in another? Values of local control compete with values of area efficiency. A consideration of what is desirable in the way of organization ought to take into account the full range of problems. Intangibles—for example, the suburbanite's satisfaction in remaining apart from the central city—should be accorded some value.

Viewed in these terms, the present "Balkanization" of government in a metropolitan area may have many advantages for a people who enjoy having a wide freedom of choice. But even if it presents notable disadvantages, the substitution of an all-purpose government appears often to be politically infeasible. In the last thirty years there have been one hundred or more surveys of metropolitan organization but few surveys were followed by adoption of any of the major recommendations. The reason, Banfield and Grodzins say, is that central cities tend to be lower-income, Catholic, Negro, and Democratic. The suburban areas tend to be higher-income, Protestant, white, and Republican. The Democrats of the central cities are unwilling to turn over central-city functions to area-wide administrations which would dilute their political power. And likewise the Republicans, who have working control of the suburbs and with it a favored position vis-à-vis the state legislature, are not likely to vote for reorganization plans that would give central-city politicians a voice in suburban affairs. There is much evidence to support this argument. In 1959, voters in Cleveland and St. Louis turned down proposals for area-wide government. The Cleveland plan was opposed by Negroes who, reportedly, feared the proposed changes would weaken their strength in the city council, where they held eight of thirty-three seats. But other experts assert that these differences apply only to a dozen or more of the largest metropolitan areas, principally those in the North Atlantic and Middle West states, and that even in these areas religious and ethnic distinctions between cities and suburbs are much less strong than they were formerly.

The inevitable conclusion, in the view of many persons, is that some degree of unification is not only possible but likely in some metropolitan areas. If localism blocks metropolitanism we will surely see state and Federal controls over the metropolitan area rise in alarming degree, first in transportation and education and later in other fields including local zoning. If the suburbs, according to this view, cling too long to their cherished local rights by resisting collaboration within the metropolitan area, they may find that the price is a far less attractive shifting of these rights to even more remote levels of government. In the meantime, metropolitan communities may have engendered so vast a spread of urban areas as to compel ever larger proportions of our economy to be devoted to transportation with less and less resources available for other social and economic purposes.

Suburbia—The Self-Defeating Dream?

The suburban dream that lured millions of families away from the cities has dimmed since the day of their first down payment. Those who were looking for a house set in a country landscape found the open country was soon swallowed up by tract developments, highways, and shopping centers. Those who were seeking a socially exclusive neighborhood found that nothing that attracts many millions of people remains exclusive for long. Most families expected to find good schools and services and low taxes, but the stubborn facts of local government finance often frustrated their hopes.

Although residential areas, whether in the city or in the suburbs, are a major source of local tax revenue, they are also a major cause of local expenditures. They require streets, sewer facilities, water, storm drainage, schools, recreation places, health and welfare services, police and fire protection, ambulance services, libraries, and many other things that cost money. As long as the population density is low, as long as the area is occupied mainly by families who prefer and can afford private services, only a few public services are essential and a very low standard of services is acceptable. But the situation changes as soon as the population starts to expand. A few people scattered throughout the countryside may put sewage into the ground and safely pump water out of the ground; add a few hundred and it becomes risky; add a few thousand and public health requires the installation of sewerage and water systems.

Most suburbanites regard good schools as the most essential local government service. But a superior school system costs $400 to $500 per child per year. Thus the new suburban family with two or three children may cost the locality $800 to $1,500 per year, when it expects to pay no more than $200 or $300 per year in local taxes. Indeed, many new suburbanites in rapidly growing areas do pay such low taxes at first. But a single elementary school is not a school system; as the population increases, taxes will be doubled and often doubled again. The tax rate of some suburbs is higher than the tax rate of the central cities they adjoin.

The relation between the costs of servicing residential areas and the tax revenues provided by them is a matter of increasing concern. Studies conducted over the last twenty-five years suggest that most residential areas do not provide direct tax revenues to municipal government equal to their costs. These relationships vary widely with the density, state of development, and fiscal and population characteristics of the community in which development occurs.

Inevitably, the central city shares the fiscal and other problems of its suburbs. True, such cities have industrial plants, central business districts, large wholesaling and market areas upon which to draw for taxes. But they also must serve larger low-income populations and at the same time provide streets and highways for the suburbanite to travel over, and colleges, museums, zoos, hospitals, and many other metropolitan services which no single suburb can afford for itself.

Other important services may be wholly lacking, however, or poorly performed. Who can control the flow of traffic on highways? Not the central city, which daily receives thousands or hundreds of thousands of suburban commuters; not the suburbs, where the commuters come from and where they return. Who can provide transit? Who is reserving the land in the metropolitan area for future industrial growth and for future airports or expressways? Who is acquiring land for metropolitan parks to serve the population of the future? Who is controlling air pollution or the pollution of streams and river valleys? These and a score of other problems go unsolved.

In Search of Solutions

As our cities have grown to metropolitan size, the principal devices suggested in the past to bypass the limitations of local government in land-use control, finance, and public services are annexation, federation of municipalities, merger of districts or authorities.

ANNEXATION

Many specialists on urban problems agree that where necessary state laws should be changed to make it easier for central cities to annex their adjoining areas. It is difficult at present, however, for central cities to annex other than unincorporated areas. So long as the jurisdictions that might be annexed have the power of veto over a proposed annexation, they will usually exercise it to preserve their autonomy. Only in a few Southern cities has there been any substantial amount of annexation since World War II.

FEDERATION

The most successful federation in this hemisphere is in Toronto where thirteen federated municipalities have surrendered to the higher level of government control over such matters as water supply, sewage disposal, arterial highways, certain health and welfare services, housing and redevelopment, metropolitan parks and metropolitan planning. The federation also controls the transit system, allocates funds for school sites and construction, regulates bond issues of member municipalities, and sets a uniform assessment rate for both metropolitan and local taxation. However, the Toronto federation was created by a provincial government over the opposition of smaller municipalities in the area. Major changes in law would be needed in many states to permit this sort of federation in this country.

THE URBAN COUNTY

More than one hundred metropolitan areas in this country are within a single county. A single county encompasses a large segment of each of most of the other metropolitan areas. The complete merger of municipalities with a county government has a number of historical precedents: New Orleans, Boston, and Philadelphia, for example. Few present-day proposals call for such wholesale mergers. The transfer of some functions to county governments is more probable.

SPECIAL-FUNCTION DISTRICTS

The independent school district is almost universal in this country, and in the last twenty-five years this principle of governmental organization has been widely authorized by state governments and adopted by local governments to carry on new functions, as in the case of housing, renewal, port, airport, and bridge authorities. The special district appeals to political leaders and the public because it usually avoids local debt limits, rarely uses taxing powers, and appears to take the problem "out of politics." These very limitations, however, prevent the use of special districts for functions which require tax revenues, involve regulation of property, or necessitate important political decisions regarding priorities in public expenditures. A few special districts have become multi-functional, but most are confined to one revenue-producing function. Since boards of special districts, other than schools, are usually appointive, it is difficult for them to assume functions traditionally vested only in elective officers or bodies. Nevertheless, several communities are exploring the possibility of creating multi-purpose metropolitan special districts with elected boards to assume major functions.

POSSIBILITIES

The location, size, and ultimate density of a city are dictated largely by limitations on transportation for people and goods and by the level of wealth. In the metropolitan cities of the twentieth century these imperatives have changed much of their force. People can live at a distance from the central city and yet rely on it for many social and economic offerings.

The tremendous expansion of the suburbs which surround the great central cities has carried in its wake many of the same problems that plague the central cities themselves. In many suburbs (the newest of course excepted) there is evidence of considerable blight and physical deterioration. The suburbs are no longer exclusive or wealthy; they are attracting millions of families of very modest income, and any efforts permanently to exclude such people will certainly fail. One of the most significant demographic changes since 1930 is the small increase in the migration of Negroes to suburban areas. Moreover, the future growth of population will accentuate the already acute problems of finding adequate land to accommodate homes, shops, and community facilities.

Local governments are remarkably inventive in creating new specialized agencies (like housing or port authorities and like metropolitan water or park districts) to perform new functions or to handle problems that cut across municipal boundaries. But even as they are inventive, they jealously guard old prerogatives and powers. The powers of the new agencies are limited: usually the agencies must pay their way and rarely are they allowed to regulate or control what was previously a wholly municipal function.

But otherwise local governments engage in a bloodless civil war over functions and responsibilities which overlap their jurisdictions. They fight any suggestion for metropolitan organization. They compete for state grants-in-aid. They impose regulations which benefit one community at the expense of another. And they seek to push each problem of housing or transportation or utilities over into their neighbors' jurisdiction. When unilateral action compounds problems too far, the combating jurisdictions pledge mutual cooperation. In New York, Washington, D.C., and five other metropolitan areas in the country, councils of elected local and county officials are making some headway with this kind of effort.

"Local autonomy," "freedom from central city domination," "home rule"—these are the slogans under which existing jurisdictions fight metropolitan influence. They reflect deep-seated social, economic, and political differences that have become infused with emotion and fixed in local institutions. Some suburbanites fled "big city politics" in search of local government closer to the popular will. But if this was true, it has lost much of its validity as many central cities enjoy reform governments and many suburbs develop one-party machines. Some suburbanites sought "exclusively residential communities" but such communities now frequently look for industry to strengthen their tax bases. Other suburbanites in their new neighborhoods sought escape from minority groups, blighted areas, urban congestion or decay, traffic hazards, and poor schools. But each of these reasons for escape has followed those who sought to escape. Today there are even blighted suburbs fighting to preserve their freedom from blighted central cities.

Other, more tangible interests have a stake in a divided metropolis. Tax and assessment rates vary widely. Some communities have poor government services and correspondingly low taxes. Others are rich enough to enjoy good services. But there are communities which have high tax rates and poor services. These differentials are capitalized: houses have been bought and factories have been located to take advantage of favorable suburban tax situations. Some communities have attracted large industries and thus are rich in tax resources. They naturally defend their favored position. Others may have secured a grant-in-aid formula which is especially favorable. Any change in status would be costly to them.

Political machines have also become vested interests. Having developed within a municipal boundary, they resist change. Elected officials fear the loss of jobs or influence; their colleagues or representatives in the state legislature share the same fear. With local jobs or favors to confer and local power to exercise, public officials resist consolidations of jurisdictions or functions which might reduce their power or position.

Nevertheless, how will the large metropolitan areas respond to the consequences of what may be a doubling of population? The pressure for Federal aid to education has been intensifying steadily. As school-age population mounts, it is not unreasonable to presume that local tax rates in suburban areas may double within the decade without additional state or Federal assistance.

Are the independent suburbs willing to accept the prospective state and national intervention in education, or will they try to go it alone with sharp increases in local taxes? To date, the evidence is that the suburban populations are strongly disposed to sacrifice local control in order to obtain state aid. But in addition to their loss of control, suburban governments in some states are being milked as a price for this aid. Because of the rural bias of state legislatures, urban areas pay in state taxes 50 to 100 per cent more than they receive in state benefits. The price of state aid is often that urban areas entirely support rural school systems.

Similarly, we may consider the social and economic consequences of continued localism in suburban zoning. Local suburban governments may be expected to respond quite naturally to the desires of their inhabitants to preserve the low-density, open character of suburban residential areas. They can do this, within limits, by zoning under present local powers so as to confine residential growth to high-income families who can afford lots of one, two, or three acres or even more. These local zoning powers, while scarcely more than forty years old, have become among the most cherished of local rights and are likely to be defended with vigor by local governments. It is appropriate to ask whether the states or the courts will long support the exercise of a local power in such a way as to seriously inhibit the opportunities for suburban homes of the next fifty million Americans. Yet if present trends continue, the effect of local zoning may be to ring metropolitan centers with a band of suburbs five to fifteen miles deep zoned so as to admit only those who can afford $25,000, $30,000 and $40,000 houses, thus compelling the newly

formed families of the metropolis and even the second generation of suburbanites to go out fifteen or more miles into
the country to find a place for modest homes.

Will American metropolitan areas continue under the present
multiplicity of local governments? What price will they have to
pay to continue this localism? There is no question that the preferences of most suburbanites are overwhelmingly for their present systems of government if they can continue to afford them.
If the price is too high, however, the residents of metropolitan
areas may sacrifice some of their preferences.

If present trends continue we may expect that city-county
consolidation, annexation, and limited forms of federation may
resolve many of the problems of metropolitan services in some
of the smaller metropolitan areas. In the larger metropolitan
areas, however, those that shape the economic and cultural
character of our nation, the prospects are very unclear.

If, in the next ten or twenty years, the population increase in
metropolitan areas is as great as forecasts indicate, the question
is whether attachments to the local autonomy of the small unit of
local government and to the benefits that derive from differential
levels of services in the same area can persist in the face of
mounting costs. It may be that one of the real economies in
housing, for example, can come from land planning developments of such magnitude that single developments will be larger
than any one political jurisdiction. Economies in governmental
operations, such as code enforcement, may be possible through
technological change in data-processing methods if they are
employed on a metropolitan basis.

If the costs of maintaining separate political jurisdictions in the
housing market, and for any number of other private and public
activities, begin to outweigh the benefits, business, civic, and
even political leaders may unite in efforts to reorganize local
government in metropolitan areas. The great danger is that the
cause of structural change may blind these leaders to the problems that are not organizational in nature—they may be
economic or social—and that will exist despite changes in structure.

Chapter 18

OPPORTUNITIES

If urban communities and their housing are to be made more efficient, satisfying, and attractive, the business, civic, and governmental leaders of America must act to improve the market system in housing and community development. This task is not easy for there is no single step or even a simple pattern of steps to overcome the frictions in the system.

Any dramatic increase in the effective demand for new and improved housing requires marked changes in consumer behavior. Yet one of the best ways to alter consumer expectations and expenditures is to change producer behavior. When offered a demonstrably better product through improved manufacturing and merchandising, most consumers are likely to be more generous with their housing dollars. However, the builder, the architect, and the manufacturer—who with others produce housing—are not completely free to woo consumers. Their decisions depend upon decisions made by the investor, the capital supplier, local government through its building codes and subdivision regulations, and the Federal government through its credit regulations. For their part, the investor and lender will not underwrite heavy investments in new designs, building processes, materials, and research without assurances of steady growth in residential construction, assurances which in the presently mixed economy of housing depend upon consistent public policy.

The pattern of steps to improve the market system comes to full circle with the expectation of the producer, the consumer, and the investor that their commitments to the future will be matched by the community's commitments. They look to local government—and to some extent to state government—to recast the urban environment for housing in a more livable, efficient, and pleasing form. More satisfactory housing will depend as much on the willingness of the governmental leaders of America's urban communities to provide schools and other public facilities or to enforce housing codes as it will on changes in the housing industry itself.

Because of the interrelations of possible policies and programs, this chapter suggests four broad areas for future attention by those who make decisions for housing and community development. These are first, the resources needed for urban investment; second, programming for housing and renewal activities; third, knowledge for housing and renewal decisions; and fourth, a new diversity and experimentation in urban development and housing offerings. These are not responsibilities which can be readily assigned to any one group. They do not belong to only one level of government; nor are they matters for public decision alone. Each of the groups identified as major participants in housing and community decisions—the producer, the investor, the consumer, the Federal government, and the community—must be willing to explore separately and together those actions which will provide better housing in better communities.

Resources for Urban Investment

Civic leaders can accomplish much more than at present simply by pursuing present stated renewal objectives with more vigor. But they cannot accomplish enough to renew entire metropolitan areas unless they as businessmen and public officials are ready to make a tremendous new investment in plant and services. They cannot be expected to do so unless the consumer is ready to pay by means of increased personal expenditures and taxes.

The renewal of American cities is a gigantic economic task because it entails rebuilding or new building for almost every aspect of urban life and for more than half of the population. There is much room for debate as to the standard of renewal the people of each area can afford. What level of expenditure is possible, for example, for the repair and maintenance of existing buildings as against investment in new houses, stores, factories, and community facilities?

No one can say exactly how much investment in urban renewal will eventually be required to achieve an efficient and attractive urban environment. Tastes and aspirations keep changing; so do levels of prices; so do urban problems or at least the perceptions of them. Although it seems clear that modest standards of improvement and new development are manageable within current and future economic capacity, there will nonetheless have to be substantial increases in the proportion of the annual output that goes to capital investment, both public and private, and a correspondingly lower rate of growth for other forms of expenditure, if a national goal of a greatly superior urban environment is to be achieved in a generation.

The achievement of such a goal will call for a high level of investment in new housing. In addition to homes for new families, dwellings that are now substandard and those that will be demolished or become deteriorated in the next ten to twenty years will require replacement. While they are being replaced, new demands will have accumulated. If deteriorated dwellings are to be removed within a generation, as many as a million new dwellings a year may have to be built just to replace them.

Furthermore, an expanding economy should provide a reasonable number of vacant units to give families more choice in the market. It should also permit the undoubling of a million families, permit some of the millions of single- and two-person families that do not now occupy their own dwellings to have separate housing accommodations, and provide larger homes for a million or so families that appear to be overcrowded at present. Moreover, if American families continue to desert older, more crowded areas of central cities for suburban areas with lower densities, market forces could produce additional new demands not foreseen by purely arithmetic summations of housing requirements.

But housing is only part of urban renewal. Another part is a higher level of replacement of stores, factories, and other industrial and commercial buildings, and of a wide range of community facilities. It is here that the gravest problems exist. Years of depression and war created large backlogs for schools, highways, sewer, water, health, and recreation facilities which the postwar population boom increased tremendously. When these capital sums are totaled they suggest large increases in public investments for community facilities.

The report of the Rockefeller Brothers Fund in 1958, *The Challenge to America: Its Economic and Social Aspects*, states that current expenditures for public works of $9.5 billion per year should be at least doubled to $20 billion per year during the next decade, and that it would be advantageous if the total rate were to be tripled to $27 billion per year. When these expenditures are coupled with requirements for new residential construction ranging from $15 to $30 billion per year, for new private nonresidential investment of $30 to $60 billion per year, and for residential rehabilitation expenditures of $8 to $16 billion per year, some idea is gained of the total magnitude of the investment.

In a more recent analysis of renewal and development cost, *Capital Requirements for Urban Development and Renewal*, published in this series of books, John W. Dyckman and Reginald R. Isaacs estimate the capital requirements for a sample American city and its environs, and reach a total investment figure of $2,374.1 million. When they project their model for all metropolitan areas and urban places in the country, they reach a national figure of over a trillion dollars. Dyckman and Isaacs rest their estimates on three arbitrary considerations: (1) The time period is set at twelve years, although they do not believe the job can necessarily be accomplished within that short a time. (2) The definition for urban renewal which they use is one formulated by ACTION in 1954: "The total of all public and private actions which must be taken to provide for the continuous sound maintenance and development of urban areas." This program is broader, they believe, than any that is likely to be adopted by conscious public decision. And (3) they base their cost figures on "modest" standards. That is, "safety and comfort in housing, highways, and public places, and availability of full utilities and community facilities, including police, fire, and health protection. . . . All slums would be cleared and all existing structures would be replaced, renovated or repaired, and all new structures maintained in standard condition" over the twelve-year period.

The specific questions Dyckman and Isaacs set themselves to answer are: What would the investment bill be for a fairly typical central city and metropolitan area with a population of around 250,000 for the city and 300,000 for the metropolitan area, and what would it amount to if all American cities were renewed at the same level of standards as those set for the "case city"? Can we muster this investment, and if so what may be the repercussions on the national economy? The accompanying table shows how they arrive at their investment bill for the case city. The total assumes a ratio of 7 to 1 of private spending to public spending. It should be noted that their figures include all "normal" public and private investments and maintenance costs, plus those required for anticipated population growth, plus those required for renewal, and would require an investment or expenditure rate 20 to 25 per cent above that currently being made.

TABLE 11. TOTAL 12-YEAR TREATMENT AND MAINTENANCE COSTS, CASE CITY, SUBURBS AND METROPOLITAN AREA (in millions of 1958 dollars)

Facility	Case city	Suburbs	Metropolitan area
Residence................	$381.3	$515.4	$896.7
Industry.................	282.4	396.3	678.7
Commerce...............	233.4	182.5	415.9
Education, public and private...............	46.1	72.4	118.5
Park and open space......	26.3	37.1	63.4
All other................	80.5	120.4	200.9
Total.................	$1,050.0	$1,324.1	$2,374.1

The following table is an extrapolation of the case city estimates to provide an estimate of total urban renewal requirements for all the country's cities.

The total cost of urban renewal in the case city area—approximately $600 per person per year—appears to be within grasp because the net addition to property values would be great enough to permit the financing of public improvements

TABLE 12. ESTIMATED EXPENDITURE REQUIREMENTS FOR 12-YEAR PERIOD,
TOTAL RENEWAL OF AMERICAN CITIES
(in billions of 1958 dollars)

	Average annual expenditures	Total, 12-year period
Metropolitan areas[a].............	$ 65	$ 800
All urban places[b]................	110	1,300

[a] An urbanized county or group of counties with a central city of at least 50,000 persons.

[b] All places with population of 2,500 or more.

with a somewhat reduced over-all effective tax rate. The additional investment in property would almost equal the present investment in real estate, adding to property rolls at the rate of 6 per cent per year. Success of such a renewal program would depend on the magnitude of incentives offered to private enterprise for investment.

The alternatives for stimulating this level of investment in cities and suburbs are more sharply drawn when viewed from different points of national economic policy. Supposing the case city's modest renewal standards were extended throughout the country on the basis of the same timetable, and assuming a 3 per cent a year growth rate for the national economy, could such standards be met without curtailing the discretionary spending power of consumers? Or would they become possible only if the Federal government is able to cut down its domestic agricultural costs and its military and foreign aid programs? Can they be met at all with so modest a growth rate?

There are a number of ways of planning to meet future spending targets. One way is to calculate probable future product, under certain growth assumptions, and then to divide this product into various objects of expenditure. Another is to assume constant shares for the various recipients of income and objects of expenditure, and to plan for the growth anticipated to meet targets under this set of assumptions. But since in a dynamic economy shifts in allocation have effects on the total output achieved, some mixture of these approaches is most often used.

A contrasting emphasis may be observed between the Dyckman-Isaacs book and the Rockefeller Brothers Fund report in this matter. The former takes a conservative model for purposes of illustrating renewal prospects. The conservative model embodies the judgments that a gross private investment rate of 15 per cent of Gross National Product (GNP), such as was reached in 1959, is slightly higher than can be maintained over a twelve-year pull; that government expenditure over the same period should not rise as a share of all spending, but should settle down at about 20 per cent of GNP; and that a growth rate of 3 per cent per annum in *real* national product is consistent with these judgments. The arithmetic suggests that the spending levels are not beyond reach, even in a twelve-year period, but that they could be attained only at the expense of other programs, and after substantial changes in consumer preferences, political choices, and investment opportunities, and after subsequent reallocations.

The Rockefeller Brothers Fund report, on the other hand, emphasizes the need for higher growth rates if such welfare targets as urban renewal and improved collective services are to be achieved. It rules out certain reallocations (such as reduced arms spending), and accepts a higher rate of government participation in national product and higher total (public plus private) investment in order to achieve a 4 to 5 per cent growth rate. There is no disagreement between the various approaches on the possibility of making vast sums available for renewal out of the difference between the "high growth" and "low growth" models, whatever the difference in view of the reasonableness of high or low growth expectations. The *annual* difference in output between the 3 per cent growth model and the 5 per cent growth model amounts to $140 billion by 1967 and almost $50 billion per year more than that by 1970. The *total* renewal bill, which includes most of the ongoing investment in physical facilities, could be met out of the *difference* between the high and low growth projections in this period.

But even with more moderate growth assumptions, renewal

targets are not beyond reach if certain reallocations are made in the economy. Dyckman and Isaacs point out that a crash development program, in which consumption is held down and investment maintained at a high level, would produce the required outcome even from lower growth totals. But they question the ability to attract this investment from private sources in such a growth context. The Rockefeller Brothers Fund report assumes the necessity for government action to bring about not only the needed expenditures but growth itself. In this report, the *governmental* renewal contribution is increased from $700 million per year in 1957 to $7 billion per year in 1967, or 1,000 per cent, in the high (5 per cent) growth model. Such investment is expected to act to employ resources more fully, and through its multiplier effect, to swell total income. Thus renewal is made part of a more massive government effort to speed growth than we have yet seen in America.

The sheer arithmetic of economic growth, then, provides the possibility for achieving comprehensive city rebuilding in a single generation if the economic incentives can be created, or if we are willing to allow the economy to be "forced." In either event, however, we may expect that the programs for achieving this ambitious reconstruction will place severe strains on existing institutions and ways of doing business.

The economy is not depression-proof, but it is less depression-prone than ever before in this country's history. The fear of depression may not have lifted sufficiently from the housing industry for producers to mechanize persistently. Nevertheless, we have achieved a state of confidence where consumers do not curb their spending drastically in face of dips in the economy, nor have there been snowballing retrenchments on the slope of downward trends. If international tensions ease and confidence in the internal economy is sustained, urban development and renewal could be a major replacement for defense spending. It has many of the same attractions for business that defense work has—there is constantly re-created demand and the expenditures permeate the economy with an extraordinary multiplier effect. Moreover, it has attractions that defense spending does not have;

urban renewal can enhance the investments of businessmen and property owners in built-up areas and protect the future investments of those in developing fringe areas.

But even if goals of urban renewal and development are feasible in terms of the national economy, they must, nevertheless, be translated into specific local programs before they can have more than hypothetical meaning.

Programming for Housing and Renewal Activities

Urban renewal programs must set specific conditions to produce effective private action, because in the long run they cannot succeed if they involve uneconomic or personally unrewarding investments. To be politically attainable, they must also ensure that the public expenditures necessary for urban renewal are advantageous to many or most groups within the community and come within the resources which elected officials are willing to provide. Furthermore, public urban renewal expenditures are expected generally to improve or establish some minimum level of social welfare for the community.

Recognizing these requirements, a wide range of means are available for urban renewal programs. These include the normal investments private investors make in new construction in the community and such additional investments as can be induced by community pride and stimulated by public investments. Another equally important means is the maintenance and repair of all types of property by their owners. If owners are induced or persuaded to maintain properties in good condition, to modernize as promptly as markets permit, to remodel structures to meet changing demands and changing neighborhood circumstances, the private side of the economy will carry a very large share of urban renewal.

So far, most cities have merely been dabbling in housing and renewal activities. Occasional projects here and there have failed miserably in the attempt to make cities less dreary and more convenient. Dramatic exceptions in a few cities demonstrate that if the quantitative and qualitative levels of housing and community development are to improve, community leaders and officials must concentrate their efforts on realizable objectives, specifying what they want to accomplish and within what time periods. And they must marshall the necessary resources to set about obtaining these objectives. Machinery must be put into working order whereby alternative community renewal objectives may be brought to public attention, may be clarified through public discussion, and implemented through private and public action.

The organizational machinery for planning and programming already exists in many communities. Its components are a community-planning agency, a renewal agency, provisions for coordination, and a broadly representative citizen organization.

This organizational structure may seem cumbersome for the smallest communities, but it is not for the large ones. The task of coordinated renewal requires both a division of labor and multiple opportunities for public debate. Each group in the community will be affected by urban renewal; each has its own ends and interests which it seeks for itself and often seeks to impose on the community.

Programming involves an analysis of what public and private resources will be available this year and in each of a series of following years to move toward stated objectives. Here private resources and potentialities become of critical importance. The estimated volume of new private investments in homes, factories, and stores is one of the most important limiting factors. It will do a community little good to clear an area on the outskirts of the central business district for new buildings if there is unlikely to be a demand for them and private investors will be unwilling to invest in such structures. A renewal program which contemplates the demolition of 500 homes a year will grind to a halt someday unless someone, somewhere, is actually making available 500 homes a year to rehouse the displaced families at prices or rents and in locations meeting their requirements. Similarly, the programming process must take account of the availability of public capital resources.

The main policy question is what set of public actions will evoke the largest possible amount of private investment and maintenance activity? Some early urban renewal programs undertook to clear the worst slum areas in the city first. This action was justified upon the grounds that since these areas were in the worst possible condition they should be the ones to be cleared and replaced first. In some communities, however, these cleared slum sites proved to be unmarketable for years. Private investors did not want them for housing or for any other purposes. Moreover, when there was an insufficient supply of housing for relocation, the effect of the displacement of population from clearance sites was often to force the migration of slum families into other areas, thus accelerating their overcrowding and deterioration. Here one of the unanticipated consequences of urban renewal has been to increase slum areas rather than to reduce them.

In other communities code enforcement efforts have been initiated on a demonstration basis in slums that were fit only for clearance. Too often, a seemingly successful code enforcement program has been unable to resist the deteriorating influences imposed by the surrounding environment. As a consequence, a few years after the completion of the demonstration program the areas have reverted to something approximating their former status. In one community the worst slum area, as measured by the American Public Health Association's rating scale, proved to be one in which a rehabilitation and code enforcement program had been conducted a few years earlier.

These comments should not be taken to indicate that urban renewal to date has been generally unsuccessful. But they are intended to suggest the importance of systematic analyses of successes and failures in urban renewal. These analyses should be undertaken locally and nationally before vast new expenditures are made.

The programming process now provided for by the Federal government in subsidies for Community Renewal Programs is a means for balancing requirements against resources. If the programming process is to succeed, localities will require competent personnel and sufficient information on which to make public decisions. Even more important is a political climate in which it is possible to reach agreement on objectives for urban renewal and development. These objectives may lead to lesser or to greater public expenditures.

Every community is constantly replacing old plant with new houses, new businesses, new schools, new incinerators, new office buildings; every community is constantly converting its land to different uses and patterns. If only these normal public and private expenditures and changes can be directed toward specific, agreed-upon renewal goals, instead of being dissipated, the total effect will surpass any renewal achievements yet experienced. No city has a level of programming and political agreement which can orchestrate the related public and private actions.

Federal activities themselves, in housing and urban renewal, often nullify or jeopardize each other's effects. Federal agencies often compete with local ones for scarce professional personnel. Because of the identification of particular housing and renewal programs with particular interest groups, even a Cabinet post for housing and urban affairs would not automatically result in the elimination of actions at cross-purposes to each other, nor in a democracy should it be expected to do so.

Knowledge for Housing and Renewal Decisions

Among the potential achievements, however, of a Cabinet post for housing and urban affairs is a research program to provide more penetrating knowledge of urban requirements and opportunities. At a time when research activities are expanding for almost every other type of endeavor, research in housing and urban renewal is scanty and scarce. More research on drugs is being conducted by individual drug firms today than the total of private and public research on drugs ten years ago. Yet almost universally cities are unable to record even the basic changes taking place within their boundaries, let alone analyze subtle relationships within and among the forces influencing change. Individual housing firms can do little more than sporadic materials research. Research funds in such national agencies as the Housing and Home Finance Agency are almost nonexistent. For example, in 1960 the HHFA spent only $15,000 for research while all other parts of the Federal government spent more than $7 billion for research and development.

Without sound market information on consumer behavior and

attitudes, producers, investors, and government officials are grop-ing in the dark. Without large-scale efforts to test new systems of building, only minor technological improvements are taking place. Without an understanding of the normal processes of urban growth and change, intelligently directed change is impos-sible. Practical information is as necessary as basic information; knowledge of an intensely local nature is as necessary as knowl-edge of typical, widespread, and national problems. Local gov-ernments and organized private groups have a major responsibil-ity in providing information on which to base public and private decisions. Since the concerned groups are so diverse, research should not be left only to Federal initiative.

Other undertakings, like a continuing national housing market analysis, should be cooperatively supported by government, business, and labor. Not only does such an analysis require the collation of quantities of data from many public and private sources, but its findings must be communicated at regu-lar intervals to a wide range of public and private users—to pro-ducers, financial institutions, government officials, and con-sumers.

The cost of broadening the base of knowledge and making it widely available will be only a small fraction of the cost of lost opportunities and dissipated resources if research is neglected.

Diversity and Experiment in Housing and Renewal

The consumer can be neither sovereign nor hopeful in a housing and renewal market where the same products are turned out with dreary monotony. If America suffers from conformity in the behavior of its people, as its critics maintain, it suffers more from conformity in its urban offerings. In the housing market, dwellings are built almost exclusively for the mythical average family of a father, mother, and two or three small children. The nontypical families of the widowed and the divorced, of the working mother and the aged, of those with no children and those with many children, of those with relatives or those who live alone, families that crave privacy and families that seek built-in services—all of these are largely ignored by the building economy. Each nontypical family (or even each typical one with nontypical tastes) is expected to be content with stereotyped housing and community facilities and services.

Many minority tastes in the commodity market have boosted sales beyond all expectations. Those for compact cars, hi-fi sets, and skiing equipment are examples. In the housing and community development market, minority preferences have been ignored. A major task of public policy should be the conscious fostering of innovations in housing and community development as a means of stimulating a quest for superior quality and a greater range of choices. Diversity and experiment in the design and site planning of all types of housing are desirable, as are diversity and experiment in community facilities and services, in density arrangements, in traffic solutions, and in community appearance.

Questioning, innovating, trying out alternatives, experimenting—these are the means by which communities discover the diverse requirements of their people. Small communities cannot easily make large capital experiments. They cannot with impunity scrap existing investments in school plant, for example, and teach everyone at home via television. But they can easily make administrative or design experiments. Even the large community might be unwise to adopt an experimental program at full-scale when testing more than one idea may be indicated.

Indeed, it is imperative to avoid an all-or-none, sink-or-swim set of public policies. We ought to re-examine the sweeping policies already instituted; for example, the ways of providing housing to low-income and other minority groups. Even under the most optimistic assumptions about the national economy, certain groups will continue to be disfranchised in the housing market. Some people, because of their physical and other disabilities, because of circumstances leading to their unemployment or underemployment, because of disruption of their families by death or other circumstances, will not be able to compete for decent housing. Rent subsidies, often proposed as a means of providing housing for people like these, have been attacked many times as a way of subsidizing slums. But why not try out the idea in a community where new housing is being produced at a satisfactory rate and where a housing code is being rigorously enforced with respect to existing housing?

Similarly, we have not seriously experimented with alternative methods of redeveloping blighted areas. Instead of purchasing land, razing buildings, and reselling or leasing the land for reuse, we might use taxation as a real incentive or sanction. For example, real property taxation might be related to earning capacity in order to penalize deteriorated buildings with unjustifiably high returns. Or the blighted areas might be ignored except for code enforcement while the community stimulates new development on land on its outskirts, thus encouraging by competition the eventual fall in revenue and land costs of inner blighted areas so that they can be rebuilt through market forces.

Among other experiments should be ones for new types of dwellings and groups of dwellings. We have not made serious and imaginative efforts to experiment and record experiments in public policy. Instead we have seized and pursued a particular policy, later modifying or repealing it or setting up countervailing policies to it. Citizen organizations are particularly well placed to prod public agencies and officials into questioning past procedures.

In Conclusion

This chapter has suggested four changes in the housing and community development situation which, if they were brought into being, would help improve cities and shelter. These, and other changes suggested throughout this book, need no magic, no extraordinary burst of power, no utopian behavior. But each of them requires a series of economic and organizational and attitudinal shifts.

The suggestions for making the urban housing market work recognize the mixed nature of that market and thus are often directed to national and local government. A caution about government is in order, however. Few economic activities in the United States have become more dependent than housing upon governmental bulwarking. While the fusion of private and public enterprise can have beneficial results, it can also have pernicious ones. In some aspects of housing, by what amounts to the socialization of loss, governmental policies have encouraged inefficiency. Just as governmental action has sometimes encouraged the marginal producer in agriculture, so has it in housing.

The various suggestions to improve cities and the supply and production of housing are based on the premise that private enterprise and public effort must complement each other to get better housing and to bring about desirable community development. Government in its legitimate concern for housing must not eliminate competition as a major means for achieving housing welfare.

Private enterprise must be encouraged to achieve that scale of operation, that integration of functions, and that mechanization of activities which will refute the charge that housing is the industry capitalism forgot. Unless this happens, shelter and neighborhood environment will continue to fall behind the rest of the American dream, despite increases in real income and leisure. Housing must be made competitive with other industries in the scale and rationalization of its production, its financing, and its merchandising to the consumer. Types of accommodations must be varied; there must be rental housing as well as sales housing, inlying locations as well as outlying locations, rehabilitated and conserved units as well as new houses.

At the same time, all levels of government, in helping make the market work, should provide those services and controls that private enterprise cannot. Government should provide the technical and economic information and research necessary for housing production and improvement—information which could be provided by no private group; should protect the economy against severe fluctuations which inhibit housing activity; should protect health and safety in housing through codes and other regulations; and should make direct provision for those people who because of chronic economic, social, or physical incapacity, disability, or discrimination cannot compete successfully in the housing market.

For thirty years, scores of organizations and special-interest groups have made literally hundreds of recommendations which they sincerely believed would improve cities and the supply and quality of American housing. To these are now added the suggestions in this book for the kinds of action that will help the housing market to work more effectively in a mixed economy. But practical suggestions are not by themselves sufficient to obtain better housing in better communities. The people who can convert the suggestions into actions—the consumers, the investors, the producers, the government and political officials, and the citizen leaders—must first persuade themselves that changes are desirable and feasible for them and for the general well-being.

LEGISLATIVE NOTE

On June 30, 1961, after this book was in press, President John F. Kennedy signed into law the Housing Act of 1961. Because of the importance of the act to the subjects with which the book deals, the main provisions of the law are summarized below. These provisions are relevant to many parts of *Housing, People, and Cities,* but especially pp. 70, 71, 74, 161, 194, 195, 202–206, 208, 209, 211, 213, 221–240, 262–265, 299–301, 311, and 312.

Changes in FHA Mortgage Requirements for New and Old Sales Houses

The terms under which the Federal Housing Administration will insure home mortgages have been altered. The following provisions apply to FHA's main program, Section 203, but also to Section 220 and Section 809.

Down payments are reduced to 3 per cent of the first $15,000 (instead of $13,500) of appraised value, 10 per cent of the value between $15,000 and $20,000 (instead of between $13,500 and $18,000), and 25 per cent of the value above $20,000 (instead of 30 per cent of the value above $18,000).

Maximum mortgage amounts are increased from $22,500 to $25,000 on a one-family home mortgage and from $25,000 to $27,500 on a two-family home mortgage.

Maximum mortgage duration is extended to thirty-five years (instead of thirty) for new construction, but the thirty-year maximum continues to apply to mortgages on existing construction (houses more than one year old). For the buyer of a new house, these changes mean lower capital and monthly payment costs but an increase in interest charges over the life of the mortgage.

New FHA-insured Improvement Loans

FHA may insure home improvement and rehabilitation loans of up to $10,000 per dwelling unit, to be repaid within twenty years.

When added to other outstanding debt against the property, the loan may not exceed the limits of a mortgage which can be insured by FHA. The loan must have security "satisfactory to the [FHA] Commissioner" (in some states this might be a second mortgage, in others non-real-estate collateral). To be eligible, properties must either be at least ten years old or require major structural changes or corrections of defects which were unknown when the house was completed, or which were caused by fire, flood, or other casualty. (FHA seeks to discourage mere upgrading of equipment and to encourage improved livability or conversion or expansion.) The interest rate is to be set by the Commissioner but may not exceed 6 per cent; no discounts are allowed.

Structures within urban renewal areas may qualify more easily for loans than those outside. Within urban renewal areas, but not elsewhere, loans are available for multi-family structures (those with at least five families). In renewal areas total indebtedness can be figured as the sum of the estimated cost of repair and rehabilitation and the FHA's estimate of the value of the property before repair; elsewhere, loans must be "economically sound." In renewal areas, defaults can be paid by FHA in cash; elsewhere, insurance claims will be paid in ten-year debentures.

Continuation of FHA Title I Property Improvement Program

This program of property improvement loan insurance is extended four years to October 1, 1965.

Expansion of FHA Section 221 to Apply to Moderate-income Families Generally as Well as to Displaced Families

FHA Section 221 mortgage insurance, formerly designed to aid low-income families displaced by urban renewal activities, has been made available on more liberal terms and broadened to include moderate-income families as well as low-income families. However, relocatees will receive more favorable terms than other families. The program for sales and profit-making rental housing for moderate-income families is due to expire in two years, and that for low-interest housing is on a four-year trial basis; no termination is set for the displaced families program.

The dollar limits on insurable mortgages on new and existing sales housing have been raised. For example, the limit for a one-family house in a normal-cost area, which was $9,000, is now $11,000; in a high-cost area, where it was $12,000, it is now $15,000. Two-, three-, and four-family house mortgages are available only to displaced families. Closing costs may be included in the mortgage; down payments for displaced families are $200 per dwelling unit, and for other families are 3 per cent of acquisition and closing costs. Mortgages may run for 40 years for displaced families, 35 years on new housing for other families (but this may be extended to 40 years if FHA determines that the purchaser cannot afford the higher monthly payments), and 30 years on existing housing for other families.

The rental housing program in Section 221 is amended to provide a "below market" interest rate for new and rehabilitated housing of five or more units. Long-term mortgages at 100 per cent of estimated replacement cost will be available to nonprofit corporations, limited dividend corporations, cooperatives, or public agencies which are not engaged exclusively in public housing. Interest rates cannot be lower than the average market yield of outstanding marketable United States obligations. FHA may reduce or eliminate the insurance premium, and FNMA may purchase the mortgages.

The maximum mortgage amount (for projects under profit-making as well as non-profit sponsorship) is to be computed as a function of the number of rooms rather than dwelling units. The effect of this will be to increase the loan limits.

Other FHA Provisions

Section 233 provides for a new program of insurance for experimental sales or rental housing; the terms will be the same as under the main sales and rental programs, except that FHA need only find the project to be an acceptable risk rather than to be economically sound.

Section 234 authorizes FHA to insure a mortgage covering an owned family unit in a multi-family structure and an undivided interest in the common areas and facilities of the structure. This *condominium* device is restricted to structures that are or have been covered by FHA-insured mortgages (other than cooperative housing mortgages).

Maximum amounts for FHA-insured mortgages for the elderly are raised under Section 231, and required equities for nursing homes are reduced from 25 to 10 per cent under Section 232.

New Investment Opportunities for Federal Savings and Loan Associations

Federal Savings and Loan Associations are authorized to invest 5 per cent of their assets in each of the following: (1) eighteen-month nonamortized 80 per cent loans (not exceeding $35,000), to facilitate the financing of trade-in housing; (2) thirty-year 90 per cent loans on nursing homes or housing for the elderly; (3) the shares of urban renewal investment trusts, set up by two or more federally insured savings institutions (this enables several institutions to supply the capital for costly urban renewal projects). Savings and loan associations may also invest 0.5 per cent of their outstanding loans, or $250,000, whichever is smaller, in business development credit corporations.

Federal National Mortgage Association

New authorization of $750 million is provided for FNMA's special assistance program, and $200 million of unused authorization from the Housing Act of 1958 is continued. Another $140 million per year for the next four fiscal years will be available from the management and liquidation portfolio.

For the first time, FNMA is authorized to make 80 per cent, one-year loans (renewable for one year) with FHA or VA mortgages as security. FNMA can also purchase insured loans and mortgages from local public agencies under the Section 221 low-interest-rate rental housing program.

Urban Renewal

HHFA is authorized to grant $2 billion for urban renewal in addition to the $2 billion allotted since 1949; $25 million of this may be used for mass transportation demonstrations. The Federal share of the write-down of land acquisition and clearance costs is increased from two-thirds to three-fourths in communities of less than 50,000 population, or less than 150,000 population in economically distressed areas. The local non-cash contribution may include expenditures (retroactive for seven years) by hospitals for land acquisition and clearance near urban renewal areas, just as college expenditures are credited by the Housing Act of 1959.

The amount of renewal funds that may be used for nonresidential projects is raised from 20 to 30 per cent. A $3,000 ceiling on relocation payments to business is removed, and payments are authorized for displaced nonprofit organizations. Displaced businesses are made eligible for low-interest loans from a special $25 million fund of the Small Business Administration. Cleared land for moderate-income housing may be resold at fair value (without bidding) to certain classes of developers.

Urban Planning and Public Works Planning

The Federal share of the "701" urban planning grant program is raised from one-half to two-thirds and the authorization of Federal expenditures is raised from $20 million to $75 million. Urban transportation planning is specifically made eligible for planning assistance grants.

To encourage comprehensive planning, the HHFA Administrator is authorized to provide technical assistance to state and local governments and to make studies and publish information.

An additional $10 million (above the $48 million previously authorized) is allowed for advances for public works planning. No advances will be given unless the proposed project conforms to an over-all state, local, or regional plan, and will be constructed within a reasonable time.

Housing for the Elderly

As mentioned above, limits are raised on mortgages for the elderly under FHA's Section 231.

HHFA's Section 202 is amended to authorize low-interest, fifty-year loans for cooperatives, public agencies not exclusively devoted to public housing, and nonprofit organizations which build units for the elderly. Loans may be for 100 per cent of costs (previously 98 per cent), and the loan authorization is increased from $50 million to $125 million.

Public housing agencies now may obtain an additional subsidy from the Public Housing Administration of up to $120 per year for each unit occupied by elderly persons if low rents threaten the solvency of the project. They may also spend $500 more per room (new limit, $3,000) on construction for the elderly, and they are no longer required to hold rents for the elderly or for relocatees below those in the private market. (This will open public housing to some families which hitherto were disqualified because their incomes were too high.)

Public Housing

The remaining balance of the $336 million annual contribution authorized by the Housing Act of 1949 is made available, permitting construction of approximately 100,000 additional public housing units. Local housing agencies are given more discretion in setting admission policies. They may permit tenants whose income exceeds the limit to remain in public housing at a higher rent if private housing is not available at a price the tenants can pay.

The act repeals a requirement that local housing agencies repay subsidies when projects are sold or amortized. The act also authorizes the HHFA Administrator to grant $5 million for demonstrations of new or improved means of housing low-income persons and families.

Open Space

Local and state governments may obtain 20 per cent of the cost of acquiring public open space (30 per cent if this is done on a regional basis) under a new $50 million program of Federal grants. The grants will be made only if comprehensive planning is being carried on for the urban area, and if the local governing body is preserving a maximum of open space with a minimum of cost, with devices such as special tax, zoning, and subdivision provisions. Open space acquired with Federal assistance may be converted to other uses provided the HHFA Administrator finds that this conversion is essential to the orderly development of the urban area, and that other open space of equivalent value is substituted.

Community Facilities

The act expands and liberalizes the community facilities loan program: the aggregate authorization of the revolving fund is increased by $500 million to $650 million of which $50 million is designated for mass transportation loans. Eligible borrowers are municipalities, or political subdivisions such as water and sewer districts, of less than 50,000 population (or less than 150,000 population in economically depressed areas). The interest rate is the average of all Treasury obligations, plus 0.5 per cent (except in depressed areas, where it is lower). Also, the HHFA Administrator may permit communities with rapid population growth to postpone for ten years paying half the interest of any public facility loan when the loan does not exceed half the cost of the project.

Urban Mass Transportation

The act aids urban mass transportation in three ways, all of which have been mentioned already:

Planning assistance. Comprehensive planning for mass transportation is made specifically eligible for Federal funds under the "701" program.

Demonstration grants. The urban renewal program provides $25 million for demonstration projects to improve mass-transportation service or reduce urban transportation needs. The grants cannot exceed two-thirds of the project costs and cannot be used for major capital improvements.

Loans. A sum of $50 million is authorized for low-interest loans to public bodies for new transportation facilities and equipment. (This is a part of the community facilities loan program, but transportation loans are not restricted by the size of the community population.) The loan authority expires in 1963. No loan may be made unless a program is developed for a comprehensive mass-transportation system, and unless the proposed facilities or equipment are required for such a system.

SOURCES

Housing, People, and Cities is the final and summary volume of the ACTION series in housing and community development. As such, its main sources of data are the seven preceding books in the series listed at the beginning of the bibliography below. The sources for the other books are documented in the footnotes in each volume. However, only the specialist need refer to the annotations in the other volumes in the series since the bibliography below covers the most relevant books and articles for this volume. Studies specifically cited in the text are identified in this bibliography by the pages in this book and the pages from the source; these page citations are in parentheses. Also, the reader will find statistical sources footnoted in the tables and charts in the text. Information from official releases in annual and other reports is cited below if the reference has wide applicability; otherwise it is identified in the text by date and agency.

Banfield, Edward C., and Morton Grodzins: *Government and Housing in Metropolitan Areas*, McGraw-Hill, New York, 1958, 192 pp.

Dyckman, John W., and Reginald R. Isaacs: *Capital Requirements for Urban Development and Renewal*, McGraw-Hill, New York, 1961, 334 pp.

Foote, Nelson, Janet Abu-Lughod, Mary Mix Foley, and Louis Winnick: *Housing Choices and Housing Constraints*, McGraw-Hill, New York, 1960, 450 pp.

Haar, Charles M.: *Federal Credit and Private Housing: The Mass Financing Dilemma*, McGraw-Hill, New York, 1960, 408 pp.

Kelly, Burnham, and Associates: *Design and the Production of Houses*, McGraw-Hill, New York, 1959, 428 pp.

Nash, William W. (directed by Miles L. Colean): *Residential Rehabilitation: Private Profits and Public Purposes*, McGraw-Hill, New York, 1959, 272 pp.

Winnick, Louis: *Rental Housing: Opportunities for Private Investment*, McGraw-Hill, New York, 1958, 295 pp.

355

Abrahamson, Julia: *A Neighborhood Finds Itself*, Harper, New York, 1959, 370 pp.

Abrams, Charles: *Forbidden Neighbors: A Study of Prejudice in Housing*, Harper, New York, 1955, 404 pp.

————: *The Future of Housing*, Harper, New York, 1946, 428 pp.

American Institute of Planners: "Steinberg on the City," *Journal of the American Institute of Planners*, vol. 27, no. 3, part 2, August, 1961, entire issue. (*See* for frontispiece of *Housing, People, and Cities*, hereinafter noted as *H,P,&C.*)

American Public Health Association, Committee on the Hygiene of Housing: "Planning the Home for Occupancy," Public Administration Service, Chicago, 1950, 56 pp.

————: "Planning the Neighborhood," Public Administration Service, Chicago, 1948, 90 pp.

American Society of Planning Officials: "Migration, Minorities, and the Implications for Planning," in *Planning 1961*, Chicago, 1961, pp. 52–74.

Architectural Forum Editors: *Building, U.S.A.*, McGraw-Hill, New York, 1957, 150 pp. (*See* p. 54 for quotation on pp. 119–120 of *H,P,&C.*)

Banfield, Edward C.: *Political Influence*, Free Press, New York, 1961, 354 pp.

Bator, Francis M.: *The Question of Government Spending: Public Needs and Private Wants*, Harper, New York, 1960, 167 pp.

Bauer, Catherine: *Modern Housing*, Houghton Mifflin, Boston, 1934, 330 pp.

Bemis, Albert F., and John Burchard: *The Evolving House*, Technology Press, M.I.T., Cambridge, Mass., 1933–1936, 3 vols.

Bendix, Reinhard, and Seymour Lipset: *Class, Status and Power*, Free Press, New York, 1953, 725 pp.

Beyer, Glenn H.: *Housing: A Factual Analysis*, Macmillan, New York, 1958, 355 pp.

Board of Governors of the Federal Reserve System: "1955 Survey of Consumer Finances: Housing Arrangements of Consumers," *Federal Reserve Bulletin*, vol. 41, no. 8, pp. 856–868.

Brazer, Harvey E.: *City Expenditures in the United States*, Occasional Paper 66, National Bureau of Economic Research, New York, 1959, 82 pp.

Burns, Arthur F.: *Prosperity without Inflation*, Fordham University Press, New York, 1957, 88 pp.

Clark, Colin: "Urban Population Densities," *Journal of the Royal Statistical Society*, vol. 114, no. 4, pp. 490–496, 1951.

Colean, Miles L.: *American Housing: Problems and Prospects,* Twentieth Century Fund, New York, 1944, 466 pp.

————: *The Impact of Government on Real Estate Finance in the United States,* National Bureau of Economic Research, New York, 1950, 171 pp.

————: *Renewing Our Cities,* Twentieth Century Fund, New York, 1953, 181 pp.

———— and Robinson Newcomb: *Stabilizing Construction: The Record and Potential,* McGraw-Hill, New York, 1952, 340 pp.

Commission on Race and Housing: *Where Shall We Live?—Conclusions from a Three-year Study of Racial Discrimination in Housing,* University of California Press, Berkeley, 1958. (*See* reference on p. 81 of *H,P,&C* taken from Commission's "Working Paper," February, 1958.)

Connery, Robert H., and Richard H. Leach: *The Federal Government and Metropolitan Areas,* Harvard University Press, Cambridge, Mass., 1960, 275 pp.

Dean, John P.: "Housing Design and Family Values," *Land Economics,* vol. 29, no. 2, pp. 128–141, May, 1953.

————: "The Myths of Housing Reform," *American Sociological Review,* vol. 14, no. 2, pp. 281–288, April, 1949.

DeForest, Robert, and Lawrence Veiller (eds.): *The Tenement House Problem,* Macmillan, New York, 1903, 2 vols.

Deutsch, Morton, and Mary Evans Collins: *Interracial Housing: A Psychological Evaluation of a Social Experiment,* University of Minnesota Press, Minneapolis, 1951, 173 pp.

Dewhurst, J. Frederic, and Associates: *America's Needs and Resources: A New Survey,* Twentieth Century Fund, New York, 1955, 1148 pp. (*See* p. 221 for reference on p. 39 of *H,P,&C*.)

Dobriner, William M. (ed.): *The Suburban Community,* Putnam, New York, 1958, 416 pp.

Donahue, Wilma (ed.): *Housing the Aging,* University of Michigan Press, Ann Arbor, 1954, 280 pp.

Duncan, Beverly, and Philip M. Hauser: *Housing a Metropolis: Chicago,* Free Press, New York, 1960, 278 pp.

Duncan, Otis D., and others: *Metropolis and Region,* Johns Hopkins Press, Baltimore, 1960, 587 pp.

———— and A. J. Reiss, Jr.: *Social Characteristics of Urban and Rural Communities,* Wiley, New York, 1956, 421 pp.

Festinger, Leon, Stanley Schacter, and Kurt Back: *Social Pressures in Informal Groups: A Study of Human Factors in Housing,* Harper, New York, 1950, 240 pp.

Firey, Walter: "Sentiment and Symbolism as Ecological Variables," *American Sociological Review*, vol. 10, no. 2, pp. 140–148, April, 1945.

Fisher, Ernest M.: *Urban Real Estate Markets: Characteristics and Financing*, National Bureau of Economic Research, New York, 1951, 186 pp.

——— and Chester Rapkin: *The Mutual Mortgage Insurance Fund*, Institute for Urban Land Use and Housing Studies, Columbia University Press, New York, 1956, 162 pp. (*See* pp. 146–156 for reference on p. 260 of *H,P,&C*.)

Fisher, Robert Moore: *Twenty Years of Public Housing: Economic Aspects of the Federal Program*, Harper, New York, 1959, 303 pp.

Gans, Herbert J.: "The Human Implications of Current Redevelopment and Relocation Planning," *Journal of the American Institute of Planners*, vol. 25, no. 1, pp. 15–25, February, 1959.

Gilmore, Donald R.: *Developing the "Little" Economies: A Survey of Area Development Programs in the United States*, Committee for Economic Development, New York, 1959, 200 pp.

Glick, Paul C.: *American Families*, Wiley, New York, 1957, 240 pp.

Grebler, Leo: *Experience in Urban Real Estate Investment*, Columbia University Press, New York, 1955, 277 pp. (*See* esp. pp. 112–122 for reference on p. 199 of *H,P,&C*.)

———: *Housing Issues in Economic Stabilization Policy*, Occasional Paper 72, National Bureau of Economic Research, New York, 1960, 129 pp.

———: *Production of New Housing: A Research Monograph on Efficiency in Production*, Social Science Research Council, New York, 1950, 186 pp.

———, David M. Blank, and Louis Winnick: *Capital Formation in Residential Real Estate: Trends and Prospects*, National Bureau of Economic Research, Princeton University Press, Princeton, 1956, 519 pp. (*See* esp. pp. 44, 106–123, 333, 334 and 426 for information on pp. 22–27, 34 and 63–65 of *H,P,&C*.)

Grier, Eunice, and George Grier: *Privately Developed Interracial Housing: An Analysis of Experience*, University of California Press, Berkeley, 1960, 264 pp.

Haar, Charles M.: *Land-use Planning: A Casebook on the Use, Misuse and Re-use of Urban Land*, Little, Brown, Boston, 1959, 790 pp.

Haber, William, and Harold M. Levinson: *Labor Relations and Productivity in the Building Trades*, University of Michigan Press, Ann Arbor, 1956, 266 pp. (*See* p. 243 for quotation on p. 119 of *H,P,&C*.)

Handlin, Oscar: *The Newcomers: Negroes and Puerto Ricans in a Changing Metropolis*, Harvard University Press, Cambridge, Mass., 1959, 171 pp.

Hawley, Amos H.: *The Changing Shape of Metropolitan America: Deconcentration since 1920*, Free Press, New York, 1956, 177 pp.

Hoover, Edgar M., and Raymond Vernon: *Anatomy of a Metropolis*, Harvard University Press, Cambridge, Mass., 1959, 345 pp.

Hoover Commission on Organization of the Executive Branch of the Government: *Reorganization of Federal Business Enterprises*, A Report to the Congress, Government Printing Office, Washington, 1949, 129 pp. (*See* pp. 25–33 for reference on p. 267 of *H,P,&C.*)

Hoyt, Homer: *Structure and Growth of Residential Neighborhoods in American Cities*, Federal Housing Administration, Government Printing Office, Washington, 1939, 178 pp.

Hurd, Richard M.: *Principles of City Land Values*, 4th ed. (1st ed., 1903), Record and Guide, New York, 1924, 159 pp.

Katona, George: *The Powerful Consumer: Psychological Studies of the American Economy*, McGraw-Hill, New York, 1960, 276 pp.

Kelly, Burnham: *The Prefabrication of Houses*, Technology Press, M.I.T., Cambridge, Mass. and Wiley, New York, 1951, 466 pp.

Kennedy, Robert C.: *The House and the Art of Its Design*, Reinhold, New York, 1953, 550 pp.

Kinnard, William N., Jr., and Zenon S. Malinowski: *The Impact of Dislocation from Urban Renewal Areas on Small Business*, University of Connecticut, Storrs, 1960, 89 pp.

Klaman, Saul B.: *The Postwar Residential Mortgage Market*, National Bureau of Economic Research, Princeton University Press, Princeton, 1961, 301 pp.

Lintner, John: *Mutual Savings Banks in the Savings and Mortgage Markets*, Harvard University, Graduate School of Business Administration, Division of Research, Boston, 1948, 559 pp. (*See* for reference on p. 258 of *H,P,&C.*)

Long, Clarence D., Jr.: *Building Cycles and the Theory of Investment*, Princeton University Press, Princeton, 1940, 239 pp.

Lynch, Kevin, and Lloyd Rodwin (eds.): *The Future Metropolis*, American Academy of Arts and Sciences, *Daedalus*, vol. 90, no. 1, Cambridge, Mass., Winter, 1961, 216 pp.

Maisel, Sherman J.: *Housebuilding in Transition*, University of California Press, Berkeley, 1953, 390 pp. (*See* p. 190 for information on p. 113 of *H,P,&C.*)

————: "Variables Commonly Ignored in Housing Demand Analysis," *Land Economics*, vol. 25, no. 3, pp. 260–274, August, 1949.

Margolis, Julius: "Metropolitan Finance Problems," in *Public Finances: Needs, Sources, and Utilization*, National Bureau of Economic Research, pp. 229–293, Princeton University Press, Princeton, 1961.

McCaffree, Kenneth M.: "Union Membership Policies and Labor Productivity among Asbestos Workers," *Industrial and Labor Relations Review*, vol. 14, no. 2, pp. 227–234, January, 1961.

McEntire, Davis: *Residence and Race*, Commission on Race and Housing, University of California Press, Berkeley, 1960, 409 pp.

Merton, Robert K.: "The Social Psychology of Housing," in Wayne Dennis (ed.), *Current Trends in Social Psychology*, University of Pittsburgh Press, Pittsburgh, 1948, pp. 163–217. (*See* esp. pp. 209–214 for citation on p. 84 of *H,P,&C*.)

Meyerson, Martin, and Edward C. Banfield: *Planning, Politics and the Public Interest*, Free Press, New York, 1955, 353 pp. (*See* esp. pp. 115–118 for information on pp. 279–280 of *H,P,&C*.)

————, Barbara Terrett, and Paul N. Ylvisaker (eds.): *Metropolis in Ferment*, American Academy of Political and Social Science, *The Annals*, vol. 314, Philadelphia, November, 1957, 231 pp.

Millspaugh, Martin, and Gurney Breckenfeld: *The Human Side of Urban Renewal*, Fight-Blight, Inc., Baltimore, 1958, 233 pp.

Morton, J. E.: *Urban Mortgage Lending: Comparative Markets and Experience*, National Bureau of Economic Research, Princeton University Press, Princeton, 1956, 187 pp.

Morton, Walter A.: *Housing Taxation*, University of Wisconsin Press, Madison, 1955, 216 pp.

Mumford, Lewis: *The City in History*, Harcourt, Brace & World, New York, 1961, 657 pp.

————: *From the Ground Up*, Harcourt, Brace & World, New York, 1956, 243 pp.

Myrdal, Gunnar: "Public Housing Policies" and "Housing Segregation" in *An American Dilemma*, Harper, New York, 1944, pp. 348–353, 618–622.

National Association of Home Builders: "The NAHB Membership Survey: A Study of Builders and the Homes They Build," vol. I, Washington, 1959. (*See* pp. 13, 48 and 49 for reference on p. 105 of *H,P,&C*.)

New York Temporary State Housing Rent Commission: "Prospects for Rehabilitation," directed by Morton J. Schussheim, New

York, 1960, 114 pp. (*See* esp. pp. 1–4, 40–51, for information on p. 182 of *H,P,&C.*)

Owen, Wilfred S.: *Cities in the Motor Age*, Viking, New York, 1959, 176 pp.

Park, Robert E.: *Human Communities*, Free Press, New York, 1952, 278 pp.

Perloff, Harvey S. (ed.): *Planning and the Urban Community*, University of Pittsburgh Press, Pittsburgh, 1961, 235 pp.

President's Advisory Committee on Government Housing Policies and Programs: *Recommendations on Government Housing Policies and Programs*, 1953, 377 pp. (*See* esp. pp. 11–13 and pp. 348–366 for reference on pp. 234–235 of *H,P,&C.*)

President's Commission on National Goals: *Goals for Americans*, Prentice-Hall, Englewood Cliffs, N.J., 1960, 372 pp.

President's Conference on Home Building and Home Ownership: *Reports*, 1932–33, 11 vols. (*See* for reference on p. 221 of *H,P,&C.*)

Rapkin, Chester, and William G. Grigsby: *The Demand for Housing in Eastwick*, Institute for Urban Studies, University of Pennsylvania, Philadelphia, 1960, 83 pp. (*See* for reference on p. 80 of *H,P,&C.*)

———, and ———: *Residential Renewal in the Urban Core*, University of Pennsylvania Press, Philadelphia, 1960, 131 pp.

Ratcliff, Richard U.: "Filtering Down and the Elimination of Substandard Housing," *Journal of Land and Public Utility Economics*, vol. 21, no. 4, pp. 322–330, November, 1945. (*See* for information on pp. 9–10 and pp. 42–45 of *H,P,&C.*)

———: Daniel B. Rathbun, and Junia Honnold, *Residential Finance, 1950*, Wiley, New York, 1957, 180 pp.

Reid, Margaret G.: "Capital Formation in Residential Real Estate," *The Journal of Political Economy*, vol. 66, no. 2, pp. 131–153, April, 1958.

Riemer, Svend, and Nicholas J. Demerath: "The Role of Social Research in Housing Design," *Land Economics*, vol. 28, no. 3, pp. 230–243, August, 1952.

Rockefeller Brothers Fund: "The Challenge to America: Its Economic and Social Aspects," in *Prospects for America*, Doubleday, Garden City, 1961, pp. 249–333. (*See* esp. pp. 320–333 for references on pp. 332–336 of *H,P,&C.*)

Rodwin, Lloyd: *Housing and Economic Progress: A Study of the Housing Experiences of Boston's Middle-income Families*, Harvard University Press and Technology Press, M.I.T., Cambridge, Mass., 1961, 228 pp.

Rosow, Irving: "Home Ownership Motives," *American Sociological Review,* vol. 13, no. 6, pp. 751–756, December, 1948.

Rossi, Peter: *Why Families Move: A Study in the Social Psychology of Urban Residential Mobility,* Free Press, New York, 1955, 220 pp.

Saulnier, Raymond J.: *Urban Mortgage Lending by Life Insurance Companies,* National Bureau of Economic Research, New York, 1950, 180 pp.

Schaaf, A. H.: *Economic Aspects of Urban Renewal: Theory, Policy and Area Analysis,* Real Estate Research Program, Institute of Business and Economic Research, University of California, Berkeley, 1960, 51 pp.

Schnore, Leo F.: "The Separation of Home and Work: A Problem for Human Ecology," *Social Forces,* vol. 32, no. 4, pp. 336–343, May, 1954.

Seeley, John: "The Slum: Its Nature, Use and Users," *Journal of the American Institute of Planners,* vol. 25, no. 1, pp. 7–14, February, 1959.

Shattuck, Lemuel, and others: *Report of the Sanitary Commission of Massachusetts, 1850,* facsimile edition, Harvard University Press, Cambridge, Mass., 1948, 321 pp. (*See* esp. pp. 153–167 for reference on p. 292 of *H,P,&C.*)

Shevky, Eshref, and Wendell Bell: *Social Area Analysis,* Stanford University Press, Stanford, 1955, 70 pp.

Silk, Leonard S.: *Sweden Plans for Better Housing,* Duke University Press, Durham, 1948, 149 pp.

Slayton, William L.: "Conservation of Existing Housing," *Law and Contemporary Problems,* vol. 20, no. 3, pp. 436–462, Summer, 1955.

"Social Policy and Social Research in Housing": *Journal of Social Issues,* vol. 7, nos. 1 and 2, 1951, 185 pp.

Sogg, Wilton S., and others: "Urban Renewal," *Harvard Law Review,* vol. 72, no. 3, pp. 504–552, January, 1959.

Stein, Clarence S.: *Toward New Towns for America,* University of Liverpool Press, Liverpool, England, for Public Administration Service, Chicago, 1951, 245 pp.

Twentieth Century Fund, Inc.: *1956 Annual Report* (Director's Report), New York, 1956. (*See* p. 9 for quotation on p. 95 of *H,P,&C.*)

United Nations, Economic Commission for Europe: *Government Policies and the Cost of Building*, Geneva, Switzerland, 1959, variously paged.

U.S. Bureau of the Census: "Local Government in Standard Metropolitan Areas," *1957 Census of Governments*, vol. 1, no. 2, 1958, 47 pp. (*See* for reference on p. 316 of *H,P,&C.*)

——: "Mobility of the Population of the United States, April 1958 to 1959," Current Population Reports, ser. P-20, no. 104, Sept. 30, 1960, 28 pp. (*See* for reference on p. 89 of *H,P,&C.*)

——: *1956 National Housing Inventory*, 1958–59, 3 vols. (*See* esp. for information on pp. 33–39 of *H,P,&C.*)

U.S. Bureau of Labor Statistics: *Construction During Five Decades, Historic Statistics 1907–52*, Bulletin 1146, 1954, 75 pp.

——: *Population and Labor Force Projections for the United States, 1960 to 1975*, Bulletin 1242, 1959, 56 pp. (*See* p. 8 for information on pp. 73 and 206–207 of *H,P,&C.*)

—— and Wharton School of Business and Finance: *Study of Consumer Expenditures*, University of Pennsylvania, 1956, vol. 18. (*See* esp. Tables 1–2, 4, and 10 for pp. 53–61 of *H,P,&C.*)

U.S. Commission on Civil Rights: *1959 Report*, 1959, 668 pp. (*See* p. 538 for quotation on p. 80 of *H,P,&C.*)

——: 1961 Report 4, *Housing*, 1961, 206 pp.

U.S. Federal Public Housing Authority: *Public Housing Design: A Review of Experience in Low-rent Housing*, 1946, 294 pp.

U.S. House of Representatives, Select Committee on Lobbying Activities: *Housing Lobby*, Hearings, part 2, April 19–May 17, 1950, 1950, 1411 pp. (*See* for information on pp. 272–280 of *H,P,&C.*)

U.S. Housing and Home Finance Agency: *Housing the Elderly: A Review of Significant Developments*, 1959, 38 pp.

——: *A Summary of the Evolution of Housing Activities in the Federal Government*, 1950, 23 pp.

——: *What People Want When They Buy a House*, 1955, 126 pp.

——: *Workable Program for Community Improvement*, 1961, 43 pp.

U.S. National Resources Committee: *Housing: The Continuing Problem*, 1940, 220 pp.

U.S. Senate, Subcommittee on Housing, Committee on Banking and Currency: *Housing for the Aged*, 1956, 70 pp.

——: *Study of Mortgage Credit*, 86th Congress, 2d Session, Dec. 22, 1958, revised July 11, 1960, 481 pp.

U.S. Temporary National Economic Commission: *Toward More Housing*, 1940, 223 pp. (*See* reference on p. 135 of *H,P,&C.*)

Unwin, Sir Raymond: "Land Values in Relation to Planning and Housing in the United States," *Journal of Land and Public Utility Economics*, vol. 17, no. 1, pp. 1–9, February, 1941.

Urban Land Institute: *New Approaches to Residential Land Development*, Technical Bulletin 40, Washington, 1961, 151 pp.

"The Urge to Own," *Architectural Forum*, vol. 67, no. 5, pp. 370–378, November, 1937. (*See* esp. p. 374 for information on p. 84 of *H,P,&C.*)

Vernon, Raymond: *Metropolis 1985*, New York Metropolitan Regional Study, Harvard University Press, Cambridge, Mass., 1960, 252 pp.

Walker, Mabel L.: *Urban Blight and Slums*, Harvard University Press, Cambridge, Mass., 1938, 442 pp.

Walker, Robert A.: *The Planning Function in Urban Government*, University of Chicago Press, Chicago, 1950, 410 pp.

Wallace, Anthony F. C.: *Housing and Social Structure*, Philadelphia Housing Association, Philadelphia, 1952, 120 pp.

Weaver, Robert C.: "Class, Race and Urban Renewal," *Land Economics*, vol. 36, no. 3, pp. 235–251, August, 1960.

———: *The Negro Ghetto*, Harcourt, Brace & World, New York, 1948, 404 pp.

Wheaton, William L. C.: "American Housing Needs, 1955–1970," *Housing Yearbook*, National Housing Conference, Washington, 1954, pp. 5–23.

——— and Morton J. Schussheim: *The Cost of Municipal Services in Residential Areas*, Housing and Home Finance Agency, 1955, 105 pp.

Whyte, William H.: *The Organization Man*, Simon and Schuster, New York, 1956, 429 pp.

——— and other *Fortune* editors: *The Exploding Metropolis*, Doubleday, Garden City, 1958, 177 pp. (*See* esp. pp. 2, 19, 30 for quotations on pp. 91–92 of *H,P,&C.*)

Winnick, Louis: *American Housing and Its Use*, Wiley, New York, 1957, 143 pp.

Wirth, Louis: "Housing as a Field of Sociological Research," *American Sociological Review*, vol. 12, no. 2, pp. 134–142, April, 1947.

Wood, Elizabeth: "Knowledge Needed for Adequate Programs of Public and Private Housing," in Donald Bogue (ed.), *Needed Urban and Metropolitan Research*, Scripps Foundation, Oxford, Ohio, 1953, pp. 51–61.

Wood, Ramsay, Eliot J. Swam, and Walter F. Stettner: *Housing, Social Security and Public Works*, Board of Governors of the Federal Reserve System, Washington, 1946, 94 pp.

Wood, Robert C.: *Suburbia, Its People and Their Politics*, Houghton Mifflin, Boston, 1959, 340 pp.

Woodbury, Coleman (ed.): *The Future of Cities and Urban Redevelopment*, University of Chicago Press, Chicago, 1953, 764 pp.

—— (ed.): *Urban Redevelopment: Problems and Practices*, University of Chicago Press, Chicago, 1953, 525 pp.

Charts

Tables

Index